Volume 18
Si/Stan

THE WORLD OF
AUTOMOBILES

AN ILLUSTRATED ENCYCLOPEDIA
OF THE MOTOR CAR

PURNELL REFERENCE BOOKS
Milwaukee ● Toronto ● Melbourne ● London

Executive Editor: Ian Ward
Editorial Director: Brian Innes
Assistant Editors: Laurie Caddell
Mike Winfield
Charles Merullo
Art Editor: David Goodman
Art Assistant: John Heritage
Picture Editor: Mirco Decet
Cover Design: Harry W. Fass
Production Manager: Warren Bright

contributors
DAVID BURGESS WISE:
Siata
Siddeley
Simplex
Singer
Sizaire
Sommer
SPA
Spyker
Standard
Stanley
LAURIE CADDELL: Specialist Cars
ERIC COUSHION: Sound System
TONY DRON: Sponsorship
BRYAN JONES: Simca
Skoda
MIKE KETTLEWELL:
Silverstone
South African Grand Prix
Spa
Spanish Grand Prix
L. J. K. SETRIGHT:
Skidding
Spark Plug
Sports Cars
IAN WARD: Signals and Signalling

HILARY WEATHERLEY:
Sports Car Racing
MIKE WINFIELD: Siffert
JONATHAN WOOD: Squire
WORDSMITHS LTD:
Sound Insulation
Speedometer
Spring

Picture acknowledgments
Page 2041:Quattroruote—2042:
Quattroruote—2043: Quattroruote—2044:
Quattroruote; G. Goddard—2045: Tony
Stone Associates—2046: Quattroruote—
2046-7: Tony Stone Associates—2047:
Quattroruote; C. Burgess Wise—2048: C.
Burgess Wise—2049: Quattroruote—2050:
J. Spencer Smith—2051: Quattroruote—
2052: Highway Code—2053: Quattroruote;
Quattroruote; National Motor Museum—
2054: I. Ward—2054-5: National Motor
Museum—2055: G. Goddard; L. J. Caddell
—2056: Quattroruote—2057: Quattroruote
—2058: Quattroruote—2059: Quattroruote
—2060: Quattroruote—2061: Chrysler—
2062: Quattroruote—2063: Orbis—2064:
Quattroruote—2065: Quattroruote; National
Motor Museum—2066: Quattroruote—
2066-7: C. Burgess Wise—2067: National
Motor Museum—2068: National Motor
Museum; Quattroruote—2068-9: National
Motor Museum—2069: Quattroruote;
National Motor Museum—2070: Quattroruote—2070-1: Keystone Press Agency—
2071: National Motor Museum—2072: L. J.
Caddell; National Motor Museum—2073: J.
Spencer Smith—2074: National Motor
Museum—2075: National Motor Museum—
2076: Papetti—2079: Fiat—2080: ACI—
2081: Quattroruote—2082: Quattroruote—
2083: Quattroruote—2084: Quattroruote—
2085: Quattroruote—2086: Quattroruote—
2087: Phipps; Quattroruote—2088: L. J.
Caddell/Orbis—2089: C. Posthumus;
Quattroruote; C. Posthumus—2090: Fiat—
2091: General Motors—2092: Quattroruote
—2093: Quattroruote; Ceci; Autovox—
2094: Quattroruote—2095: Philips;
Autovox; Autovox—2096: London Art Tech
—2097: London Art Tech—2098: London
Art Tech—2099: Quattroruote—2100:
Quattroruote—2101: Quattroruote—2102:
—Quattroruote—2103: Quattroruote; Phipps
—2104: Attualfoto—2105: Quattroruote—
2106: F. Lini—2107: London Art Tech;
Quattroruote—2108: London Art Tech—
2109: Papetti—2110: Papetti; Marelli/
Quattroruote—2111: Champion; Papetti—
2112: Papetti; T. Nesta—2113: J. Spencer
Smith; A. Morland—2114: National Motor
Museum—2115: J. Ross; L. J. Caddell; A.
Morland—2116: National Motor Museum—
2117: National Motor Museum—2118:
Quattroruote; A. Morland—2119: A.
Morland—2120: L. J. Caddell—2121:
Papetti—2122: A. C. Delco; Fiat; Papetti—
2123: Quattroruote—2124: A. Morland; Di
Santo; Boroli; I. Ward—2125: A. Morland—
2126: D. Goodman; L. J. Caddell—2127:
N. Bruce—2128: N. Bruce—2130: N. Bruce
—2131: N. Bruce—2132: Belli; N. Bruce—
2134: N. Bruce—2135: M. Decet; N. Bruce
—2136: Quattroruote—2137: Quattroruote;
Zagari—2138: Attualfoto; Quattroruote—
2139: Attualfoto—2140: Quattroruote—
2141: Papetti; Papetti; Papetti—2142:
Ford; Ford; Ford—2143: British Leyland—
2144: Milleruote; Milleruote—2145:
National Motor Museum—2146: National
Motor Museum—2147: Thouroughbred &
Classic Cars; J. Wood; J. Wood—2148: J.
Wood—2148-9: J. Wood—2149: J. Wood
—2150: Quattroruote; National Motor
Museum—2151: National Motor Museum;
National Motor Museum; Quattroruote; G.
Goddard—2152: National Motor Museum;
National Motor Museum; National Motor
Museum—2153: A. Morland; National
Motor Museum—2154: National Motor
Museum; A. Morland—2155: A. Morland;
A. Morland; Quattroruote—2156:
Quattroruote—2156-7: Dona de Carli—
2157: Quattroruote—2158: Italfoto—2159:
Belli—2160: National Motor Museum—
cover: J. Spencer Smith; G. Goddard; J.
Spencer Smith; National Motor Museum

Reference Edition © 1977, Purnell Reference Books, a division of Macdonald-Raintree, Inc.

Library of Congress Number: 77-10138

Printed and bound in the United States of America

Library of Congress Cataloging in Publication Data

Main entry under title:

World of automobiles.

Includes index. pp. 2615-2640
1. Automobiles—Dictionaries. 1. Ward, Ian,
1949-
TL9.W67 1977 629.2'03 77-10138
ISBN 0-8393-6009-6 lib. bdg.

© Orbis Publishing Ltd, London 1974
© Quattroruote/Domus, Milan & Istituto
Geografico De Agostini, Novara 1972

Contents

TUNING EQUIPMENT AND SPORTS CARS

Siata made a reputation building tuning 'goodies' for Fiat before entering the market whole heartedly with their own sports cars

Top: a 1934 Fiat 508S Ballila Spyder Sport; after being thrashed by the MG Magnettes during the 1933 Mille Miglia, Siata's supercharger pushed the car's bhp from 36 to 55

Above: the Siata Gran Sport 750 was derived from the 1937 Fiat 500

THE Societa Italiana Auto-Trasformazioni-Accessori was founded in 1926, manufacturing go-faster equipment for popular Italian cars in its works in Turin. There was always a close link with Fiat, and the new Fiat Tipo 508S Ballila Spyder Sports which ran in the 1933 Mille Miglia had Siata ohv cylinder heads and Siata four-speed gearboxes, neither of which adjuncts prevented the cars from being thrashed by the more powerful (and more expensive) MG Magnettes. The ohv conversion pushed the Ballila's power output from around 30 bhp to 36 bhp: in 1934 Siata announced a supercharger for this car which raised the engine's

potential to 55 bhp. They built a blown single-seat Ballila which could achieve around 95 mph: and when the diminutive 500cc Fiat Topolino appeared, Siata turned their attention to the apparently unrewarding task of turning it into a competition car.

In the touring class of the 1937 Mille Miglia, a Topolino with Siata ohv conversion driven by Spotorno and Besana covered 1615 km of the course at an average speed of just under 50 mph. In the 1938 Mille Miglia, an open two-seater Topolino-Siata (quite a good-looking little car with faired pontoon wings and inset headlamps) was converted into an odd-looking coupé with the addition of a streamlined hardtop by the flying ace Renato Donati: another curious touch was a third headlamp mounted cyclops-fashion above the radiator grille.

In its most developed form, an aerodynamic coupé with full-width bodywork and enclosed rear wheels, the Siata version of the Topolino had an engine increased in capacity to 596cc, developing 30 bhp at 5500 rpm; maximum speed was around 75 mph. And in 1938 one of these coupés set a 24 hr class record, averaging 70 mph throughout the run; a full-width open-two-seater with a long tail was also available, and known as the Pescara.

After the war, Siata announced an intriguing little sports car called the Bersaglieri, which had a light-alloy four-cylinder twin overhead camshaft engine displacing a mere 750cc mounted at the rear of a tubular chassis independently suspended all round on coil springs. The light-alloy body had an exposed, aircraft-type radiator, and seated three with the driver in the centre. A very advanced self-locking differential was

another feature of this unorthodox model.

Alongside it was offered a Siata cast in a more orthodox mould, known as the Amica, and available in 500 cc and 750 cc form.

Once again, the power unit was the Fiat 500 engine but with extensive modifications. Though the 500 cc version retained the standard Fiat two-bearing crank, the bored-out 750 cc Amica had a special Siata fully-balanced crankshaft with three main bearings; also fitted were oversize valves with multiple springs and a specially-profiled camshaft, again of Siata's own make. Claimed output of the 500 cc version was 22 bhp at 4400 rpm, and of the 750 cc 25 bhp at 4500 rpm, a surprisingly small improvement in view of all the modifications. The Amica had a tubular chassis with independent front suspension by transverse leaf springs and wishbones, though the standard Fiat rear axle with reversed quarter-elliptic springs was retained.

Standard wear for the Amica was a two-seater sports body, though a sporting coupé was also available, and a four-speed gearbox was fitted, though a five-speed transmission was used on the special 42 bhp Amica 750 which won the Italian championship in 1948 with a speed of 95 mph. In normal trim the 500 cc Amica could achieve 62 mph, and the 750 71 mph.

Another model, the Daina, appeared the following year. This used the Fiat 1400 as a basis, in conjunction with a sheet-steel box section chassis, and had a claimed top speed of over 90 mph, thanks to several modifications which boosted the engine power output from 44 bhp to 65 bhp; included among these were a

Top: the Siata 36 single-seater record breaker

Above right: the chassis of Siata's Amica of 1949

Above left: the Siata Amica; two body styles were available, a two-seater sports and a sporting coupé

twin-carburetter manifold and an increase in the compression ratio.

Another Fiat 1400-based model, the Rallye tourer, was announced in 1951: this was a blatant attempt to cream off some of the success of the MG sports car line, and was a close stylistic copy of the MG TD, even down to the radiator and separate headlamps, though a five-speed gearbox was something that Abingdon did not offer.

Now Fiat themselves decided to get in on the high-performance, limited-production formula, and Siata were called in to help with the development of a new 1996cc V-8 model, which was launched at the 1952 Geneva Show. All-round independent suspension by coil-springs was a feature of the Fiat 8-V, and Siata used this chassis as a basis for some handsome sporting coupés with five-speed transmissions and Vignale or

veloped a puny 12.2bhp, sufficient to propel the little two-seater coupé along at speeds far lower than usually associated with Siata products. One unusual feature of the design, however, was all-round independent suspension by torsion bars.

Another venture during the 1950s was the fitting of American power units into Siata chassis; engines as diverse as the 720cc Crosley and V-8 Chrysler appeared in Siata guise, as well as the more common Fiat 600 and 1100 motors.

The year 1960 saw a link-up between Siata and Abarth, though both companies continued to operate as separate entities.

By 1964, 1400 cars a year were passing through the Siata factory in Turin's Via Leonardo da Vinci, though most of these were just hotted-up versions of the Fiat 1500 saloon that had been fitted with Siata

Left: the 750cc competition Siata Fiat TC of 1948; like most Siatas of the 1940s and 50s, it was based on Fiat mechanical parts extensively modified by the small Torinese firm

Left: Siata, in collaboration with Fiat, introduced the Siata 208S America coupé at the Geneva Show in 1952. It was powered by a 1996cc, V8 Fiat motor and had a top speed of about 125mph. The car had all-round independent suspension by coil springs and a five speed transmission system

Bertone coachwork; typical was the Tipo America roadster 208S, which looked rather like an AC Cobra. Alternatively, there was a 208S Spyder, a stark open two-seater with flared wings and external exhaust, which scaled only $17\frac{1}{2}$cwt.

Top speed of the Siata 208S coupé was said to be over 125mph, though the Spyder's bluff snout slowed the maximum of this model somewhat.

Totally different in concept was the 1953 Siata Mitzi, a tiny minicar essayed in 1953–54. Purely utilitarian in appearance, the Mitzi had a rear-mounted twin-cylinder power unit of only 328cc, which de-

twin-carburettor manifolds.

However, there was also a GT model, the TS 1500, which acquired a 1600cc power unit and a 109mph maximum speed in 1966.

But perhaps the best-remembered Siata of recent years was the 'spider', launched in 1967, which used the mechanicals of a Fiat 850 in a boxy open two-seated body which was intended to recapture the spirit of the 1930s; there was even an MG-inspired dummy radiator. This rather ugly little car appealed greatly to Italian youth, who liked its 'vecchio stile' concept; it was marketed as the 'Spring'.   DBW

THE MANY CARS OF J.D. SIDDELEY

John Davenport Siddeley had his fingers in many motoring 'pies' in the early years of the century

YOUNG JOHN DAVENPORT SIDDELEY was one of the early advocates of the pneumatic tyre for motor vehicles. By the turn of the century he had become managing director of the Clipper Pneumatic Tyre Company, of Aston Cross, Birmingham, whose products were claimed to be 'Best for all forms of Automobile Cycles or Carriages.' To prove their worth, Siddeley had a set of his tyres fitted to a Parisian Daimler, which competed in the 1900 Thousand Miles' Trial: and apart from a handful of punctures caused by the appalling road surfaces en route, the tyres proved quite reliable. Siddeley himself had taken part in the trial at the tiller of his 6 hp Daimler (with solid tyres), and had gained joint second prize in the class for cars selling between £300–£500.

Within a couple of years, however, Siddeley had become convinced that there was a brighter future in the manufacture and sale of motor cars than tyres, and began, initially, to import Peugeot cars from France, then, backed by Lionel de Rothschild, approached the mighty Vickers, Sons & Maxim armaments group, which was already producing Wolseley cars, to see whether they would be prepared to build cars to Siddeley's design under licence. The Vickers brothers were becoming increasingly dubious of the merits of the horizontal-engined vehicles which Herbert Austin was producing for them, and decided that production of vertical-engined cars of the type proposed by Siddeley could be a sound insurance for the future. So the Siddeley Autocar Company was established in 1902, though it seems likely that the first cars to bear the Siddeley name were merely re-radiatored Peugeots. Then came a 6 hp light car, which seemed to go against all Siddeley's design philosophy with its horizontal engine. Apart from its square-cut radiator and bonnet, this was identical to the contemporary small Wolseley, and was built in Wolseley's Crayford, Kent, factory.

The 6 hp Siddeley was, it seems, distinctive enough to stand on its own merits, winning a first class award and gold medal in the 1904 ACGBI Small Car Trials at Hereford for 'general excellence of design, construction and workmanship, and for hill-climbing': but the larger-engined Siddeleys, though obviously Peugeot-inspired, were entirely different from anything that Wolseley had so far manufactured.

The 12 and 18 hp had vertical engines, channel steel chassis and chain final drive. An advanced feature was the use of overhead inlet valves, with pushrod operation 'after the manner of this year's De Dietrichs and last year's Mercedes . . . fulcrummed in a small block, which can be raised or lowered at will by means of a small lever on the steering wheel': varying the lift of the inlet valves in this way gave a somewhat empiric form of throttle control by altering the amount of petrol/air mixture drawn into the cylinders.

The 12 hp Siddeley had a two-cylinder pair-cast engine, was one of the earliest cars to be supplied for War Office use, and achieved 998 marks out of a

Right: the two-seat 6 hp Siddeley of 1904, which was built in Wolseley's factory

Above: another 1904 light Siddeley; this picture was taken at the end of the 1974 London –Brighton run

possible 1000 for a non-stop run from Glasgow to London in 1904; in early 1905, John Siddeley drove a 12 hp on a 5000-mile observed reliability run in a snowstorm. The 16 hp, with a four-cylinder engine, was claimed to be 'perfectly silent-very powerful', and was capable of recording over 20 miles per gallon under ACGBI observation. At this period, the Siddeley Autocar Company were also agents for Birmingham-built Mulliner coachwork.

Early in 1905, Siddeley built a monstrous 100 hp racing car to the order of Lionel de Rothschild, which was entered for the Gordon Bennett Eliminating Trials in the Isle of Man, to be driven by Sidney Girling. It followed the design of the company's touring cars,

Above: the 1903 Siddeley, which was really little more than a re-radiatored Peugeot

with inlet valves operated by pushrods and rockers, and had dual ignition by magneto and coil systems. Engine and transmission were three-point-suspended in the frame, there was a multi-plate clutch, and the three-speed gearbox drove the rear axle through side chains. 'The new Siddeley is said to have shown an extraordinary turn of speed during its trial runs,' commented *Country Life*: but though the car proved as fast as any of its rivals in the eliminating trials, it failed to stay the distance.'

Four days before the eliminating trials, on 26 May, 1905, a meeting of the board of the Wolseley Tool & Motor Car Company, Douglas and Albert Vickers announced that they were forming a committee of investigation to look into the possibility of Wolseley absorbing the Siddeley Autocar Company: not long after, the takeover took place, and Siddeley became manager of Wolseley, a move which soon resulted in the resignation of Austin, who left in a huff to set up on his own.

Siddeley lost no time in impressing his personality on the company, and the cars were known indifferently as Wolseley-Siddeleys, Siddeley-Wolseleys or just plain Siddeleys: new models designed by Charles Rimmington appeared.

In the 1906 Coupé du Matin, a 6000 mile reliability trial which encompassed both the Alps and the Pyrenees, two 32 hp Siddeleys were the only British competitors, and were successful in the Large Car class, which necessitated a total weight of 47 cwt and an average speed of 28.13 mph.

Commented *Motoring Illustrated*: 'Le Matin, under whose auspices this trial took place, has nothing but praise for the behaviour of the two British cars, and states that their performance has been quite a revelation to French makers of what a British-built car is capable of doing.'

Shortly afterwards an 18 hp Siddeley won a gold medal in quite a different type of competition, the Town Carriage contest held in London. The award was made for 'the all-round usefulness . . . general

successful company—it was only the Vickers millions which kept it from foundering irrevocably. A profit had only been made in two years since the company's formation, 1902 and 1903, since when the annual losses had been mounting up. The pattern continued at first under Siddeley's direction, with the annual loss mounting to £60,000, then falling back to £36,000. In 1909 Siddeley resigned, and the management was taken over by E. Hopwood.

Siddeley now joined Captain H. H. P. Deasy, formerly well-known as the importer of Martini cars, who had been a manufacturer in his own right since the end of 1906 building a 'moderate-priced car on

Above: a 100 hp racing Siddeley of 1905, which was very fast, but failed to last in the Gordon Bennett Eliminating Trials; this was one of the last cars made before the merger with Wolseley

Right: a Wolseley-Siddeley landaulette of 1906

design (chassis and body) and all the numerous details of construction and accessories which are desirable in forming the most comfortable, smooth-running and generally satisfactory town carriage.'

The spring of 1907 saw a 40 hp Siddeley undertaking a 10,000 mile reliability trial, and meeting snow as deep as the wheels in the Spittal of Glenshee, where 'the official observer decided further progress to be undesirable, and took the car back to Dundee'. A notable feature of the car was the fact that the tyres were filled with Elastes, a noxious mixture which was supposed to eliminate punctures. However, far from eliminating punctures, the Elastes caused them in profusion. Explained the Wolseley company: 'It appears that the Elastes fillings, which were used in conjunction with Michelin outer covers throughout the trial, are made on tyres fitted to rims, and the rims used for this purpose differ in regard to the shape of the bead from those employed on the car. In consequence of this, the Elastes, which is naturally less adaptable than air, was altered in form when fitted to these new rims, causing a sawing action to arise at the head of the bead and cutting through the sides of the tyre. The greater number of covers used on the trial were damaged from this cause, and the result cannot, therefore, be in justice taken as reflecting on the durability of the Michelin tyre in normal use.

'In regard to the time spent in adjustments to the car itself, the makes point out that, taking the cost of the work on the ordinary repair shop basis of 2s 6d per hour, the result shows a total of 29s for the 10,000 miles, while the new parts required to put the car in perfect repair were new bushes and pins to the front spring shackles at a cost of 1s 10d.'

In that year's Coppa Florio (and other Italian events) Wolsit cars were in evidence: these were Wolseley-Siddeleys built under licence in Milan by the Fabbrica Italiana Automobili Legnanese, who went out of business in 1908.

At this period, Wolseley was not a particularly

up-to-date lines' designed by E. W. Lewis, formerly with Rover. The original Deasy had been a 4½-litre model of neat appearance, distinguished by enormous brake drums, an adjustable steering column and a Rover-style camshaft brake, which slowed the engine by cutting off the lift of the valves, turning the cylinders in effect into compressors.

But by 1909, giantism had set in: the range was now headed by two huge four-cylinder models, the 8621 cc 35 hp and the 11,974 cc 45 hp. Siddeley changed all that immediately, and reshaped the company's offerings to more manageable—and saleable—proportions, with the announcement for 1910 of the new 'J.D.S.' model, a 4084 cc four-cylinder with a dashboard radiator and the power unit housed beneath a 'coffin-nosed' bonnet. Final drive was by Lanchester worm gearing, and rear suspension was on the Lanchester pattern, too, with cantilever springs and parallel-motion radius links to locate the back axle: this feature gave the J. D. S. Type Deasy its slogan—'The car that holds the road.'

measurements to the sleeve-valve model.

Fortunately, this confusion of induction gear was brought to an abrupt halt by the onset of the European hostilities, and not given a chance to recur after the Armistice, when Siddeley-Deasy merged with the Sir W. G. Armstrong, Whitworth Company.

Armstrong-Whitworth were a famous Tyneside engineering and shipbuilding concern who had entered the car industry in 1904, building the Wilson-Pilcher, which had a flat-four engine and preselective four-speed transmission.

From 1906 their Scotswood-on-Tyne car factory became increasingly concerned with the new Arm-

Left: a Siddeley-Deasy of 1912; Siddeley had resigned from Wolseley in 1909 and joined Deasy, but Wolseley incorporated his name as late as 1910

Above: a Siddeley-Deasy of 1913–4, with a strange radiator position, behind the bonnet

strong-Whitworth car, a handsome machine on Mercedes lines. In 1913 the Scotswood factory was enlarged, and a new bodybuilding and repair works opened at Openshaw, Manchester.

But with the merger, all production was transferred to the Siddeley-Deasy factory at Coventry: after the fusion of the interests of the two companies, the new firm was known as Armstrong Siddeley Motors.

The first Armstrong Siddeley car to be produced was a six-cylinder 30 hp of 5 litres and ponderous appearance. Its heavy Vee-radiator (surmounted by a Sphinx mascot) and disc wheels were massive rather than elegant, and it appeared to have been styled on the lines of an Armstrong-Whitworth Dreadnought. But it was intended for a clientele who prized comfort and reliability above all else: and in a 1921 advertisement the Armstrong Siddeley company summed up the philosophy behind the car.

'From the time of its introduction in 1919 our settled policy has been to make the Armstrong Siddeley 6 cylinder car the best car—both for performance and economy—which can be produced and to sell it at the lowest possible price. This policy still holds.

'In the period which has elapsed, the Armstrong Siddeley has proved itself a fine motor carriage of perfect comfort, costing less to buy than any other car of like capacity and achievement, and less to run. Its leading features are reliability, comfort, power, silence, ease of handling, distinguished appearance, and economy in operation.

'One result of the success of the 30 hp Armstrong Siddeley has been a strongly expressed desire from

There was soon a small 'J.D.S.', too, in the shape of the 14/20 hp of 2654 cc: 'Simply delightful,' gushed an enthusiastic owner.

Oddly enough, though Siddeley was long gone from them, Wolseley were still advertising their cars as Wolseley-Siddeleys at the end of 1910 (though they set the Siddeley name in smaller type to make the position at least partially clear).

In 1912, the Deasy Motor Car Company became the Siddeley-Deasy Motor Manufacturering Company, thus setting the seal on Siddeley's influence over their policies: co-incident with the changeover came two new models with Silent Knight sleeve-valve engines, the 18/24 of 3308 cc and the 24/30 of identical cylinder dimensions but six cylinders, which brought the swept volume to 4962 cc. Alongside these were offered two poppet-valve models, the 12 hp of 1944 cc and the 18/24 of 3308 cc (with identical bore and stroke to its sleeve-valve sister). A six-cylinder model was announced for 1914: this was the 30/36 hp of 4962 cc, another engine designed with identical cylinder

another large section of the public for a car of like advantages which shall cost even less to buy and run.

'In response to that demand we have decided—while maintaining the 30 hp Armstrong Siddeley as our leading product—to introduce a model of less power and seating capacity, but, except in the matter of dimensions and weight, of identical design and also of the same high quality. This is to be known as the 18 hp Armstrong Siddeley 6 cylinder car.'

Prices of the 30 hp ranged from £775 for the chassis to £1250 for the laundaulette; the new 18 hp model cost £575 in chassis form, £975 for the landaulette.

Early in 1922, *The Autocar* carried out a comparison test between the two models, an open tourer on the 18 hp chassis and a magnificently equipped 30 hp saloon owned by J. Davenport Siddeley CBE himself.

Commenting on the silence of the overhead valve gear and the transmission, the tester wrote: 'The first outstanding impression is the extreme ease of the pedal and hand controls, the freedom of action and the general docility of the engine, all of which characteristics engender a feeling of confidence, not to say repose, in gliding along the road . . . 33 mph would appear to be the most comfortable speed of the 18 hp model, at which rate it swoops smoothly over hill and dale, and little affected by the state of the road surface . . . the

larger car glided in silence over pot-holes that would cause a dither in every part of a light and frail vehicle . . . the steering is light and of the single-finger order . . . one fits a car such as this with the extreme ease and comfort which suggests that the bodywork was designed to suit individual anatomical standards . . . of rattles and jingles there were none, even over deserted roads that permitted with safety a high average—just one long silent swoop, using one lever only, and that the accelerator, to govern speed—no strain, unlimited reserve power, and a feeling that it could be maintained *ad libitum*.'

Against this background of estentation, Armstrong Siddeley's next venture seemed uncharacteristically plebean, for their subsidiary, Stoneleigh Motors, now offered a curious light car, with a single, central driver's seat in front, and two passengers seats behind; it was powered by a 1 litre V-twin engine claimed to be constructed from World War I radial aeroengine cylinders. The car was not a success, and production ceased in 1924.

In the summer of 1922, an 18 hp Armstrong Siddeley tourer covered 10,010 miles in 23 days, recording 24.64 mpg and using six pints of oil: it travelled 450 miles every day (but rested each Sabbath), yet spent less than two hours in the entire period being serviced

Top: a 1933 Siddeley Special; this was announced at the 1932 Motor Show and was powered by a six-cylinder engine of 4960 cc

Above: a Siddeley-Deasy 1914 model, still with the odd radiator location, but this time with a touring body

Above right: a 1936 17 hp tourer with bodywork by Maultby incorporating a hydraulically operated hood

or repaired, and retained the same four tyres throughout the trial.

In 1923 a new small Armstrong Siddeley appeared—this was the 14 hp, a 2-litre four-cylinder model which had a flat radiator instead of the marque's distinctive vee-cooler. It was a refined and silent car, and there was a rare sporting version with vee-screen and cruiser tail, which was apparently 'sporting' only in appearance, with a maximum speed of little more than 45 mph.

About this time, too, Armstrong Siddeley aero engines were establishing an enviable reputation—Sir Alan Cobham used an Armstrong Siddeley Jaguar radial for his flight from London to Capetown and back—and it was not long afterwards that the slogan 'The Car of Aircraft Quality' was adopted.

The 1924 season saw the adoption of four-wheel brakes on the larger Armstrong Siddeley models: the range continued virtually unchanged until the end of 1927, when centralised chassis lubrication and automatic ignition advance and retard became standard features of all models. And on 1 November, 1927, deliveries of a new low-priced 15 hp six-cylinder Armstrong Siddeley began. A year later, it was joined by an even smaller six, the 1236cc 12 hp, which a former owner characterised as 'sluggish beyond belief'.

Also in 1929 came the option on all models of the Wilson pre-selective gearbox, which was really a harking back to one of the roots of the company, the veteran Wilson-Pilcher. This type of epicyclic transmission was standardised on Armstrong Siddeleys in 1933.

The 'aircraft quality' slogan was really taken seriously: at the company's Parkside works, aeroengines and cars were assembled in parallel, and the same Aeronautical Inspection Department standards were applied to both: thus a 1.2 litre 12 was finished to the same strict standards as a 47.5 litre 14-cylinder Leopard radial aeroengine.

For 1931, the stroke of the 12 was lengthened, bringing the swept volume up to 1434cc, while the 15 hp was now available in a choice of wheelbase lengths, with a general tidying-up of chassis design. The Short 15 had a three-speed transmission, the long 15 four speeds.

This was the period when luxuriously equipped Armstrong Siddeleys were doing well in events like the RAC Rally and the Monte Carlo Rally: the marque was even featured in a rare murder novel, *The Motor Rally Mystery*, by John Rhode, based on the author's experiences in the 1931 RAC Rally.

At the 1932 Motor Show the chassis of a magnificent new model was shown: this was the Siddeley Special, which had a 5-litre engine cast largely from Hiduminium light alloy—crankcase, block, cylinder head and sump were all of this material, though it seems likely that the same pattern of crankshaft and connecting rod which had served Armstrong Siddeley faithfully since 1919 was used, for the cylinder dimensions were identical with the old 30 hp model. This power unit, which gave a 6–93 mph performance in top gear, was mounted in a massively-built double-dropped chassis; standard wheelbase was 11 ft, but a 12 ft wheelbase was available for closed coachwork. Chassis price was £650, to which tourer coachwork added another £300.

The car did not reach production until the end of 1933, by which time a new sporting variant of the 12 hp, which had a vee-radiator instead of the models characteristic flat front, was also available. It had attractive close-coupled coupé coachwork which, claimed the newly knighted Sir John Siddeley was designed for 'the daughters of gentlemen'.

At the 1934 Motor Show, two more new Armstrong Siddeleys were revealed—these were the Seventeen and Seventeen Sports, both with a 2394 cc six-cylinder power unit, but having different wheelbase lengths

and suspension arrangements.

Armstrong Siddeley sales were strong with annual output generally around the thousand mark and it was observed that there were now 7000 employees at the Parkside works where there had been only 500 25 years earlier, in the days of the JDS-Deasy.

The Plus Twelve was a new model for the 1936 season; this had a 1670cc power unit 'to provide a greater reserve of power for arduous conditions'.

Another new Armstrong Siddeley was launched at the 1936 Motor Show, designed to compete in export markets and rated at 20/25 hp. Its robust 3666 cc engine—a six-cylinder of course—consumed petrol at 17–18 miles per gallon, and was capable of over 80 mph performance.

In 1937, Sir John Davenport Siddeley was elevated to the peerage, as Lord Kenilworth; there was some rationalisation among the car range that year, but the Armstrong Siddeley line-up remained virutally un-changed in basics until 1939, in which year the Siddeley Special was dropped after some 400 had been produced and two new medium-powered models were announced. The new models were the 1991 cc 16/6 and the 2783 cc 20.

Production was soon resumed after the war—in which Armstrong Siddeley built around 4000 Cheetah radial aeroengines for Ansons and Oxford training) reconnaisance aircraft, as well as tank transmissions and precision equipment for the Navy—doubtless due to the old parallel production system. Using the 1939 16/6 power unit, the company brought out Britain's

first postwar models, named after some of the famous warplanes produced by the Hawker Siddeley Group, of which the company was a member. These were initially the Lancaster four-door saloon, the Typhoon two-door sports saloon and the Hurricane drop-head coupé: their 'modern smooth-flowing lines' attracted much favourable comment, as did the adoption of torsion-bar independent front suspension and the adoption of heating/demisting equipment as standard. In 1948 came the Whitley, with a 2309cc engine, which power unit was standardised throughout the range in 1950.

At the 1952 Motor Show, the Sapphire luxury model was introduced, with a 3.4 litre engine and, for a while at least, the option of manual, preselective or automatic transmission. In 1958 came the Star Sapphire, with a 4-litre engine, disc brakes and power steering, with separate heating for the passenger compartment.

It succeeded two unsuccessful models, the 234 and 236, the former with a 2.3 litre engine having only four cylinders, the latter using the old longstroke six-cylinder power unit. Their bland lines and poor sales ensured their early demise, after being on sale only from 1956–58.

The Star Sapphire was a splendid car, offered only with automatic transmission: but in 1960, as a result of the merger between Hawker-Siddeley and the Bristol Aeroplane Company, the decision was made to stop car production. That summer saw the very last Armstrong Siddeley slowly drive out of the Parkside factory into the sun—and motoring history.   DBW

Above: a 1956 Sapphire automatic; this car was fitted with a 3.4-litre engine and was offered with the option of manual, preselective or fully automatic transmission

Switzerland's World beater

FATE SOMETIMES PLAYS strange tricks on racing drivers. While few would dispute that Jo Siffert was one of the fastest Formula One drivers of his time, it was in the exacting and exhausting field of endurance sports-car racing that he excelled. Siffert was born in Fribourg, Switzerland, on 7 July 1936. He started racing motor cycles in 1957 and by 1959 was the Swiss 350cc champion. Shortly afterwards he switched to four wheels using a Formula Junior Stanguellini. In 1961, he exchanged this machine for a Lotus 22 and soon began to make his mark on the European circuits. At the end of the year he was declared joint European Formula Junior champion with Trevor Taylor and Tony Maggs.

For 1962, Siffert bought a Formula One Lotus 24 and his World Championship F1 debut was made at the Belgium GP but with little success. The following season he joined the Swiss Ecurie Filipinetti team, driving their F1 Lotus-BRM. Apart from a win in the non-championship Syracuse GP and a second in the Imola GP, he again had a frustrating season. Having broken with the Filipinetti team during the 1963 season, he bought a Brabham-BRM for the following year. Although not ultra-competitive, the car enabled him to take a fourth place in the German GP. By this time his talent had been spotted by entrant Rob Walker who drafted the slim, mustacheod Swiss into his team alongside Swede Jo Bonnier. He immediately repayed Walker's confidence in him with a third in the United States GP behind Graham Hill and John Surtees.

For the following year, 1965, Rob Walker retained both Siffert and Bonnier. Siffert began the season well by winning the Mediterranean GP at Enna, beating Jim Clark in the process. He also finished fourth in the Mexican GP but the rest of his season was punctured by mechanical failures and retirements.

Nineteen-sixty-six saw the pattern repeated. Driving Rob Walker's heavy and uncompetitive Cooper-Maserati he could manage no better than fourth in the United States GP. 1966, however, was the year that Siffert began his sports-car racing career. It was the start of a very successful period that would establish Siffert as one of the greats.

Driving Ferraris and Porsches in 1967 he finished fourth at Sebring and Daytona, fifth at Monza, second at Spa, sixth at the Targa Florio and fifth at Le Mans while in World Championship Formula One events he finished fourth in both the French and US Grands Prix.

It was obvious by now that sports-car racing was Siffert's forte yet his 1968 season is best remembered for a spectacular win in the British Grand Prix driving the privately-entered Rob Walker Lotus 49 Cosworth. Apart from being perhaps the highlight of Siffert's career, it was also one of Rob Walker's proudest moments. Siffert followed this success with a fifth in the US Grand Prix and a sixth in the Mexican Grand Prix. In the field of sports-car racing he was now a member of the works Porsche team and provided them with some remarkable successes. He won the Daytona 24-hour event, the Sebring 12-hour race and the Nürburgring 1000 kms and, single-handed, the Austrian 1000 race. In addition to these successes, he had also set fastest lap times in the British, Canadian and Mexican GPs.

In F1 in 1969 he took fourth in South Africa, third at Monaco, second in Holland and fifth in Germany. In sports cars, Siffert proved unbeatable. Sharing a works Porsche with British sports-car ace Brian Redman, Siffert won the BOAC 1000 kms, the Monza, Spa, and Nürbur-

gring events and the Watkins Glen 6-hour race. Co-driving a Porsche 917 with Kurt Ahrens, he also won the Austrian 1000kms. Apart from being his most successful season, 1969 was also his most varied. Driving a Formula Two BMW he finished second at the Eifelrennen and fourth overall in the Can-Am sports car series.

For 1970, Siffert signed to drive for the much-publicised new March Formula One team. Alas, Siffert's year proved to be a disaster with retirement after retirement. In sports cars, however, he continued to excel. Sharing with Brian Redman, he drove a Porsche 908/3 to victory in the demanding Targa Florio. He followed this with a win in the Spa 1000kms, seconds in the Daytona 24-hour and Watkins Glen 6-hour events and victory in the Austrian 1000 kms race.

Unhappy with his year at March, Siffert signed for the BRM F1 team in 1971. He finished sixth in Holland, fourth in France and then led the Austrian GP from start to finish to take his second World Championship Grand Prix victory. Later in the year he finished second in the US GP thus gaining enough points to finish joint fourth with Jacky Ickx in the World Championship table. In sports-car events he was also successful, gaining a win in the Buenos Aires 1000kms, seconds at Monza, Spa, Nürburgring and Watkins Glen and a third in the BOAC.

At the end of 1971, the Mexican GP was cancelled. To replace it, a non-championship F1 race was organised at Brands Hatch to celebrate Jackie Stewart's World Championship title victory. The event was held on 24 October 1971 and it proved to be Jo Siffert's last race. At over 130mph, the BRM left the track, cannoned into an embankment, overturned and exploded into flames, killing its driver. The race was halted and slowly the stunned spectators made their way home, mourning the loss of one of motor racing's most fearless and popular drivers. MW

Below: Swiss ace Jo Siffert driving the Formula One Yardley-sponsored BRM in 1971

LETTING OTHERS KNOW YOUR INTENTIONS

So that others can prepare for your manoeuvres, it is advisable to broadcast yours as clearly as possible

WITH THE ADVENT of winking indicators and automatic stop lights, hand signals have almost disappeared; they are used mostly during driving tests and by people who endeavour to cool their bodies by keeping one elbow out of the side window. In fact the law in Britain no longer requires that hand signals be used; nevertheless, a great deal of danger can be avoided by warning other drivers of one's intentions, especially where stopping is concerned.

In the early days of motoring, cars were not equipped with any form of warning device, so it was necessary for a driver to use his arm to warn other road users of every direction alteration or speed change he was proposing to make. Then, semaphore indicators became standard fittings on most cars, so that it was possible for another driver or a pedestrian to be forewarned of any intention to execute a turn. Unfortunately, however, the semaphore arm could only be seen by people watching from the correct side of the car, due to its diminutive size and its position on the door pillar or the scuttle. In these instances it was still well worth a driver stretching his arm out of the window and making sure that his message was reaching the right people.

It was some time after the introduction of the semaphore indicator that brake-warning lights came on to the scene. Early cars had not been fast enough or common enough to warrant this sort of luxury, although brake efficiency was limited to say the least. As speeds rose and motor cars became available to those with not a vast amount of money, some form of brake warning became desirable. The obvious answer was to fit a light or lights which were illuminated at the command of a switch connected to the brake pedal.

The main drawback with the stop light is that it only indicates that the brakes have been applied—not how hard the pedal has been pressed (except in the case of certain experimental set-ups). This means that a following driver may see a stop light in operation and assume that the vehicles to which it is fitted is only slowing gently when in fact it is stopping as quickly as possible.

A simple hand signal (a straight arm and hand raised vertically from the elbow) will tell the following driver that the car is stopping, while a straight horizontal arm, waved up and down, warns that the car is merely decelerating. If stop lights are to be relied on they must be checked regularly, as following drivers will expect them to be in working order and may well decide to inspect the car's boot if this is not the case.

Right and left-turn signals are not really necessary, now that winkers are situated not only at front and back but on the side as well, but a driving-test examiner will expect a new driver to know how to use these and to demonstrate this knowledge for the first few nervous turns of the test. Also, the examiner may ask awkward questions, such as 'How do you indicate a left turn to a person in front of the vehicle?', the answer to which

is that you should hold your left arm in a horizontal position across the car.

As a general rule, hand signals should be used at all times when they may benefit other road users, so a driver should keep a keen watch all round his vehicle and pay special attention to the mirror.   IW

Below: a page from the British Highway Code, showing how hand signals should be used on the roads of Britain

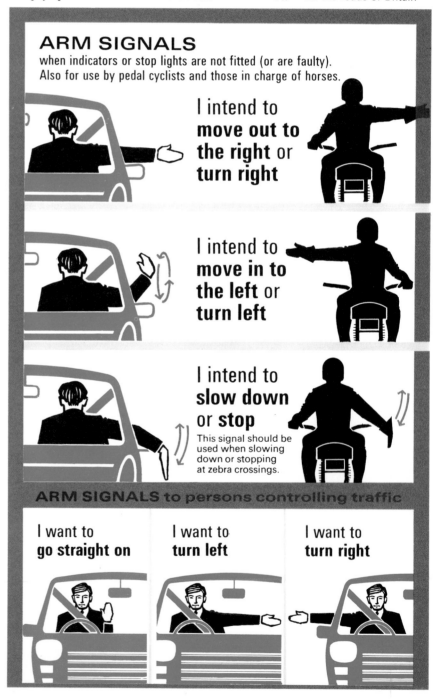

ARM SIGNALS
when indicators or stop lights are not fitted (or are faulty).
Also for use by pedal cyclists and those in charge of horses.

I intend to **move out to the right** or **turn right**

I intend to **move in to the left** or **turn left**

I intend to **slow down** or **stop**
This signal should be used when slowing down or stopping at zebra crossings.

ARM SIGNALS to persons controlling traffic

I want to **go straight on**

I want to **turn left**

I want to **turn right**

BRITAIN'S FOREMOST AIRFIELD RACING CIRCUIT

An otherwise humble ex-air force airfield has now assumed a second life as one of Britain's two premier motor-race circuits

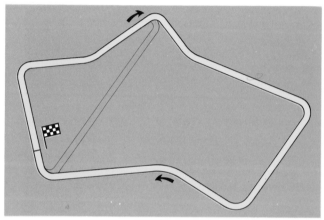

COMPARED to some luxurious venues in other countries, Silverstone is not the ideal motor racing circuit. It never was when it was first used in October 1948, and it was no better in 1975 when freak weather conditions brought a premature halt to the John Player British Grand Prix. But Silverstone is Britain's premier motor racing circuit and attracts large and enthusiastic crowds. Every two years it is the home of the British Grand Prix; it is the present venue of Europe's oldest-established race, the Tourist Trophy; it hosts major internationals for sports cars, Formula 5000 and Formula Two single-seaters and motorcycles.

When World War II was concluded in 1945 the French were quick to organise motor racing. Other countries followed suit but Britain had nowhere to organise an important meeting apart from the Isle of Man, Northern Ireland or Jersey where local laws permitted racing on public roads. In the pre-war days there were the Donington Park and Brooklands circuits, but Donington, near Derby, had been requisitioned by the government and was still covered in military equipment and Brooklands, in Surrey, had been sold to Vickers Armstrong in January 1946 and was part of Britain's aircraft industry.

The Royal Automobile Club made several attempts to locate a suitable venue for international motor racing and eventually, in July 1948, it was revealed that negotiations with various bodies had been successful. In October the British Grand Prix was to be run at Silverstone Airfield. Silverstone, straddling the border of Buckinghamshire and Northamptonshire, became an RAF station in March 1943 and was chiefly used for training crews of Wellington bombers. Four-and-a-half years later the bleak venue was abandoned, apparently disused. The surrounding land was put to good use by a farmer, but from time to time people brought their racing cars to test them on the runways . . . unofficially, of course.

No one among the huge crowd which invaded Silverstone on 2 October, 1948, could have possibly imagined the old airfield as Britain's top racing circuit.

Mud, Nissen huts, barbed wire and pieces of old aircraft provided the background to the circuit which was a combination of the perimeter track and inside runways lined with straw bales to provide a slow, 3.67-mile circuit. The start/finish line and the pits were situated on the straight between Abbey Curve and Woodcote and the circuit followed the perimeter to Copse where cars turned sharp right up the runway. A sharp left took cars back to the perimeter road after Maggots. Then it was round Becketts, Chapel Curve and down the Hangar Straight to Stowe where a very tight right-hander took cars up the runway. A hairpin left then took cars to Club Corner and then it was back up to Abbey Curve and the start/finish area. The two corners on the infield runway were known as Segrave and Seaman, named after Britain's two pre-war Grand Prix winners.

The first post-war British Grand Prix was dominated by works Maserati 4CLT/48 drivers Luigi Villoresi and Alberto Ascari, the Italians scoring an easy 1-2 victory despite having to start from the back of the grid through lack of practice. Loudly cheered was

Top left: Alberto Ascari's Ferrari Sport at Silverstone in 1950

Top: from this map, one can clearly see why Silverstone is a fast track

Above: the start of an historic-car meeting in the 1970s

Britain's Bob Gerard who took a gallant third place in his pre-war ERA.

Plans were quickly drawn-up for the 1949 Grand Prix to be run at Silverstone on May 14. The circuit layout was revised, however. Gone was the interior runway, leaving just the perimeter road with a slow, 15 mph chicane at Club Corner which meant a lap distance of 3 miles. Swiss driver Emmanuel de Graffenried (Maserati 4CLT/48) was the winner from Gerard's ERA. Another full-scale international meeting, sponsored by the *Daily Express* and organised by the British Racing Drivers' Club, was scheduled for 20 August and this time the Club chicane was removed, reducing the circuit length to 2.972 miles.

Silverstone was growing up. For 1950 Club, Copse and Stowe corners were eased to reduce the lap length further to 2.8886 miles and the scene was set for the 'Royal Silverstone'. HM King George VI, Queen Elizabeth and other members of the Royal Family attended the Grand Prix on 13 May. It was the first time a road race in Britain had been attended by a reigning monarch; it was also the first time *Grand Prix d'Europe* had been granted to a British race; and it was the firstever race anywhere to qualify for the newly-instigated World Championship of Drivers. Alfa Romeo, making a return to racing in what turned out to be a successful attempt to win the World Championship, scored a 1-2-3 success, Giuseppe Farina leading home Luigi Fagioli and Reg Parnell. Britain's great hope, the V16 BRM, was unready, making a parade lap only. The BRM was due to make it's race *début* at the *Daily Express* Trophy meeting three months later but, as is embarrassingly well-recorded in motor racing history, it broke a drive-shaft on the line.

Perhaps Silverstone's greatest short-coming has been its flatness and consequent poor drainage. The 1951 *Daily Express* Trophy had to be halted after six laps after a torrential downpour which completely flooded the track, not to mention the cockpits of the racing cars. The problem recurred several times after, at both international and small club meetings, most notably at the 1975 John Player British Grand Prix when no fewer than 10 cars crashed within seconds following a sudden downpour. The race had to be red-flagged to a stop with 56 of the scheduled 67 laps run.

From 1949 the circuit became increasingly regularly used by amateurs and semi-professionals for club meetings and in 1951 the first of a long series of six-hour relay races was held. At first a 2.4-mile layout using part perimeter road and part runway was employed, but soon a 1.608-mile affair was utilised, one which remains to the present. The Club Circuit comprises the perimeter road from Woodcote to Becketts and a runway which links them.

In 1952 the RAC handed over operations of the circuit to the British Racing Drivers' Club and several improvements were made prior to the start of the season, including easier access to and from the public enclosures and protective earth banks. Grandstands which had been erected between Woodcote and Copse Corners in 1950 now overlooked a new start/finish line and pits and with a slight modification to Woodcote the lap length was increased to 2.927 miles, the official figure which remained until 1975.

Shortly before the 1975 John Player-sponsored British Grand Prix it was announced that a chicane would be laid-out at Woodcote corner in an attempt to reduce speeds. This was as a result of comments made by Grand Prix constructors about the safety of spectators in the grandstands. Woodcote had become

a 160 mph corner and drivers considered it to be one of the most difficult in the world. However, should a car go into a spin there was a chance that its aerodynamic aids—ie, the rear wing—could have the opposite effect if the car went backwards. Instead of giving the car extra bite, it could cause it to take off. A debris fence had already been erected, but this was not considered strong enough to arrest a Grand Prix car. The chicane reduced speeds to 120 mph, adding $3\frac{1}{2}$ seconds to lap times, but Silverstone—now 2.932 miles long—remained Britain's fastest circuit, except the lap record was now 130.47 mph instead of 135.96 mph.

Lap speeds rose dramatically in the 1960s. Before

Above: a Connaught leads a Cooper-Bristol in one of Silverstone's famous historic-car races

later when his Brabham BT7-Climax conquered Hill's BRM P261 in similar fashion. For drama in front of a packed grandstand, little can equal the flaming multiple accident after one lap of the 1973 John Player British Grand Prix? Eight cars were eliminated in spectacular fashion, yet there was only one injury as Italian driver Andrea de Adamich left the race with leg injuries.

The face of Silverstone continually changed. Oil drums which marked the corners were replaced with low concrete walls and in 1970 these, in turn, were scrapped to give way to plastic marker cones. Following two fatal accidents in 1963 the pit area was completely rebuilt for the following season, being elevated and reached via a ramp. Eleven years later these were pulled down to be replaced by one of the largest and most sophisticated pit areas in the world, reputedly costing £120,000. Over the years other modifications have included a press/television tower at Woodcote, spectator and vehicles bridges, permanent buildings and a ring-road to ease spectator entrance and exit. Silverstone has also kept pace with constant demands for safety improvements by drivers, including better run-on areas, catch-fencing and guard-rails.

With the growth of post-war motor racing in Britain it was inevitable other circuits would wish to take the Grand Prix from Silverstone. The RAC, indeed, gave the date to Aintree in 1955, 1957, 1959, 1961 and 1962 and from 1964 the Grand Prix has been run every two years at Brands Hatch. (In order to allow the circuits to plan well ahead, the RAC agreed the British Grand Prix should alternate between Silverstone and Brands Hatch until the end of the 1970s.)

The annual *Daily Express* Trophy meeting has been run for Formula One cars on all but three occasions; in 1952 and 1953 it was for Formula Two and in 1961 for Inter-Continental Formula cars. The list of winners includes such names as Ascari, Farina, Hawthorn, Gonzalez, Moss, Behra, Collins, Brabham, Clark, Stewart, Hulme, Hill, Fittipaldi, Hunt and Lauda. From 1960 to 1974 Martini sponsored a major race at Silverstone, usually for sports cars, while GKN backed Formula 5000 cars. The Tourist Trophy found a home at Silverstone in 1970 and but for 1971, when it was cancelled, has been run to its original format for production cars. A major Formula Two international was due to be held in 1975.

Silverstone has a long, interesting and intriguing background. Many have been the surprise victories, the heartbreaks, the grandstand finishes. It is an ever-changing place. Gone are the relics of the aircraft; in their place are the trimmings of a full-scale international motor racing circuit. It is difficult to believe that what used to be an old wartime airfield could evoke nostalgia, but Silverstone has a unique atmosphere that has to be sampled to be appreciated. It is a circuit loved by the motor racing enthusiast. MK

Far left: Carlos Pace's Brabham leads a stream of 1975 F1 GP cars through the Woodcote esses; this 'chicane' was added in 1975 to reduce speeds through the almost flat-out corner, where cars entered at nearly 165 mph. It was thought that in the unfortunate case of a car going out of control at that speed, catch fencing and Armco would do little to restrain it from the grandstands

Near left: a group of mid 60s F1 cars come off the Hangar straight into Stowe; one can see the flat, airfield nature of the circuit

Above: World Champion for '74, Emerson Fittipaldi, hounds Lauda at Beckett's corner in the 1975 *Daily Express* Trophy race; the two were as close as this at the finish line

the 1960 *Daily Express* Trophy meeting the lap record stood at 105.37 mph; after the race winner Innes Ireland (2.5-litre Lotus 18-Climax) had raised this to 111.86 mph and by the end of the decade the 120 mph barrier had been well and truly cracked and 130 mph was in easy reach. (But for the introduction of the Woodcote chicane, 140 mph laps were a possibility before the end of the 1970s.) In the 1960s and 1970s Silverstone saw many more exciting motor races. There was Graham Hill's determined and successful chase of Jim Clark in the 1962 *Daily Express* Trophy where Hill's BRM P56 literally pipped Clark's Lotus 24-Climax on the finish line. Ironically enough, Jack Brabham meted out the same treatment two years

CHRYSLER'S FRENCH OUTPOST

Simca started building Fiats under licence but soon took to building their own, typically French, cars

THE FRENCH SIMCA COMPANY was founded in November 1934 by Henri-Theodore Pigozzi to manufacture Fiat cars for the French market. The name Simca is taken from the initials of the original company, Ste. Industrielle de Mecanique et Carrosserie Automobile which had its headquarters and factory at Nanterre on the Seine in Paris.

The factory in which the company first began production had previously been owned by SA des Automobiles Donnet, a company which from 1924 until its demise in 1934, had built a number of cars under the names of Donnet and Donnet-Zedel, including a 7CV Type G which had a side-valve four cylinder engine of 1100cc and a four speed gear box in 1924 and a 750cc two stroke model in 1932.

Simca's first efforts were virtually identical to their Italian counterparts with the first model being the Tipo 508 Balilla powered by a three bearing, short stroke 995cc engine. The car had hydraulic brakes, a four speed synchromeshed gearbox and four door pillarless saloon bodywork. Simca also produced their version of the Fiat 1.9 litre 518 model and this went into production in the French factory in 1935.

Shortly afterwards Fiat introduced the legendary 500 Topolino and Simca manufactured this in France as the Simca Cinq. The Cinq had a 570cc side valve four cylinder engine mounted in front of the radiator; hydraulic brakes; synchromesh box, independent front suspension and a two seater fabric roll top convertible body. At that time, in France it sold for 9,900 francs.

A year later, in 1937, after Fiat had introduced the 508C Millicento with a 1,089cc ohv 32hp engine and four door body, Simca again produced their version in France and called it the Huit.

It was the Simca Huit which Amedee Gordini developed in the 1930s into a car which was capable of winning, with him at the wheel, the Index of Performance at Le Mans in 1939. Gordini had previously developed more highly tuned versions of other models of the 508 and of the Simca Cinq, raising its output to 28bhp. Gordini was also responsible for Simca versions of the 508 range winning the small sports car race at Rheims, the Bol d'Or and the Paris to Nice Rally in the same year.

Between 1936 and 1939 Simca's production rose steadily to a peak in 1938 and achieving Pigozzi's ambition of producing 20,000 cars in a single year. In 1936 the company built 7,283 Simca Cinqs; in 1937 this rose to 12,925 Cinqs and 318 Simca Huits. The 1938 production figures were 14,194 Cinqs and 6,739 Huits. A pre-war production record, it was achieved despite a 45 day long strike which totally paralysed production at the Nanterre factory and left the entire company in a financially precarious situation as it entered the year of 1939.

Nevertheless in 1939 Simca managed to produce 12,131 Simca Cinq models and 7,680 Simca Huits. Until July production averaged 2,000 cars a month,

The first Simca cars were built under licence from Fiat; *above*, is the F11, based on the Balilla and built in 1935, while, *left*, is the French company's version of the famous 500 Topolino, named the Simca Cinq

but in August, as the clouds of war began to gather, over the European continent, it slumped to 760 cars per month.

In September 1939 Germany invaded Poland and France declared war on Germany. In June 1940 German armed forces entered Paris and a week later the French surrendered. Little damage was done to the Simca factory and, indeed, the French company continued to produce cars in gradually decreasing numbers throughout the war years. In 1940 they produced 3,604 Cinqs and 1,911 Huits; in 1942, 632 Cinqs and 2,217 Huits; in 1944 23 Cinqs and 180 Huits and in 1945 47 Cinqs and 65 Huits.

In 1942 Simca had joined Baron Petiet's Groupe Francaise Automobile selling consortium together with Delahaye and Delage, but the company terminated this arrangement at the end of the war.

By 1947 Simca surged ahead with 3,733 Cinqs and 8,053 Huits and introduced the Simca Six, an overhead valve equivalent of Fiats 500C and in that year built 11 of them. In that year Simca were building six

Top: a Fiat-engined 1100 cc Simca racer seen in 1938; only a few examples of this model were built

Above: the Simca Huit of 1949 was available in six different versions, although all used the 1200 cc engine

Right: also based on the Topolino theme was this Six of 1949

versions of the Huit, the Decouvrable, the Berline, the Coupé, the Break, the Fourgonnette and the Camionette. In 1948 production had risen to 3,901 Cinqs, 14,074 Huits and 191 Sixes but the company were not to see production top the pre-war 20,000 mark until a year later.

In 1949 the Cinq was gradually being phased out of production and that year the Simca company produced only 221 units of the car which had been in production for 13 years. That year's final production figure of 26,614 units was largely made up with 15,580 Huits and 10,813 Sixes and in 1950 production went over the 30,000 mark for the first time when 26,258 Huits and 5,497 Sixes rolled out of the factory.

Gordini resumed his development and racing work with Simca after the end of the war and continued to breed race winning machines until 1951 when he came out from underneath the Simca umbrella and set up as a manufacturer of high performance cars in his own right. In 1947 Gordini had developed for Simca a 1100 cc single seater sports car which had a

number of successes on circuits including first, second and third places in the Coupé des Petites Cylindrees at Rheims.

The following year saw the cars with five bearing crankshafts and a victory in the Bol d'Or and a class win in the 1948 Belgian 24 Hour Race. Gordini's later efforts for Simca saw the cars equipped with $1\frac{1}{2}$ litre power units and their victories culminated in Trintignant's victory in the Albi Grand Prix in 1951.

1949 had seen the introduction of a Sport Cabriolet version of the Huit and 1950 the introduction of a Sports Coupé version. In 1949 a Cabriolet Sport type won its class in the Alpine Rally, while the following year two standard Huits took a brace of class wins in that year's Monte Carlo Rally.

The following Spring a new model was shown in secret to the Simca management—the Simca 9. Although the 45 hp engine which powered it was a modified form of the engine which had powered the Huit, the rest of the car was entirely new and incorporated coil and wishbone independent suspension at the front and hypoid final drive. Much discussion followed the presentation of the car to the Simca board as to a suitable name for their new creation, and, eventually, they decided on the name 'L'Aronde'. This name was chosen because the symbol of the Simca marque was the swallow and the ancient French word for swallow was L'Aronde.

In June the model was launched to the public and production began in earnest in the October after the factory at Nanterre had been extensively modernised and new mass production machinery installed. With production of the Six terminating at the end of the previous year, Simca turned their efforts towards producing nearly 30,000 L'Arondes in the short time left to them in 1951 to add to the 20,568 units of the only other model they were still producing, the Huit.

From the moment of its launch the Aronde was a startling success and at the end of 1952, when production of the Huit had been phased down to a mere 27 before ending completely, production of the Aronde had reached a staggering 69,028 units. In 1953 and 1954 the Aronde was the only car which Simca were building, with production rising from 61,567 units in 1953 to 92,432 units in 1954 by which time there were six versions of the Aronde available including a Coupé de Ville model which had a 5 km per hour faster top speed than the standard 1,221 cc version. In 1954 the Aronde was put on the British market at a list price of £896.

In 1953 an Aronde achieved the startling performance of completing 100,000 kilometres at a constant speed of 100 km/hr. Production of the Aronde continued until 1964 when only 21 units were built, with the 500,000th Aronde being delivered in January 1957 and the 1,000,000th in February 1960. In 1955 the Aronde had been the first Simca car to take their production in a year over 100,000 mark. Altogether Simca manufactured just under $1\frac{1}{2}$ million Arondes in its twelve year production history.

In the meantime Simca had bought Unic in 1951 a company which had been founded in 1904 to build private cars but which ceased production with the outbreak of World War II, and Ford's subsidiary in France in 1954, giving them what is still their largest manufacturing plant at Poissy, Seine-et-Oise sind the rights to manufacture the Ford Vedette.

The Vedette had been introduced by Ford after World War II and was a fastback powered by a 2.2 litre 63 bhp V8 first introduced in 1936. Ford had also introduced, prior to the takeover, a Comete version with a sports coupe type of body. The 1953 models had

Left: the Grand Large two-door version of the Aronde which was produced in 1957; it featured a 1221 cc engine

Below left: another version of the Aronde, this being the 1962 Elisée

Right, from top to bottom: the 944 cc, four-cylinder 1000 of 1961;

a later version of the 1000;

the 1301 saloon of 1970. This car was also available in 1501 and estate-car versions;

the Special version of the 1100; this car had an engine of 1294 cc, despite its title

'notch' backs and the 1954 models a 3.9 litre V8 power unit and when Simca took over the 1955 models were given an 80 bhp version of the 2.2 litre V8 which continued in production as Simca Vedettes.

Gradually the Poissy factory began to take over production of all Simca models which in 1955 consisted of versions of the Aronde and the Vedette, with the company producing 115,646 Arondes and 42,349 Vedettes that year. The Nanterre works were eventually turned over to Citroen in 1961.

In 1956 Simca also bought the French subsidiary of Saurer, a company which had been established in Switzerland in 1897 to build motor cars but which had turned to the development of diesel engines and trucks in the first year of World War I.

In the following year Simca introduced the Ariane 4, a development of the Aronde and powered by the same 1290 cc power unit, but with the bodywork of the V8 Vedette Berlines.

In 1959 Simca bought their last company, Talbot, a company financed by Englishmen but producing in a factory in Suresnes. With an enviable list of competition successes behind them prior to the Simca takeover, the Suresnes factory continued to compete in races with the Ford V8 engine. Although a coupé Talbot appeared at the Paris Salon in 1960 powered by a Simca Aronde engine the car did not go into production and the Talbot name has ceased to be used by Simca.

A year earlier, in 1958, Simca themselves sold 15 per cent of their shares to the Chrysler Corporation of America and took the first step towards their eventual complete takeover by the American company. Chrysler achieving their share in Simca by purchasing the shares which had been attributed to the Ford Motor Company when the Simca-Ford S.A.F. merger took place. At the same time Chrysler announced that their Australian factory in Adelaide would build Arondes under licence for the Australian market.

Again in the same year the Simca Vedette was given a 84 bhp 2351 cc power unit and so was the Ariane. Production of the Vedette continued until 1961 when units built totalled 166,895 though at least two versions were being built under licence in Brazil until 1967.

Development work had also been continuing throughout the financial negotiations on the Aronde range with a 1090 cc 6CV model being introduced in 1959 together with a 1290 cc 7CV version and the 1290 cc P60 versions. Models of the Aronde continued in production until 1964, as did also models of the Ariane of which 159,418 units had been built by the end of its production life.

In 1960 the first Société Simca was split into two companies: Simca Automobiles and Simca Industries, with Simca Automobiles receiving from the old Simca company all assets and facilities regarding the production of passenger cars and in particular the Poissy manufacturing plants.

Two years later Simca Automobiles produced their first new car under the new structure, the Simca 1000. A 944 cc rear engined saloon, the 1000 had a five bearing crankshaft, all round independent suspension,

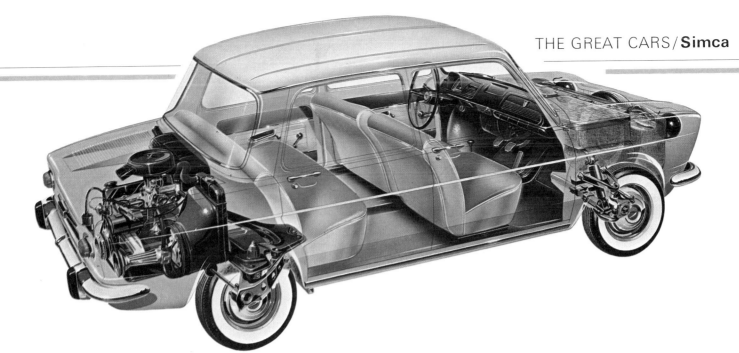

a four speed all synchromesh gearbox and had the radiator mounted alongside the engine. Production had begun at the end of 1961 with an initial stock of 9,670, but by the end of 1962 Simca had produced a further 154,282 and by the end of 1973 the company had constructed a total of 1,417,825 units. When the car first went on sale in France it was cheaper than Citroën's Ami 6. The saloon was quickly joined by a Bertone styled coupé using the same power unit and technical specification.

In 1963 the Simca 900 was added to the range which was also powered by the 944 cc unit, and this model was joined by a 1300 version powered by a 1290 cc unit and a 1500 version powered by a 1475 cc engine. The following year a 'brake' version was added to the range.

It was also in 1963 that the Chrysler Corporation increased their interest in Simca to a majority share holding of 64 per cent and in which M. Georges Hereil was named President-Director General of Simca. The following year Henri-Theodore Piggozi quietly passed away.

Also in 1964 work began on a new production plant for Simca cars at La Rochelle and operations began there in 1965. Today that plant produces front and rear suspension, components for engines and gear boxes as well as shock absorbers. At the end of 1965 Simca Automobiles handed over all their assets to a new company, called Société des Automobiles Simca. Later on, Simca Industries contributed to Société des Automobiles Simca the shares they held in Société de Metallurgie Automobile and in this way the basic products plant came back under the control of Simca Automobiles. The Simca 900 ceased production in the same year.

In 1966 the Simca 1000 became available with the option of a Ferodo three speed semi-automatic gearbox and the 1500 with a Borg Warner fully automatic box, and the Simca 1000 van was introduced. The Chrysler Corporation increased their share in Simca to 77 per cent in 1967. That year also saw the introduction of uprated versions of the 1300 and 1500 to become the 1301 and 1501 and the addition of the Simca 1200S coupé which was powered by a 1204 cc unit.

A year later Simca introduced their transverse engined, front wheel drive 1100. Powered by a 1118 cc engine, the car was available in two- and four-door versions and various standards of trim, in addition to two 'brake' versions. Production of the 1100 passed the one million mark in 1973.

1969 saw the introduction of the austerity Simca 4CV which was powered by a 777 cc engine which gave the car a top speed of 121 km/hr; of the 1000 Special with an 1118cc unit; of the 1100 5CV with 944cc unit of the Simca 1000; and of the 1501 Special using the same 1475cc unit as before but with greater performance. The same year Simca took Matra Sports srl into the fold, the company which had been founded by Engin Matra to run Renault engined sports cars inherited from the defunct Rene Bonnet concern and updated Cosworth-Ford engined Formula Three racing cars. That year Simca's car production amounted to 351,403 units compared with 206,751 in 1958, an increase of 69 per cent in eleven years.

By the time the Chrysler Corporation had increased its share holding in Simca to 99.3 per cent, in July 1970, and changed the name of the company to Chrysler France, Simca had embarked on one of the biggest investment programmes in their history. At Poissy extensions were made to the pressing machine plant and the assembly lines as well as to the electroplating, paint and trim workshops; at Vernon a new commercial vehicle spare parts depot was built; at Carrieres-sous-Poissy a new research centre was built to supplant the previous one at Argenteuil and a complete modernisation programme was carried out at the company's Mortefontaine proving ground. In addition the La Rochelle plant was doubled in size and the decision was taken to start work on a new assembly plant at Valenciennes.

All Simca cars since 1967 carried the Chrysler Penta-

Below: the Chrysler 180 which was built by Simca; the car featured an 1812 cc four-cylinder engine

Bottom: the 1307 and 1308 Simcas, which were marketed under name Chrysler Alpine in Great Britain

star symbol but in September 1970, the first Chrysler named model, the 160, was launched. Originally designed by Rootes, the Chrysler company decided to export the design and the jigs to France and then re-import the 160 into Britain. Three versions were available, one powered by a 1639cc engine and the other two by a 1.8 litre engine.

In September 1971 M. Gwain H. Gillespie was appointed President-Director General of Chrysler France. The following year saw the introduction of the Simca 1000 Rallye 1 with a 1294cc engine and of Simca 1000 and 1100 Specials. 1972 was also the year that the Simca Racing Team was formed and in June that year a Matra-Simca was driven to victory at Le Mans by Graham Hill and Henri Pescarolo—a feat which was repeated again in 1973 with Pescarolo again at the wheel but with Larrousse as co-driver. In the September of 1972 the Simca Rallye 2 was introduced. In December the total production figures for a year long period passed the 500,000 mark for the first time in Simca history.

Early in 1973 G. H. Gillespie was succeeded by Franklin M. Rogers as President-Director General and a month later, in the February, the Chrysler 2 litre automatic was introduced. This was joined the following month by the three seater, two door Matra Simca Bagheera which was powered by a 1294cc transverse mid-engine. The same year the new factory at Valenciennes went into production, and the number of Simca 1100s built passed the one million mark. In the December it was announced that Matra-Simca had won the Manufacturer's World Championship, and Simca's total car production since its formation reached six million.

At the end of 1973 Chrysler France were producing six versions of the Simca 1000; eight versions of the Simca 1100; two versions of the 1301 and two of the 1501, together with the Chrysler 160, 180 and 2 litre. This range carried on into the energy crisis year of new models. Nineteen-seventy-five promises for a new automobile looked more than usually interesting from Chrysler's European operations but political considerations made themselves evident and were presenting particularly difficult obstacles and generally hampering its launch.   BJ

1307/1308

Mid July 1975 saw the introduction of the 1307/1308 Simcas, known in Britain as Chrysler Alpine GL and S, respectively.

The cars are very loosely based on the Simca 1100 series, although there have been many improvements, including an impressive new body.

Two power units are available for the Alpine; a 1294 cc engine for the GL and a 1442 cc one for the S, both pushrod fours. In smaller form, it produces 68 bhp and 79 lb ft of torque. This gives a top speed of 92 mph, enables it to accelerate to 60 mph from rest in 15.5 secs. The GL's fuel consumption is 33 mpg. In larger S form, the engine produces 85 bhp and 93 lb ft of torque. Top speed for this version is 101 mph; the acceleration from 0–60 mph takes 13.5 secs and it returns 30 miles for each gallon of petrol.

The Alpines use independent suspension all round and, with their front-wheel drive, corner quite quickly. With long, double-acting dampers and a large (8 in) ground clearance, the cars provide their passengers a soft ride on even the bumpy minor roads of France. Steering is by rack and pinion, while braking is by discs all round. There is a neat load-sensitive control valve, linked to the suspension, valve on the rear brakes.

A sleek, aerodynamic five-door, six-light body clothes the Alpines and gives it a competitive modern look as any of its competitors. If necessary, the rear seat can be folded down to make an exceedingly large luggage platform.

Altogether, this new car, designed at Coventry, England and built at Poissy, France, is practical, elegant and very roomy.

ENGINE Front-mounted, water-cooled straight-four, transversely mounted and inclined 41° rear-wards. 76.7 mm (3.02 in) bore × 70 mm (2.76 in) stroke = 1294 cc (79 cu in) (GL), or 76.7 mm (3.02 in) bore × 78 mm (3.07 in) stroke = 1442 cc (87.9 cu in) (S). Maximum power (DIN) 68 bhp at 5600 rpm (GL), or 85 bhp at 5600 rpm (S); maximum torque (DIN) 79 lb ft at 2800 rpm (GL), or 93 lb ft at 3000 rpm (S). Cast-iron cylinder block and light-alloy head. Compression ratio 9.5:1. 5 main bearings. 2 valves per cylinder operated, via pushrod and rockers, by a single camshaft, side.

TRANSMISSION Single-dry-plate clutch and four-speed manual gearbox. Ratios, 1st 3.906, 2nd 2.315, 3rd 1.524, 4th 1.080, rev 3.77:1. Spiral-bevel final drive. Ratio, 3.706.

CHASSIS Integral.

SUSPENSION Front—independent by wishbones, longitudinal torsion bars, an anti-roll bar and telescopic dampers, rear—independent by wide-based trailing arms, coil springs, an anti-roll bar and telescopic dampers.

STEERING Rack and pinion. Turns from lock to lock 4.

BRAKES Servo-assisted front discs and rear drums.

WHEELS 5 in × 13 in steel.

TYRES 155SR × 13.

DIMENSIONS AND WEIGHT Wheelbase 102.5 in; track—front 55.7 in, rear—54.7 in; length 167 in; width 66 in; height 55.1 in; ground clearance 8 in; dry weight 2314 lb; turning circle between walls 34 ft; fuel tank capacity 13.25 gals.

BODY 5-door, 5-seater saloon.

PERFORMANCE Maximum speed 92 mph (GL), or 101 mph (S). Acceleration 0–60 mph 15.5 secs (GL), or 13.5 secs (S). Fuel consumption 30–33 mpg.

LIMOUSINES & RACING CARS

Simplex started as low-priced limousines, but these were soon adapted successfully for use in racing

IF YOU WANTED TO BUY an elegant, expensive imported car in New York at the turn of the century, *the* place to go was Smith & Mabley, Incorporated, of 513–519 7th Avenue, who were agents for Mercedes, Panhard and Renault. For $12,750 they would sell you a 28/32 hp Mercedes with 'Vedrine King of the Belgians' bodywork complete with canopy, windscreen, wicker luncheon baskets and umbrella holder and paint it any colour you chose. But out of that $12,750, a swingeing 40 per cent was an *ad valorem* import duty: and, reckoned Messrs Smith and Mabley, anything Europe's finest makers could do, they could manage to equal—at a lower price.

So, in 1904, they began building an 18 hp luxury car which they called the S & M Simplex; with a four-cylinder engine, angle steel chassis and coachwork in the latest Roi-des-Belges style, including exaggerated ploughshare front mudwings. The S & M Simplex followed contemporary European practice in design of car and coachwork (an individual touch was the provision of an elegant little chest of drawers built in under the front seat).

During 1904 the engine size was increased to 30 hp (5.2 litres); fully equipped the S & M Simplex cost $6750, which showed that Smith & Mabley had got their sums right.

There was also a 'special 75 hp' racing car of 14.7 litres: Smith & Mabley, perhaps wanting to keep the plate glass windows in their showroom unbroken, supplied one of these to young Frank Croker, whose father ran the city's corrupt Tammany Hall political organisation. Liberally drilled to bring it inside the weight limit for the 1904 Vanderbilt Cup Eliminating Trials, the Simplex folded in the middle during the race, and finished with its gearbox dragging in the road. Croker took the car—with a new chassis, of course—to the Ormond Beach speed trials in January 1905, where he wrote off the car (and himself) in spectacular fashion. Photographs of the wreck show that the axles were still hollowed out to a ridiculous

extent, the whole assembly apparently consisting of more air than metal. . . .

There was no racer in the 1905 catalogue, just a wide range of bodies on the 30 hp chassis: side-entrance coachwork in the latest style was now available, at prices ranging from $750 to $2000 (the latter sum being approximately the price of a fully-equipped Franklin touring car).

There was nothing to quibble about in terms of quality in the Simplex though admittedly the design of its radiator was somewhat clumsy; but nevertheless, Smith & Mabley went out of business in 1907, the victims of a general recession. A man named Herman Broesel obviously thought the Simplex name worth saving. He acquired the moribund company and began manufacture of a new Simplex, this time a Mercedes-inspired car designed by Edward Franquist.

Cylinders and pistons of the new model were of the finest 'gun iron', while frames were pressed from Krupp's chrome nickel steel: just about everything was made in the Simplex factory, save for tyres, electrical components and of course coachwork, which was supplied by the finest and most fashionable bodybuilders of the day.

Best known of the new Simplexes was the 50 hp model, with a 10-litre T-headed engine: its speed potential was apparent from the fact that the company

Below: the American driver Ralph de Palma at the Indianapolis Speedway in a Simplex

frequently entered stripped chassis in endurance races. One of the first they entered was the 24-hour Morris Park event in 1907.

In 1908, Joe Seymour's Simplex was the highest-placed American car in the Savannah Grand Prize Race (though its eleventh place was hardly earth-shattering). In October 1908, George Robertson's Simplex won the 24-hour race at the Brighton Beach one-mile dirt-track on Coney Island, New York, setting a new record distance of 1177 miles, at an average of 49 mph, despite collecting a track police-man in the process.

The marque's best racing year was 1909, in which George Robertson was again triumphant at Brighton Beach, though this time his average was down to 45.9 mph over a distance of 1091 miles: however, the winning car was fifty miles ahead of any other competitor . . .

On 8 September that year, a 50 hp Simplex, again with George Robertson at the wheel, won the National Stock Chassis race over the twisting Merrimac Valley course at Lowell, Massachussets, covering 318 miles in 352 minutes, an average of 54.20 mph, while Robertson, this time at the wheel of a 90 hp Simplex, took first place in the Founder's Day Race in Fairmount Park, Philadelphia, covering 200 miles in 218 minutes (55.05 mph). These achievements were certainly very significant factors in earning George Robertson the American Automobile Association National Championship that year.

In 1910, Mitchell's 10,492 cc Simplex was the biggest car in the Vanderbilt Cup race, but could only finish seventh, but at Brighton Beach Al Poole (who had been Robertson's co-driver in the 1909 race) and Charles Basle won the 24-hour race, averaging 47.7 mph but missing the 1908 record by a mere 32 miles. Also at Brighton Beach, George Robertson, driving the 90 hp Simplex *Zip* (which had left-hand-drive for dirt-track racing) beat Ralph de Palma's Fiat in a five-mile match race: the car was subsequently acquired by Louis Disbrow, and was still in good racing form five years later.

Franquist then introduced two new touring models 7.8 litre, a 38 hp shaft-drive touring car in 1911 and a massive 10-litre, chain-drive 75 hp sporting chassis in 1912, almost certainly the last new chain-driven car to be introduced in America—and it was probably the last chain-drive automobile to remain in production anywhere, which it did until 1914.

In the interim, Simplex had undergone another change of ownership, passing into the hands of a triumvirate called Goodrich, Lockhardt and Smith, who also took over the Crane Motor Company of Bayonne, New Jersey, and appointed Henry M. Crane in place of Franquist. The Crane Motor Company had been building a high-quality six-cylinder 9.2 litre car which cost $8000 in chassis form, and at the end of 1914 this became the Crane-Simplex—costing $10,000 as a chassis!

The Crane-Simplex was one of America's out-standing luxury cars, but lacked the thunderous glamour of the earlier Simplex models. It was built until 1917, when the factory turned to making V8 Hispano-Suiza aeroengines for the war effort, and a few chassis were assembled from existing components after the Armistice.

Then the company was acquired by ex-Packard Salesman Emlen S. Hare, who was attempting to form a motor manufacturing empire, which also included Mercer and Locomobile, and a few Crane-Simplex chassis were manufactured in 1923–24. The company failed to survive the collapse of Hare's Motors in 1924; however, it enjoyed a renaissence in attenuated form many years later when automobile collector Henry Austin Clark, owner of the Long Island Automotive Museum, acquired the name and whatever goodwill remained of the old Simplex company. But the proud Simplex badge recalled the long history of the famous company only as decoration emblazoned on humble Zippo cigarette lighters presented by Clark to his business and social visitors at the museum.   DBW

Below: a Simplex landaulet of 1909, powered by a four-cylinder 1340 cc engine

A CAR FOR EVERY PURSE AND PURPOSE

George Singer started in industry by making sewing machines, but he soon went on to build cycles and then a great variety of cars

Left: a Singer tricar of 1905; this vehicle replaced the earlier unstable three-wheeler with a single driven front wheel, two rear wheels and an outrigged seat

Below left: a 10 hp model of 1914; this line was introduced in 1912 with a 1096 cc four-cylinder engine and was the first really successful car to come from this company

SUSSEX BORN GEORGE SINGER'S first years as a mechanic were spent with the marine engineering firm of John Penn & Sons of Lewisham before he was drawn into the sewing machine industry by Newton, Wilson & Company. He soon moved from London—and Newton, Wilson—to join James Starley at the Coventry Sewing Machine Company. Starley, works manager of the Coventry firm had come a long way from his days as a gardener on Jon Penn's estate.

When Starley and his backer, Josiah Turner, had set up on their own, they had recruited several of the more able mechanics of Newton, Wilson & Company to place the venture on a sound engineering basis; it was a move which eventually had great influence on the just nascent Coventry motor industry. For apart from Singer, the mechanics included William Hillman and William Henry 'Tubby' Herbert, two of the original partners in the Hillman Company as well as Bayliss (of Bayliss-Thomas). The Coventry Sewing Machine Company itself was the progenitor of Swift . . .

In November 1868 at the age of 21, George Singer had risen to become a foreman when Josiah Turner's young nephew, Rowley Turner, newly returned from Paris, panted up to the Cheylesmore Works astride the latest novelty from France, a Michaux velocipede, ancestor of the bicycle, with the suggestion that his uncle's firm should begin making similar machines for sale in France. He had already been sounding out the market, and could promise firm orders for 400 of these 'boneshakers'.

As the sewing machine industry was then in something of a recession, the company jumped at the scheme with alacrity, and altered its name to the Coventry Machinists' Company to signify its change of direction. Production of velocipedes started in 1869, but expected French sales evaporated when the Franco-Prussian War broke out (Rowley Turner escaped from Paris on his velocipede), and the company was forced to turn to the home market, but, happily,

called George Dominy, from Weymouth, in Dorset, had the idea of producing a 'safety' bicycle which would eliminate the tendency of the old Ordinary to tip over forwards should the big front wheel hit a stone or rut, though his design, patented on 24 October 1878, did retain the big driving wheel and small trailing wheel of the original type. Singer's basic concept was remarkably simple, and can still be seen on modern cycles: he was the first to propose raking the front forks so that a line drawn through the steering centres would strike the ground at the point of contact of the front wheel, which not only made the machine more stable, but also gave self-centring castor action to the steering. In order that the rider could sit low on the machine, keeping the centre of gravity low while retaining the big driving wheel, Singer invented a treadle drive which replaced the rotating action of the pedals: this proved invaluable when in 1890 George Singer built a cycle for his brother Robert, who had one leg shorter than the other, and thus could not ride a pedal cycle: one of the new machines, which were christened 'Xtra Ordinaries', was built with one treadle higher than the other to compensate for Robert's infirmity.

Top: the 1916 version of the Singer 10, with electric lights and a modified screen

Above: a side view of the 1914 10 hp model pictured opposite

they did this with considerable success.

Starley and Hillman broke away from the Coventry Machinists' Company in 1870 to produce the Ariel, the first Ordinary (or 'penny-farthing') cycle, designed jointly by the two men; Singer, too, resigned in 1875 to start his own company, in which he was aided by his brother-in-law, J. E. Stringer.

Singer, apparently inspired by an amateur cyclist

In 1879 Singer built a tricycle with a large rear wheel and small front wheels which could be folded inwards to allow the machine to be wheeled through narrow passages: in 1885 an improved design of tricycle with one front wheel appeared, with chain drive to a rear axle with differential unit and a band-brake patented by Singer and his associate, R. H. Lea. Around 1888 the company began building diamond-

Below: the Singer Junior introduced at the Motor Show of 1926 with an 848 cc overhead-camshaft engine which produced 16.5 bhp at 3250 rpm

Bottom: the sporting version of the Singer 10, which won the 200 miles at Brooklands in 1921 in the hands of W. Bicknell; on the same circuit, this car established a Brooklands lap record of 74.42 mph

framed safety cycles with both wheels of 30 in diameter: the type was named the 'Rational', as it was felt that the new design would logically prevent 'headers' over the handlebars. It must be admitted, however, that the plodding Rational achieved its safety at the expense of performance. Yet the design proved popular with touring cyclists, and featured such 'modern' touches as a detachable handlebar and adjustable ball-bearing steering head and slotted rear forks to facilitate removal of the rear wheel.

In 1895 the Singer Cycle Company was the subject of a £600,000 flotation by that egregious company promotor Terah Hooley, but managed to survive the sudden slump in the cycle trade which hit Coventry in 1898 and swept away many of the companies floated or refloated by Hooley and his associates, including H. J. Lawson. By now, George Singer was a local citizen of some consequence, holding many civic positions including Mayor of Coventry three years in succession from 1891–3.

Considering its links with the Hooley/Lawson empire, the Singer Company was late in entering the motor industry. It finally did so in 1901 by acquiring the rights to the Perks & Birch Motor Wheel, a self-contained power pack in which a single-cylinder engine and drive gear was contained in an aluminium-

spoked wheel, which could be fitted between the front forks of a tricycle or the rear forks of a bicycle. It was a device whose virtues were about equalled by its inherent failings, as the pioneer motorcyclist B. H. Davies recalled: 'Alone among motors of that day, it had a reliable ignition, consisting of a low tension magneto with make and break inside the cylinder. Moreover, it had a transmission devoid of

belts, for the engine drove the back wheel direct by spur gears.

'That the noise of its progress would have put a worn-out threshing machine to the blush was no oddity in those days. I liked this mount much. But it passed from my ken when its owner snapped two or three of the back wheel spokes, and had to *carry* it three miles to his home.'

There was also an unstable-looking three-wheeler, the Tri-Voiturette. Stated Singer: The front part of the machine is practically the same as the Tandem Tricycle, but the rear part is designed to carry a second rider, or rather a passenger, the steering and management being effected from the front saddle. The engine is of $2\frac{1}{2}$ bhp. The machine is made in two forms, the No. 1 with the passenger looking backwards, and the No. 2 with this position reversed.'

As the seat was outrigged well behind the rear axle, the stability of the machine must have been a nebulous quantity with a full load: but there was worse to come . . . At the 1902 Cordingley Show at the Agricultural Hall, Islington, Singer showed 'two specimens of the Singer Motor Carrier, one fitted up as an ordinary Tradesman's Carrier and the other especially adapted for Dairymen, having a large churn and a basket fitted'. Imagine having to carry *that* home if the spokes snapped . . .

This somewhat unsatisfactory device was soon replaced by a tricar of more substantial type, with two front wheels and a rear driving wheel, plus a

more powerful engine and a coachbuilt body with a proper seat for the passenger, who was now, however, seated nearest the accident, rather than being the probable cause of it . . .

Then, in 1905, Singer acquired the licence to build a car which was then being manufactured by R. H. Lea, who had been a Singer employee for 17 years and his partner Graham Ingleby Francis. The most remarkable feature of the Lea-Francis car was its engine, designed by Alex Craig; its 15 hp horizontal three-cylinder power unit had an overhead camshaft and connecting rods three feet long to gain the advantages of a long-stroke engine without imposing excessive side-thrust on the pistons. Smooth-running the Craig engine may have been: but the design was obviously too unorthodox and in 1906 the Singer range was entirely reconstituted, and now contained

two light cars, both with White & Poppe engines, a 7 hp twin and a 12/14 hp four, and two touring cars, with Aster power units, a 12/14 and a 20/22 hp. There was also a three-cylinder White & Poppe-engined Doctor's Brougham. Shaft drive to a live axle was standardised throughout the range, and the cars were equipped with 'hinged body, and other features that must appeal to the practical motorist'.

When George Singer died in January 1909, the company was reorganized. The new Singer cars had a rather clumsy design of radiator with a circular brass motif on the honeycomb, intended, it seems, to symbolise a cycle wheel. This motif was retained until 1911. The principal model was the White & Poppe engined 16/20.

'If you want a really smart, speedy car, luxuriously comfortable, easy to drive and economical to keep up, 'eulogised the Singer Motor Company,' a car in which every part is as handy and reliable as master engineers can make it, you want a 1910 model 16/20 Singer car. It has low front seats, well-removed from the dash; the footboards are sloped to suit the high wind doors, which are included; and the rear seats provide ample accommodation for three passengers. The engine has dual ignition and, being hung direct from the main frame, instead of from an underframe, is perfectly accessible in every part.'

In 1912, after experimenting with a transverse-engined air-cooled cyclecar, Singer introduced an excellent 1096 cc four-cylindered light car, marred

Below left: a 10/26 of 1926; this went on to become the Senior and had a 1308 cc engine

Above: the 'Waterfall' 8 hp Junior Special of 1931, so named because of the shape and style of the radiator grille

Right: the 9 hp Sports coupé of 1932; it was powered by a 972 cc overhead-camshaft engine and was an immediate success in competitive events, eventually giving rise to the Le Mans

Below: two Singer 9s, after a crash in the 1935 TT caused by steering failure

only by having its three-speed gearbox built in unit with the back axle. It was one of the first 'big cars in miniature' to appear on the market, and possessed a usefully lively performance, which attracted a motor agent from Henniker Mews, Kensington, named Lionel Martin, a former racing cyclist who had recently gone into partnership with Robert Bamford. Martin was looking for a small, high-efficiency car as a foil to his Rolls-Royce Silver Ghost. He bought the 1912 show model off the company's stand at Olympia, took it back to Henniker Mews and had it completely stripped down. Fibre inserts were used to silence the tappets, and the camshaft drive was altered so that the cams could be changed merely by removing the radiator and timing cover; then the car was taken over

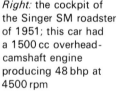

Right: the cockpit of the Singer SM roadster of 1951; this car had a 1500 cc overhead-camshaft engine producing 48 bhp at 4500 rpm

an extended test route so that the effect of various cam profiles could be compared, and the best camshaft for all-round performance could be chosen.

The Martin treatment transformed the Singer from a sedate 40 mph runabout into a lively sporting vehicle with a top speed of well over 70 mph, and as a result the Henniker Mews workshops were kept busy tuning Singers; the competition successes of Martin's original hotted-up Singer Ten, especially at the Aston Clinton hillclimb, inspired him, when he built a light car of his own design with a Coventry Simplex engine in an Isotta Fraschini chassis, to call it the 'Aston Martin'.

Another historic link came around the same time when young Billy Rootes, who had served his apprenticeship in the Singer factory became an agent for the company's products, which he sold through his mid-Kent motor and cycle agencies.

And the famous comedian Harry Tate, whose 'Motoring' sketch had topped the bill at music halls for many years, chose a Singer Ten as his personal car, and embellished it with the registration 'T8'.

The little Singer Ten continued in production after World War I, little changed save for the adoption of a rounded design of radiator shell (which had originally appeared on the few 1915 models to be built) in place of the square-cut cooler of the prewar models.

Though the engine remained unchanged, except in

detail, until the end of 1923, the chassis of the Ten was totally redesigned late in 1921.

The transmission was now of more orthodox layout, with the gearbox divorced from the back axle and mounted at the head of the torque tube in the middle of the chassis; quarter-elliptic springs replaced the half-elliptics of the earlier model, and Michelin disc wheels were standardised. Price was £395 in two-seater form, with neat drop-head 'all-weather' coachwork with windup windows.

There was, temporarily, a smaller addition to the company's range: but it was an addition by adoption, for during 1921 Singer had acquired Coventry-Premier, manufacturers of motorbikes and cyclecars, and for a while a four-wheeled Coventry-Premier with a watercooled V-twin engine of 1005 cc was offered at £250. In 1922 it acquired a Singer four-cylinder power unit, but production of this sub-marque ceased the following year.

Also new for 1922 was the first six-cylinder Singer to reach production status. It had a 15 hp engine of 1999 cc, and was designed to 'provide remarkably comfortable motoring at moderate cost'.

With a monobloc cylinder casting on an aluminium crankcase, the engine was a neat, if somewhat dated, design—after all, a non-detachable cylinder head with valve caps was a feature of Edwardian rather than vintage light car design, where the detachable head

Left: the 1500 tourer of 1954; the bodywork was evolved from that of the SM 1500

Below: the SM 1500 was introduced in 1948 and was Singer's first streamlined car; it was hoped that this model would put Singer back in the big league, but this was not to be

was rapidly becoming commonplace equipment.

Apart from semi-elliptic front suspension and cantilever springing at the rear, the chassis of the 15 hp was similar in design to the new 10 hp; it incorporated a neat luggage grid which could be slid away beneath the rear of the body when not in use.

Singer were well ahead of the fashion in offering a six of such modest capacity—in 1924 it could even be specified with Weymann fabric coachwork, again anticipating a coming vogue—and it seems as though sales during the vintage period were modest.

In 1923 the power unit of the Ten was neatly modernised with a conversion to overhead valves, operated by exposed pushrods, and the old bi-block cylinders were changed to a monobloc casting. For 1924, the pushrods were enclosed, and a Weymann saloon was available on the Ten chassis, too.

At the 1924 Olympia Show, a new light Singer, the 10/26, replaced the old Ten: with an engine enlarged to 1308 cc, it was a far more modern-looking vehicle than its predecessor, and sold well, aided by competitive pricing which ranged from £195 for the 'Popular' four-seater to £295 for the Saloon Limousine De Luxe. Singer sales soared steadily during the mid-1920s until the company became the third-biggest British car manufacturer following Morris and then Austin organization.

For 1927, the quarter-elliptic front springing of the 10/26 was replaced by semi-elliptics, the better to withstand the stresses imposed by the front-wheel brakes which had been adopted the previous year. Another high point of 1926 had been the acquisition of the moribund Calcott company, a maker of quality light cars since 1912: their factory in Far Gosford Street, Coventry, became the spares and service division of Singer.

A major step forward came at the 1926 Motor Show, with the introduction of the 848 cc Singer Junior, whose diminutive overhead camshaft engine was to be the progenitor of Singer power units for the next three decades. At first, the Junior, costing only £148 in four-seater tourer guise, had rear-wheel brakes only but four-wheel brakes came the following year. The 10/26 became the 'Senior', while there was a new overhead valve Six, basically an enlarged Senior, with a 1776 cc engine and Clayton Dewandre vacuum servo-assisted four-wheel brakes.

And the company's advertising, in keeping with the new image, took on a Somewhere-West-of-Coventry breathlessness: 'A passport to Fairyland . . . A Singer Car can be the key to untold enjoyment, the constant source of discovery of something new. Whatever the mood or fancy, the Singer will respond. Discover England afresh with a Singer, let her take you to pastures new, away from the madding crowd and the hurly-burly of everyday life. Somewhere there is a road to rolling slopes and the music of running water—to a sleepy old-world village full of charm—to the coast and the sea where you can take your fill of pure ozone. The Singer will take you safely and bring you back. There is a Singer Car waiting for you from £148 10s.'

Continuing their policy of 'a car for every Purse and Purpose', Singer carried out a comprehensive redesign of the Senior for 1928, increasing the engine capacity to 1571 cc and fitting three crankshaft main bearings instead of two (which also enabled, thanks to the increased length of the cylinder block, the valves to be arranged in line instead of staggered). The chassis had a wider track and improved braking and steering, features also to be found on the Junior and Six.

An odd sidelight on Singer history is that the redesign of the Senior apparently left several hundred 1927-type chassis surplus to requirements: fitted with a new radiator shell cast from aluminium and van bodywork, these were sold off under the guise of the 'Singer Delivery' at £180 each.

Perhaps the most interesting aspect of the restyling of the bodywork for the 1928 season was the introduction of what was then known as 'Sun' saloon coachwork, and which was later marketed under the name 'As-U-Dryve'. At first glance this seemed to be a slightly ponderous-looking form of fabric saloon, but closer inspection revealed that the top and rear of the body were made of hood material. A handle operated endless chains running all round the perimeters of the body sides winding the hood back into a recess behind the rear seats on fine days.

At the end of 1928 one of the attractive little sporting two-seater Singer Juniors set up a curious record by climbing the 1:4 Porlock Hill 100 times in 15 hours; and after that the model was known as the 'Porlock'. It was joined a year later by a Sportsman's Coupé on the same chassis, a somewhat malproportioned 2+2 which was one of the first of this type to be offered on such a small chassis.

The Senior was dropped in the autumn of 1929, to be replaced by a new Six of 1792 cc with side valves and a four bearing crankshaft: the seven-bearing ohv model was continued as the 'Super-Six', now with a capacity of 1921 cc, and a four-speed transmission, plus centralised chassis lubrication operated by a pedal in the driving compartment. 'The completeness of the equipment,' wrote *The Autocar*, 'certainly makes the car comparable with the transatlantic machine in point of value, which is saying a great deal; and the car looks well. This is, in fact, the most impressive Singer yet made.'

For 1931, the Junior acquired a four-speed transmission, and there was a new Ten, with a 1261 cc four-cylinder engine, similar in design to the sidevalve six. The range was beginning to take on an unnecessary complication, which grew to ridiculous proportions with the announcement of the 1932 range, which featured redesigned chassis, ribbon radiators and sliding sunshine roofs.

There was now a Junior Special of 972 cc in addition to the 848 cc model; the Ten continued alongside these, while there was now a new sidevalve 12/6, of 1476 cc as well as the sidevalve 18/6, with an increased engine capacity of 2041 cc and the ohv Silent-Six, now of 2180 cc. Most expensive model in the range was the vee-radiatored Kaye Don saloon, styled by C. F. Beauvais, on the Silent-Six chassis, priced at £480; the Junior Special saloon was a miniature reproduction of this model, with the same flared wings.

In 1932, a new chief engineer was appointed. He was Leo J. Shorter, who had formerly worked with Duryea, Humber, Sunbeam, Arrol-Johnston, Calcott and Coventry-Climax: in conjunction with two other designers, one of whom was A. G. Booth, formerly with Clyno and AJS, he drew up plans for a new sporting Singer Nine, which was launched at the Motor Show that year. Hydraulic brakes were standardised on all models, except the Kaye Don, which was totally restyled, and which retained the Dewandre servo-assistance. There was also a new 14 hp six, similar in design to the new Nine power unit, with a chain-driven overhead camshaft; the old Junior and Ten had vanished, though the Ten was replaced by a new sidevalve 12.

The new Sports Nine proved an immediate success in reliability trials, and a special car built for Le Mans gave the model its generic name (though the

true Singer Le Mans with fully-machined, counterbalanced crankshaft was a rather rare beast).

At the 1933 Motor Show, it was announced that the Singer 'Perm-Mesh' clutchless gearchange was to be adopted throughout the range, which now included a new 1½-litre six-cylinder sporting model.

Top: Singer's 1969 Gazelle

Above: the Singer Chamois version of the Hillman Imp

Top: the Gazelle convertible and saloon models of the 1960s

For 1935, the Nine, Eleven and 16 hp models featured independent front suspension, while Fluidrive transmissions were fitted to the two larger cars. The 1384 cc Eleven was new, as was the 2-litre 16 hp: both followed the general design of the Nine. The Eleven was available with full-width Airstream coach-work, which made it look like one of those Art Deco motorcar teapots of the era, though it should be noted that the Airstream was launched before the Chrysler Airflow made any impact on the British market.

The excellent reputation which the sporting Singers had built up was dashed to pieces in the 1935 Ulster TT, in which all three team cars were eliminated in a spectacular series of crashes due to steering failure, the cars going out on separate laps, but crashing in the same spot.

A new Singer Nine, the Bantam, was introduced at the 1935 Motor Show. The fact that Singer had lost the ability to lead the light car market was shown by the fact that body styling on this car was a blatant crib of the Ford Model Y (which Morris had already copied closely with their Eight). Priced at £127, it cost far more than either of its rivals, and falling sales soon had Singer in financial trouble again.

Sales continued their downward drift during the 1930s, and, indeed, some points of specification actually retrogressed during the period, the Nine went back to mechanical brakes for 1939.

Just before the war, Leo Shorter was working on the development of a new two-pedal transmission, though this failed to make production. For a while, the pre-war models continued in production, though Singer's ugly sporting tourer was hardly a rival to the MG TC. Shorter was by now technical director, and for 1948 he produced a new, modern Singer, the SM1500, with streamlined, full-width coachwork and coil-spring independent front suspension. But Singer had fallen too far, and the SM 1500 failed to put them back in the big league. Interestingly enough, Shorter was already looking at alternative power sources, and during the early 1950s tested a steam-driven version of the SM 1500 (though Singer vehemently denied all knowledge of it).

The de luxe Hunter of 1955 failed to save the day (and its optional extra twin ohc power unit probably never reached the public), and early in 1956 the company's former agents, Rootes, absorbed Singer. The Singer Gazelle of late 1956 was thus little more than an up-market version of another Rootes model, the Hillman Minx, although the old single ohc engine was retained—but only until 1958.

After that, Singer became a badge-engineered marque only, falling somewhere between Hillman and Humber in the Rootes Group. In the late 1960s the range consisted of the Imp-based Chamois, the Gazelle and the Vogue, but the latter two models had already been phased out when the marque was finally given its discharge in April 1970, just 95 years since George Singer had set up on his own.   DBW

TWO BROTHERS, THREE COMPANIES

Maurice and George Sizaire had a love of motor cars; between them they formed and ran three companies

MAURICE SIZAIRE TRAINED AS AN ARCHITECT but ever since he had seen a steam tricycle (possibly an early De Dion Bouton) chug in front of his house when he was around eight years old, Sizaire had harboured a secret ambition to build a self-propelled vehicle. In his early teens at the beginning of the 1890s, he began experimenting in his bedroom workshop. He set himself the task of absorbing as much as he could of contemporary cycle and motor technology. He even persuaded his younger brother, Georges, to becoming a trainee turner in a bicycle factory, so that he might have help in realising his ambition.

In 1897 the brothers rented a tiny workshop in Puteaux, near Paris, where they began construction of a single-cylinder car with a tubular chassis and three-speed belt drive. Short of funds and working only in their spare time, the brothers progressed slowly, helped latterly by their friend Louis Naudin: the car was running by 1902, but the transmission was not a success. So Sizaire devised a novel form of gearing, on which three forward speeds were provided by a propellor shaft which could be shifted so that pinions of varying diameter were forced into engagement with the long-suffering crown-wheel. It was, apparently, the first time that a car had been provided with three direct drives forward: another novelty was the use of independent front suspension by sliding pillars linked by a transverse leaf spring. But the ash chassis looked a trifle archaic. . . .

In this form the car was complete by 1904, and was shown at the Exposition des Petits Inventeurs in March 1905, where its design attracted much attention: a company was formed for its production, and a stand taken at the 1905 Paris Salon. Many orders were forthcoming for the Sizaire-Naudin light car, and by 1906, two cars a day were leaving the factory.

But it had been priced too low, and the newly-formed company ran into financial difficulties; it was bought by the Duc d'Uzès, who provided sufficient capital for the firm to indulge in some sporting activities as well as building private cars.

First fruits of this new sporting policy was the entry of three cars in the original Coupe de l'Auto race in

Below: a 1905 Sizaire et Naudin 1442 cc single-cylinder car

Bottom: Louis Naudin's 1908 racer

Seine-Inférieure — Grand Prix de l'A. C. F. - 6 et 7 Juillet 1908

NAUDIN sur voiture SIZAIRE-NAUDIN

L'Hirondelle - Paris

1906—and a victory by Georges Sizaire with a standard 1244 cc single-cylinder Sizaire in this somewhat unsatisfactory six-day event. More significant was the marque's first place in the Coupe des Voiturettes run over the tortuous Targa Florio course just before the Paris Salon of 1906, at an average speed of 21.7 mph.

A team of three long-stroke cars was specially built for the 1907 Coupe de l'Auto, with single-cylinder engines of 1178 cc equipped with steel (instead of cast-iron) pistons, which began to develop cracks during the endurance run section of the event. So the drivers were forced, on one lap, to drive into a wood and remove the cylinder to change the pistons in secret: they still maintained the required average, and the timekeepers put the delay down to a call of nature: And by virtue of this pleasant subterfuge, Louis Naudin came first, followed by Georges Sizaire. It seems as though the Sizaire-Naudin company was the first to realise that, though the regulations of the Coupe de l'Auto restricted the bore of a car, the length

of the stroke was up to the manufacturer and his engineering ability, real or imagined. It was a widely copied ploy, yet the Sizaire-Naudin racers were never tall-bonneted freaks like the Lion-Peugeots.

This first time out success with the long-stroke Sizaire-Naudin caused such consternation among the marque's racing rivals that they demanded an official examination of the cars' fuel . . . and were duly non-plussed to find them burning ordinary petrol.

The company built its largest single-cylinder racing cars for the 1908 Coupe des Voiturette at Dieppe, with 1963 cc power units developing a healthy 42 bhp. Unfortunately Naudin could manage no better than second place behind a Delage, having been delayed by a burst tyre and a leaking petrol tank.

The normal production cars built by this company were popular with the young bloods of the day, as they were one of the first cheap sports cars to offer a decent performance. Power output was progressively increased by lengthening the stroke. In mid 1908 the 9 hp, 1357 cc Sizaire-Naudin was replaced by a new 12 hp model of 1470 cc. The author and motoring journalist, Max Pemberton, was lent one of the first of these cars imported into England for an extended road test by the British agent, Charles Jarrott. He found the car 'as flexible as many a forty, and much handier.' Priced at £220, this Sizaire model was apparently selling faster than it could be imported, and Pemberton's experiences gave some of the reasons for this popularity.

'I had not driven a single-cylinder car for some time and I succeeded in stopping the engine once, but the Sizaire-Naudin is difficult to stop even by a bungler, and she can be driven down a country lane at ten miles an hour with no more effort (or considerably less) than is necessary to drive some "monsters" at fifteen. As for hills, I discovered nothing during a three-days' tour which brought her down from top.

An early 1913 example of a Sizaire et Naudin four-cylinder, Ballot-engined car; this car still has the front-suspension system of the older Sizaires

You can pick your way through crowded traffic with her and accelerate instantly to thirty miles an hour to take an opening should the necessity arise. Perhaps it would not be wise to speak of what she will do on the level, but if there be any man so dead to all sense of veneration for the police as to desire a speed of forty miles an hour in the open, then I venture to say the Sizaire-Naudin will not disappoint him.

'Now these are facts established by a car of the standard pattern just over from France and in no way tuned up. The only point of criticism I could possibly make concerned the gear-changing, which on this particular chassis was not as smooth as it might have been; but then the whole gear system is so novel on a Sizaire and possesses such amazing advantages that it would be absurd to carp at trivialities. As a general rule these gears are to be changed quietly and pleasingly. I had an unlucky specimen which would have required an hour in the works to put right.'

The tractability of a Sizaire-Naudin was all the more surprising when you consider that the speed was controlled, not by a throttle of the conventional pattern, but by a cam which varied the lift of the inlet valve, thus controlling the charge size.

The popularity of these little cars was shown in 1908 when an all-Sizaire race was organised at Brooklands. More significant was the French company's decision to opt out of racing after 1909, for the very sound reason that other companies with far greater resources were now coming into the voiturette racing field, making competition far keener, and races harder

design and Sizaire-Berwick had. After that, the Sizaire-Berwick had a shallow radiator which was, if anything, more handsome than the Rolls cooler.

Sizaire-Berwick cars were initially built at Courbevoie, near Paris; one of the apprentices seconded to the factory from London was a young man named Jack Waters, who was later to achieve fame as the actor Jack Warner.

Production was halted by World War I, and the Sizaire brothers spent the duration in the army, while Berwick established a factory in London to build aircraft.

Below: a 1924/5 2-litre chassis, now in the Malartle Museum

to win than in the period from 1906 to 1908.

A new touring Sizaire-Naudin appeared in 1909, this time with a 1583 cc engine. This was chiefly remarkable for a number of detail refinements, such as a new design of air inlet valve for the carburettor, which eliminated the characteristic jingling sounds which had formerly heralded the approach of all Sizaire cars. Another untoward noise was eliminated by the provision of ball-bearings at either end of the gearshaft, which was claimed to make the gears wonderfully silent and to do away with the grinding sound which had previously emanated from the transmission on the over-run. The clutch spring was lightened, the throttle cam was improved, and a new pattern of radiator, giving greatly improved cooling, was standardised.

However, before long, the Duc d'Uzès decided that the company was now on a sufficiently firm footing for him to dismiss Naudin and the two Sizaire brothers, even though they were under contract. The company had just introduced its first four-cylinder model, the 1847 cc 12 hp. In 1913 the last of the single cylinder models appeared, a new 1357 cc 10 hp, but the company was now tending to produce solid, respectable family cars and the sporting image waned as rapidly as the firm's fortunes.

The Sizaire-Naudin company lasted until 1921, by which time its products had become very staid.

After the rift with the Duc d'Uzès, Maurice and Georges Sizaire founded a new company in conjunction with F. W. Berwick, who was a motor agent dealing in French cars such as the La Licorne. Naudin, however, retired from work and died soon after. The new Sizaire-Berwick car, designed by Maurice Sizaire, was a well engineered, totally orthodox car, with a four-cylinder engine of 4072 cc. The radiator was of similar design to that of the Rolls-Royce, a fact which eventually caused Rolls-Royce to take legal proceedings—which were settled out of court when it was discovered that Rolls-Royce had not registered the

After the hostilities, Maurice Sizaire moved to London to design a new Sizaire-Berwick car, but found his decisions were constantly overruled by the chief engineer of the company (who was related to the man who had put up the capital to establish the business). The new 25/30 hp, 4536 cc, Sizaire-Berwick scaled almost two tons in chassis form thanks to the modifications made by this engineer in the interests of strength. Materials were on hand to build 1000 cars, but it is highly unlikely that anything like this number was ever built. In 1923, the Austin Motor Company acquired Sizaire-Berwick, and the company's principal production in its declining years were re-radiatored Austins of 12 and 20 hp, though a six-cylinder 3.2 litre model was also available.

Sizaire-Berwick were moribund by 1925, but Maurice Sizaire and his brother were working on a new model as early as 1920, for production at Courbevoie. Two prototypes were completed that year, which featured independent suspension all round. When this model reached production status in 1923, it was the first all-independent car to be sold to the general public. The design followed the broad principles of the old voiturette front suspension, but was of course considerably refined. With a two-litre power unit, the standard Sizaire Frères Type 4R1 was capable of almost 70 mph in standard form, while there was also a 16 valve sports version, which went on sale in 1926. The company enjoyed considerable success with this model, but lacked finance to expand. The board of directors demanded exorbitant licence fees from companies interested in fitting the Sizaire suspension to their products, and only succeeded in frightening them all away.

After production ceased in France in 1929. Some cars were still being built in Belgium by Georges Sizaire until 1931. In 1933 Maurice Sizaire joined the Técalémit Company as an engineer and stayed with that company until 1960, when he retired at the age of 83 to devote himself to his hobby of painting. DBW

Above left: a 1914 Sizaire-Berwick 14 hp; this 4060 cc car, which cost £745, was used as a staff car during World War I

Left: a 1921 Sizaire-Berwick 25/50 hp

LOSING YOUR GRIP ON LIFE

Considerable driving skill is required to control a skid, but such devices as anti-lock brakes can help

LIKE SO MANY OF THE BEHAVIOURAL QUIRKS of the moving motorcar, skidding is a phenomenon originating in the non-linear idiosyncracies of pneumatic tyres' behaviour. Even when a car is cornering gently, its tyres do not travel quite along the path on which they are aligned: the difference between the steered course and the actual one is called the *slip angle*. Differences in loads and duties result in the four tyres each operating at slightly different slip angles, the interaction of which determines the actual trajectory of the car, and any tendency for its attitude to depart from one that is strictly tangential to that curve. As the car is cornered harder, so will the slip angles grow larger, so that the path of the car displays a considerable drift from the course that might be inferred from the positions of the steered wheels. Despite these slip angles and that drift reaching sensible or even visible magnitudes, the car may not be skidding.

The onset of the skid occurs when the slip angle is forced to increase even further, although the tyre has already reached the point where it is generating its maximum cornering power. Slip angles then grow very quickly until they can be as much as 90°, when the tyre is sliding sideways; and on the way to reaching this extreme, the cornering power of the tyre will decrease more or less sharply according to the nature of the tyre and the surface upon which it is running.

Bias-ply tyres commonly reach maximum cornering power at fairly large slip angles, and continue to generate cornering power even when these angles are exceeded—the deterioration in grip is fairly progressive. Radial-ply tyres, although nowadays far better than in their infancy in this respect, have a more sudden breakaway, as well as operating at smaller slip angles, and their cornering power while sliding sideways can rapidly sink to almost zero.

Something similar occurs during acceleration or braking. In either case there is a creep between the tyre and the road surface which is roughly proportional to the torque transmitted by the tyre, up to a value

Below: snow is one of the most difficult surfaces on which to manoeuvre a car, especially if normal road tyres are fitted to the wheels; in countries where snow is very common during the winter months, chains or studs are fitted to the tyres to provide extra grip

determined by the limiting friction. As an approximation, the maximum effective friction force will be realised when the relative slip between tyre and road surface is about 12 per cent, although the value will vary according to the nature of the materials involved. If the relative slip is increased beyond this limiting figure by the application of more braking or tractive torque, then the frictional forces drop as the slip increases until eventually the situation is stabilised when the wheel is completely sliding—that is, it has locked under braking or is spinning wildly under acceleration. Of course there is still some residual friction between the tyre and road, the amount varying according to circumstances; but the skid may be deemed to begin when the optimum relative slip is exceeded.

Whether in cornering or in braking, it is possible for any one of the four tyres to begin to skid before the others, perhaps because its tread is inferior in condition or it has found a more slippery bit of road, or perhaps because its particular brake tends to grab. In fact most skids begin at one corner of the car, but it is common for the other wheel at that end of the car to come out in sympathy, so to speak. For all four tyres to skid simultaneously and equally is very rare indeed, and even then tends to be a transient condition.

Understanding a skid is half way towards correcting it. Better still, it is a significant part of the art of preventing it from happening. Clearly the skid can be induced by cornering, braking or accelerating too hard, in the particular circumstances of road surface material and condition and tyre equipment. It is not right to insist that the good driver never has a skid, for there are occasions when it may be reasonable and proper for him deliberately to provoke one that he can subsequently control in order to perform a manoeuvre that may otherwise be impossible, and may well be necessary to extricate himself from a dangerous situation. It is however proper to insist that a good driver never has an accidental skid, which must be *prima facie* evidence of negligence.

Whether the skid has been deliberately provoked or carelessly allowed to happen, the need to control and to correct it remains the same. Text books and instructors often make this sound easy, and sometimes it is; but there are times when it can be surprisingly difficult, and if the car has hopelessly low-geared steering that cannot be turned fast enough, or if one of the tyres has deflated and thus lost all its ability to contribute any cornering or braking force, then control and correction of the skid may turn out to be impossible. Nor is it always an easy thing to practice: the behaviour of a car on a wet and slippery road, on snow and ice, or on a specially prepared skid-

Below: the layout of the Dunlop Maxaret anti-lock braking system, as used on the Jensen FF of the 1960s

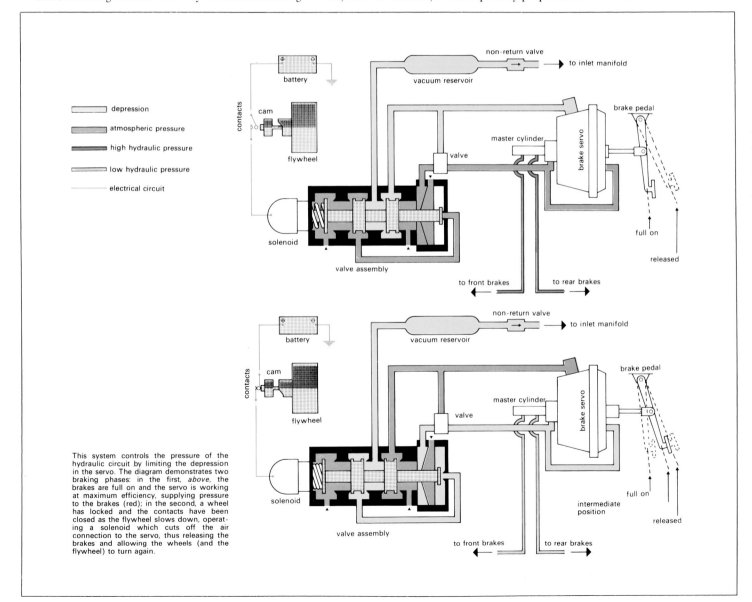

depression

atmospheric pressure

high hydraulic pressure

low hydraulic pressure

electrical circuit

This system controls the pressure of the hydraulic circuit by limiting the depression in the servo. The diagram demonstrates two braking phases: in the first, *above*, the brakes are full on and the servo is working at maximum efficiency, supplying pressure to the brakes (red); in the second, a wheel has locked and the contacts have been closed as the flywheel slows down, operating a solenoid which cuts off the air connection to the servo, thus releasing the brakes and allowing the wheels (and the flywheel) to turn again.

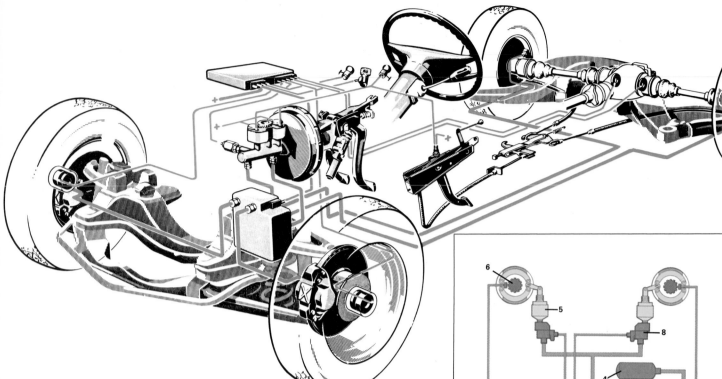

Above: an anti-lock braking system used by Mercedes; it makes use of wheel sensors which supply information about wheel velocity to an electronic analyser and this, in turn, controls the hydraulic brake pressure

Right: an anti-lock system used on commercial vehicles with pneumatic brakes

1 compressor; 2 regulator; 3 operating unit; 4 air reservoirs; 5 brake cylinders; 6 velocity sensors; 7 electronic control unit; 8 electro-pneumatic valves.

pan of the type used for teaching policemen and bus drivers, is likely to be quite different from its behaviour when skidding at higher speeds on a dry road, when the higher limiting friction level provokes more extreme roll or pitch that in turn introduces suspension deflections that may well alter the car's response characteristics completely.

Nevertheless there remain some sound general principles to be adopted. In the case of a rear wheel skid while cornering, the classic correction procedure is to pay off a certain amount of steering in the direction towards which the rear of the car is sliding, being careful not to overdo it because the sudden contraskid that will then ensue is always much more difficult to correct. Some instructors advocate lifting the foot off the accelerator or even de-clutching, but these are procedures to be viewed with suspicion because they introduce further elements of change at a time when equilibrium and therefore continuity are being sought. An obvious exception is the case of a skid produced by strong acceleration breaking traction while cornering, in which momentary or partial release of the accelerator pedal may be the only corrective procedure necessary.

If it is the front tyres that skid in a corner, the correction procedure is rather less natural and instinctive. In this condition they cannot effectively steer the vehicle, and to wind on more steering lock is likely to exacerbate the condition. Unwinding the steering until it can once again grip will eventually undo the skid, but unless there be plenty of recovery space available it may not solve the ultimate problem of getting round the corner at a speed that was clearly excessive. Allowing the skid to continue, with the front tyres scrubbing away the speed, may occasionally be sufficient when on dry roads, but as a general-purpose procedure it is better to try to unstick the rear wheels by violent acceleration, brutal gearchanging, or deft use of the handbrake: if they can be induced to skid, the front tyres will be relieved of the excessive demands being made of them, and will regain their grip, whereupon the car—by now probably travelling sideways and scrubbing off speed rapidly—can be controlled in the manner appropriate to an ordinary

rear wheel skid. In many cases the violent understeering front wheel skid is brought about by excessive tractive effort while cornering, in which case releasing the accelerator is sufficient to correct matters, and releasing it too much or too suddenly will create the oversteering skid.

A frequent cause of front wheel skids is failure to complete braking before starting to negotiate a corner. Forward weight transfer under heavy braking substantially increases the load borne by the front tyres which have less residual work capacity for cornering, the limiting condition being observed when the front wheels have been locked by braking and are thereafter incapable of doing any steering. To release the brake pedal might seem the obvious palliative, but if this is done while the steering wheels are turned to one side, then in the course of half a revolution of the

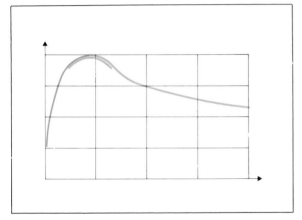

front wheels they will have recovered their full cornering power, and the effect will be to give the nose of the car an almighty and sudden shove in the direction in which they are steering. This may well prove too much for it, and the resulting swerve, if performed at high speed, may allow the driver to practice practically every kind of skid correction previously known or spontaneously invented.

Although it was not always so, nowadays more skids are provoked in ordinary road driving by hard braking than by excessively fast cornering. If the brakes are applied harshly while the car is negotiating a curve, a violent serve can be almost guaranteed, and a spin is more than likely, although tail-heavy cars on wet roads may occasionally go off in a front-end slide. In these circumstances releasing the brakes, and treating the skid as a cornering one, should be the correct drill. However, if the car was travelling straight when the brakes were applied and the two front wheels lock more or less simultaneously, the car will slide straight ahead. Delicately releasing the braking pressure until the front wheels can resume rotation will allow the maximum braking power to be recovered (at the point of optimum slip) and will restore some steering ability. If only one front brake locks, or one or both of those at the rear, the car will

become directionally unstable and it may be necessary to release the brake pedal completely and get the car straight again before resuming braking with more delicacy and caution than before.

Because forward weight transfer increases the load on the front tyres and unloads the rear tyres, it is the front brakes that are called upon to do most of the work, and it is usual for them to be made more powerful than those at the rear. This is only a first step to maintenance of the car's stability in braking, however, for any such arbitrary distribution of braking effort can only be correct for one particular rate of deceleration, and at higher rates the rear wheels will still be the first to lock. The actual value of the critical deceleration rate will vary according to how the car is laden at the time: the most extreme variations are noted in small front-wheel-drive cars in which a full payload can increase the all-up weight by 50 per cent and move the centre of gravity back by about 20 per cent of the wheelbase, thus altering the loads on the tyres and the amount of forward transfer of load under braking.

The simplest and most effective way to deal with this problem is to introduce a load-sensitive valve to inhibit the braking effort applied to the rear wheels according to the amount of load they are supporting. This can be measured accurately by reference to deflection or extension of the rear suspension, the first significant application of the technique being in the Fiat 124. By these means it can be made reasonably unlikely that the rear brakes will ever lock before the front ones, and excessively harsh braking will not rob the car of directional stability.

The ultimate extension of this principle is to measure the braking capacity of each tyre and control the braking effort applied to it in such a way that, however brutish and insensate the driver heaving at the brake pedal, none of the wheels will be able to lock. The aircraft industry contrived such a system 30 years ago with the aid of an elegant piece of trickery known as the Dunlop Maxaret: the principle was that any excessively rapid deceleration of the braked wheel could be interpreted by a mechanical sensor as a sign of

Above: part of an anti-lock system used on a Fiat commercial vehicle; the electronic centre is mounted just above the propeller shaft

Left: a graphical representation of adhesion as a function of slip; the blue line shows the adhesion available while the tyre is rotating, the green line shows the area of maximum grip and the orange line the area where the tyre begins to slip quickly over the road surface; anti-lock braking devices keep the relationship in the area of the green line

incipient locking, whereupon the sensor would open a bleed bypass valve in the high-pressure hydraulic system serving the brake, so that the tyre could recover its grip and the valve would close again to restore full braking effort. A skilled driver in an ordinary car can do the same sort of thing by pumping the brakes, alternately squeezing and relieving the pedal; but the Maxaret could do the same thing at a much higher cyclic rate, allowing a heavy aircraft to be braked to a standstill on a wet runway that might otherwise prove much too short for safety at the speeds involved.

Dunlop did experiment with a Maxaret system for cars, but found no manufacturers prepared to spend the necessary fortune on endowing their products with high-pressure powered hydraulic systems to work the brakes. Only when Jensen introduced their four-wheel-drive FF car in the late 1960s did there appear a glimmer of hope for the Maxaret: the coupling of the driven front and rear axles was done in such a way that one single Maxaret unit, acting on the central differential, was sufficient to ensure that no wheel could lock unless all four wheels were so sorely tried as to lock simultaneously, a condition rare enough to be statistically negligible. Because the actual braking system remained conventional, it was possible for the driver to override the Maxaret system by treading really hard on the brake pedal, in which case wheel-locking could be introduced; but normally it was kept at bay by the FF/Maxaret system, the driver being warned of its operation by the brake pedal kicking back gently beneath his foot.

As ill luck would have it, four-wheel drive was not a commercial success, and has been abandoned. A lock-inhibiting braking system remains desirable, however, and a good deal of effort has been expended on developing such systems that can work effectively and safely without demanding costly powered-hydraulic brake circuits. These developments have been encouraged by indications from the legislative bodies of certain countries that in due course they will make some form of anti-lock system mandatory.

Already an anti-lock system is desirable, for even the most highly skilled driver cannot allow for variations of surface friction under each wheel, and cannot therefore exploit the full braking power available. The feasibility of such a system has been enormously improved by the evolution of electronic devices that can more quickly, reliably, and cheaply sense incipient wheel lock than the purely mechanical sensors originally used in aircraft. At present the release and re-application of the brake remains a mechanical operation, but this did not deter several electronics firms from exploring the possibilities of skid preven-

tion mechanisms, Mullard demonstrating a notable one in 1970. Three years later Daimler-Benz demonstrated an essentially similar system, designed for incorporation in their S class Mercedes-Benz cars, and originally intended to be marketed as an optional extra item in the specification. Their engineers' suspicion that the system could not be made entirely fail-safe was confirmed in tests at Stuttgart, and work continues there and elsewhere without any production car yet being so equipped.

If one of this kind of lock-inhibitors is to be compatible with existing brake actuation mechanisms, one of the principal difficulties is in providing sufficient energy to reapply the brake after having released it, while allowing the driver to keep his foot hard on the pedal. The bulk of the requisite electric motors, solenoids, or vacuum actuators, has been particularly embarrassing on small cars, and a preferred solution has been to extract energy from the wheel itself. If the anti-lock system is working, the wheel cannot lock, and therefore the rotating wheel is available to provide the necessary energy. This direct nexus makes a very small unit feasible, and in the case of the Mullard apparatus the whole lot could be housed within existing brake calipers: a cam formed on the hub worked a little pump that returned bypassed braking fluid to the brake input as the wheel continued to rotate.

This example shows us that history is as repetitive as ever. In the 1930s that brilliant Frenchman Gabriel Voisin endowed some of his better cars with hydraulic brakes that were energised by tiny pumps fitted in the front wheel hubs and driven by rotation of the wheels. If the wheels stopped rotating, the pumps stopped delivering, so there was an anti-lock tendency inherent in the system. Alas, Voisin was considered a crank, and this particular effloration of his genius was much too clever and much too soon for his times.

Of course neither the electronics industry nor the likes of Daimler-Benz nor even Gabriel Voisin could devise anything that would prevent a skid developing in cornering, as opposed to the simpler kind that occurs in braking. All the major work (and for that matter the most important achievements to date) in this aspect of skid prevention is attributable to the tyre manufacturers, working sometimes with and sometimes against the road surfacers. If they continue to make progress at the remarkable rate sustained during the last fifteen years, it may be that mechanical, hydraulic, electronic and other skid-prevention devices will become superfluous; but this freedom from the danger of a skid is never likely to extend beyond countries that enjoy not only modern roads but also temperate climates.   LJKS

BEHIND THE CURTAIN

By 1975, Skoda was one of Czechoslovakia's best-known motor manufacturers and was exporting most of its production to the West

OTHER THAN THEIR alliterative value, books and bicycles are strange bedfellows, but such was the relationship which eventually led to the birth of the Skoda motor car.

When Vaclav Klement left his bookshop in the early 1890s and joined with mechanic Vaclav Laurin to found a small bicycle repair workshop in Mlada Boleslav, at that time part of the Austro-Hungarian

Below: Skoda do not only build cars, this is one of their fire tenders; 256 of these were built between 1938 and 1950

Empire, they could have had little idea that eventually they were to establish one of the biggest of the East European car manufacturers.

Business was satisfactory until Klement, chairman of the 'Club for the Promotion of Cycling' in Mlada Boleslav, discovered that it was extremely difficult to get spares for the imported bicycles which, because there were no domestic manufacturers, they were

forced to ride. The final straw came when, having written to the Dresden-based firm of Seidel and Neumann for spares to repair one of their bicycles, he received the reply: 'If you want something write in German'.

Suitably spurred, Klement determined from that time on to design and build his own bicycles and not just be content with repairing ones of other people's manufacture. As a result the first bicycle manufactured by the two partners was produced in rented rooms in the Nove Mesto district of Mlada Boleslav and was called the 'Slavia'.

Not surprisingly they met with considerable competition from the established manufacturers, especially those of Britain and Germany, but, undaunted, by 1897 they were employing 28 craftsmen and selling as many bicycles as they could produce.

In 1898 they moved their premises to a new building, the site of which now lies in the centre of the present day car factory. That same year Vaclav Klement travelled to Paris where he was particularly impressed with the Werner Brothers' motor driven cycle and the De Dion Bouton tricycle. On the return journey Klement made the decision that he would build his own motorised bicycle.

Soon the workforce was 32 strong and the battle was on to produce a satisfactory motor cycle. They struggled with no less than eight different prototypes before arriving at a solution that gave them an indelible place in automotive history.

Although motoring historians argue constantly about who did what first, the press of the day were in no doubt as to who was responsible for the first motor cycle—Laurin and Klement. In 1904, the German press proclaimed: 'The Laurin and Klement firm at Mlada Boleslav can by right be described as the makers of the powered two wheeler—without detracting any credit due to the French designers, the Werner Brothers.

'The French have attached an engine to a normal bicycle without changing its lines. In contrast, Laurin and Klement went the other way about it.

'They built around the engine and its elements a cycle. The idea was the same but the ways were different. The French emphasised the principles of the bicycle and the Czechs the principle of a motor car. And the Czechs were proved right!'

Klement and Laurin's customers apparently agreed. Motor cycle production began late in 1898 in the newly completed plant. Employing forty workmen, it was far ahead of its time in using what today we would regard as industrial production techniques. The factory had its own power station, forge, plating and paint shops, bodywork and machine shops, and a completely separate assembly bay.

The first demonstration of the Laurin and Klement type A-1.25 motor cycle came in 1899. Powered by a single-cylinder engine, it had a specially designed 'surface' carburettor, belt rear wheel drive and all the controls concentrated on the handlebars. It was also the first motor cycle in the world to be equipped with electromagnetic ignition instead of the customary hot bulb, and the first motor cycle to be built in the Austrian Empire. The first export orders for the machines, 150 for England and thirty for Germany, came towards the end of that year.

Within a short time the sporting potential of the new motor cycle was realised. Pioneer 'TT riders' straddled the Laurin and Klement machines not only in short distance events but also in bone-shaking marathons such as the Paris to Vienna race. Spurred on by their success, the two partners set about producing new and

better machines fitted with water-cooled, single-cylinder engines or twin-cylinder V-engines and eventually four-cylinder models.

In 1900, following the expansion of the factory premises to an area of 1100 square metres and an increase in the number of employees to 68, the company exhibited at the International Exhibition in Frankfurt-am-Main for the first time and took away the First Prize together with a Gold Medal, for their motor-cycles.

The following year saw the introduction of improved types of the A-1.25 motor cycle and of the B-1.75 machine. 1901 was also the year during which the BZ-2.5 boosted power, single-cylinder motor cycle was introduced and in which Laurin and Klement won First Prizes and Medals at International Exhibitions in Prague, Vienna and Hanover.

In 1902 the company introduced three more single-cylinder machines, the BZP-2.5, the L-2.75 and the LW-3. The latter having a water-cooled engine. This was the year in which the company experienced their first real successes in competition with Podsednicek and Klement himself, taking first and second places in the Exelberg Uphill Race. The Paris to Vienna Race was composed of fourteen motor cycles in 1902, eleven French machines and three Laurin and Klement bikes. At the finish there were only two French and two Laurin and Klement machines after 31 hours. The Laurin and Klement machines were ridden by top Czechoslovakian riders Riegr and Podsednicek, the latter being the only rider to pass

Top: Laurin & Klement were taken over by Skoda in 1925; this is the type A of 1905

Above: another Laurin & Klement; this is a 110A, produced between 1924 and 1928

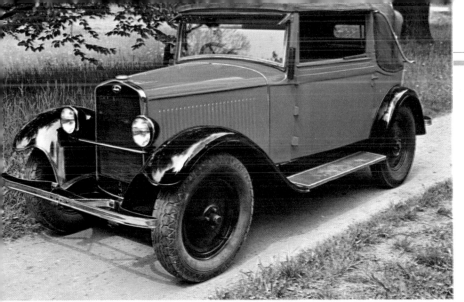

races in 1903 with 87 machines winning 72 prizes, including 32 first prizes.

In 1904 four new models were introduced, the CT-2.75, the CCD-4, the CCR-5 and the CCRW-5, the latter featuring a water cooled engine. By the end of the year Laurin and Klement had built 2000 motor cycles since their establishment and had sold a manufacturing licence to the German firm Siedel and Werner Foster. The participation of Laurin and Klement machines in thirty races that year resulted in twenty-four first places and F. Toman taking second place on a Laurin and Klement bike in the Gordon Bennet International Cup; completing his fastest lap at an average speed of 84 kilometres per hour.

The factory was again tripled in size in 1905, the production of bicycles was discontinued and the company introduced their CCCC type motor cycle which was powered by a four cylinder in-line engine developing 5 hp. In the same year a manufacturing licence was sold to the French company Alcylon.

In the unofficial world championship held that year on the elliptical track near the French town of Dourdon, the Laurin and Klement factory driver, Vaclav Vondrich stormed to victory. All the leading motor cycle manufacturers of that time entered their machines in the race, including Peugeot, Griffon, Progress, JAP, Ariel and Matchless and the victory of Vondrich on the Laurin and Klement machine resulted in him being acclaimed a national hero by the Czechs. Leading Czech composer of the day Kmoch, even went so far as to compose a piece of fiery dance music called 'On the Motor Cycle' to honour Vondrich. 1905 was, however, to be a year of even greater significance.

The Laurin and Klement factory in Mlada Boleslav had produced its first four wheeler vehicle as early as 1901 but realised immediately that it was not enough to merely apply the principles of motor cycle design to four wheels, and, although the company exhibited two prototypes of the car in Vienna, the project was handed back to the designers for further work.

For four years the Laurin and Klement engineers worked on a design for a motor car and the result in 1905, was the unveiling of the first car to be designed and produced in Austria-Hungary, the Model A Voiturette. Of entirely original design, it had a four stroke, twin-cylinder, V engine giving 3 hp, a three speed gearbox with reverse gear and a maximum speed of 30 mph. Available with two or four seats as required, the engine was not placed under the seats as was customary at that time, but was positional in front of the driver.

The following year it was joined by the Model B. Of the same design concept, the B had an increased power output to 9 hp. Its sporting *début* was at Semmering where Voiturettes took first, second and third places in their capacity class. In the same year the car also won first prize in a reliability contest which involved driving from Berlin, through Wroclaw and Leipzig, to Berlin. With an obvious success on their hands the company again set about expanding the factory to cope with the increased demand for their products.

During 1907 the entire factory was reconstructed and an extra 4000 square metres of working area added. The company went public that year with a capital of 2,500,000 Czechoslovakian Crowns—by 1920 the company's worth was estimated to be 16 million Crowns. Despite the reconstruction work the company continued to introduce new models. First the D and E Models powered by four cylinder engines, then the Type B-2 motor cab and finally one of their greatest pre-World War I models—the Type

Top: the 430 convertible of 1929

Above: the six-cylinder 2918 cc 6R Skoda Tourer of 1929

Left: the Popular 420 of 1924

Aroberk without having to dismount from his machine.

Work on trebling the size of the factory to 3300 square metres and the building of a new engine assembly shop, tinsmithy and forging shop began and was completed in 1903. That year the company introduced the first twin-cylinder CC-3 type motor cycle and, after experimenting with trailers and a seat in front of the driver, the company produced their first motor cycle and sidecar combination. These combination bikes were successfully exported to all parts of the world including Britain and Mexico where they were used as postal delivery vehicles.

Continuing their participation in competitions, Laurin and Klement motor cycles competed in 34

FF. Powered by an eight-cylinder, 4854 cc engine which produced 40 bhp, it was the first eight-cylinder engine to be cast in two parts with ignition by two magnetos to two spark plugs.

Competition successes that year included first and second places at a race held in Padua, Italy; a repetition of their victory at Semmering in the previous year and participation in the 430 kilometres non-stop race from London to Holyhead.

The factory engaged the outstanding designer and experienced racing driver, Otto Hyeronymus, in 1908, to supervise the building of their first special racing car, the Type FCR. With a valve-in-head four-cylinder engine of 85 mm bore and 250 mm stroke, the car completed ten laps of Brooklands circuit at an average speed of 72.57 mph and with a fastest lap of approximately 73 mph set a new world record for cars with a bore of up to 86 mm.

In the same year the company's products took the first nine places in a race from Petrograd to Moscow and Laurin and Klement were rewarded with massive orders from Czarist Russia which accounted for 35 per cent of their total exports. New models continued to pour from the factory during the year. The new G Type was introduced which was powered by a four-cylinder unit giving 14 hp and the Types A and B were supplemented by the twin-cylinder in-line powered Type BS.

That year the company began to manufacture commercial vehicles and omnibuses.

In 1909 the company bought a licence from a Dutch company for the manufacture of Brons stationary engines with power outputs ranging from 4 hp to 60 hp. In the same year the Type L was introduced with a four to six seat body, and powered by a 25 hp four-cylinder engine, together with the Type EN which was powered by a 46 hp unit giving the car a top speed of 85 kph.

1910 saw Otto Hyeronymus designing and building the first aircraft engine to be produced in Austria and in the same year test flights took place at Radouc near Mlada Boleslava and in Vienna. Continuing with their policy of proving their cars to the public by racing and rallying them, Laurin and Klement cars took three medals, three silver shields and the Factory Team prize in that year's Alpine Rally. Nineteen-ten also saw the introduction of the Type ENS luxury car and the Type GDN taxicab.

Sporting successes continued throughout 1911 with the most notable that year being the Petrograd to Sevastopol Rally of Czar Nicholas, in which the competitors travelled over 1600 kilometres of roads and 800 kilometres over the Russian steppes. Of the five Laurent and Klement cars entered four finished without getting any penalty points.

The Type S was introduced in 1911 and continued in production until 1925 at a production rate of 2000 cars per year. Powered by a four-cylinder, L-shaped 1766 cc engine which gave 14 hp, it was acclaimed as the most comfortable four seater appealing to the largest possible market. A Type K luxury model was introduced that year with a 32 hp engine.

In a non-stop race from Vienna to San Sebastian, through Linz, Munich, and Bordeaux, 2137 kilometres in all, an S Type Laurin and Klement took fourth place against 61 other competitors.

In 1912 the company began side-line manufacturing and were the first to build motorised ploughs in Austria-Hungary. These were sold under the name Excelsior and the first six-furrow ploughs were followed by three-furrow models. In the same year the RAF automobile factory in Liberec was incorporated

with a 4072 cc power unit which delivered 50 hp.

By 1922 official statistics showed that Laurin and Klement cars were the most popular in Czechoslovakia with a 19.6 per cent share of the total market and 42.1 per cent of those of Czechoslovakian origin. By 1923 car production was back to normal and the company introduced the Type 100, which was to become the backbone of their model range, and the Type 445. The former was powered by a 1796 cc unit giving 20 hp and the latter by a 4960 cc unit which gave 60 hp. Types 200 and 210 were also introduced as 2403 cc versions of the S Type. A year later the Type 400 was introduced powered by a sleeve-valve, 3300 cc 30 hp engine together with the Type 450 which was powered by a 4962 cc unit developing 60 hp.

With the company still suffering from the after effects of a disastrous fire in 1924, negotiations opened with a company then known as Akciova Spolecnot, today known as Skoda, with a view to the latter company taking over the assets of the Laurin and Klement company. These negotiations were satisfactorily concluded in 1925. Vaclav Klement became manager of the factory but the Laurin and Klement marque had disappeared for ever and all future models were to carry the Skoda name and emblem.

Skoda, at that time, were well known for their heavy machinery, guns and ship parts. Some of these latter

Opposite page, top: based on the Octavia saloon was this 450 Felicia of 1959

Centre: the Skoda Rapid cabriolet, which had a top speed of 70 mph

Bottom: another version of the rapid; this is a 1938 1558 cc car

in the Mlada Boleslav factory and the company bought a licence to build Knight sleeve-valve engines. Laurin and Klement cars again took the manufacturers team prize in the Alpine Rally.

A year later, in 1913, the company won the Alpine Prize and the Thurn-Taxis Industrial Award, which was awarded to the factory team which took the manufacturers' prize in the Alpine Rally three years running. That same year the company introduced Types MK and RK models, both with sleeve-valve engines.

World War I completely disrupted production at the factory and even when peace was declared it took the company a number of years to get back onto its feet. Post-war production included, however, many of the models which they had been manufacturing prior to 1914, including an updated version of the Type S. In 1918 Laurin and Klement introduced the Type MH

found their way onto ships such as the Queen Mary and Normandie. Skoda had embarked on car production in their own right in 1924 when they bought licences for the production of Hispano-Suiza cars and Sentinel steam lorries. Skoda-Hispano-Suizas were recognised as being outstanding luxury cars in their day, with many of them having specially made bodies. They were powered by six-cylinder, overhead camshaft 6600 cc engines which developed 100 bhp and gave the cars a top speed of 90 mph. Production of these cars continued at the Mlada Boleslav factory until the 1930s when the name was dropped.

Between the wars Skoda developed into one of the three biggest car manufacturers in Czechoslovakia, the other two being Tatra and Praga. As well as cars, Skoda produced trucks, tractors and aeroplane engines, with power units ranging from four up to eight cylinder.

Above left: the Popular Berlina of 1938, which featured an engine of 995 cc

Above: based on the Popular was this Montecarlo drophead of 1937

Immediately following their takeover of the Laurin and Klement car factory work began on extensive reconstruction including the building of a new mechanised assembly shop, a coach building shop, laboratories and the establishment of a research and development department.

In 1928 the first of the new models were unveiled: the 4R with a 1944 cc 32 hp four-cylinder engine and four-seater bodywork and the 6R, a 2,918 cc, 50 hp, six-cylinder, six seater. A year later these models were joined by a Type 422 four-cylinder, 1165 cc, 22 hp model, a Type 645 six cylinder, 2940 cc, 45 hp model and a Type 860 eight-cylinder, 3880 cc, 60 hp model.

In 1930 further rationalisation of the company led to the formation of the Automobile Industry Co Ltd, and annual production of 6000 cars. Production continued to concentrate mainly on the 430, 422 and 645 and the Type 633, introduced in 1931, which had a six-cylinder 1792 cc 33 hp unit, but soon the demand for a cheap and economical car led to the introduction of the Model 420.

The 420, introduced in 1933 represented a turning point in design for Skoda with the conventional frame being replaced by centre tubular chassis and rear swing half axles—a design that continued for the next thirty years.

The following year the 420 was remodelled to produce the very successful 'Popular'—Skoda's first

small, family car. Powered by a 903 cc (later 995 cc) engine developing 18 hp, it rapidly became the most successful car on the Czechoslovakian market (the Republic of Czechoslovakia had been created after the signing of peace in 1918). Exported throughout the world it also helped to put the Skoda name on the international map.

The same year saw the introduction of the six-cylinder, 1165 cc, 26 hp 420 Rapid and the six-cylinder, 2941 cc, 55 hp Superb.

In 1936 the Rapid was given a 1766 cc, 31 hp unit and the Superb a 2703 cc, 60 hp unit and the Favorit was introduced with a 1802 cc, 38 hp, four-cylinder engine. That year a Popular, driven by Pohl and Hausmann took second place in the Monte Carlo Rally in its class and finished eighth overall. A Rapid won the 1936 Olympic Games Rally.

The following year Skoda cars took third and ninth places in the Monte Carlo and two South Africans, Van Derburg and Van Vuuren, won the Nairobi to Johannesburg Rally, driving a two-year-old standard Popular. That year the Popular was given an uprated 1089 cc, 32 hp, four-cylinder, overhead valve engine; a design which was retained until the Octavia.

The year before World War II broke out saw the restyling of the bodies of the Popular, Rapid and Superb and the development of new engines all with overhead valves. The Popular was given a 1089 cc,

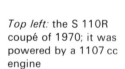

Top left: the S 110R coupé of 1970; it was powered by a 1107 cc engine

Above left: a 1969 version of the 110 saloon

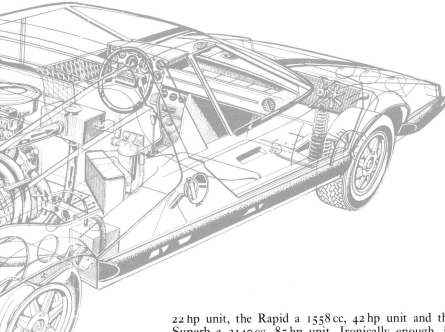

Top and above: two views of the Super Sport, which was first exhibited in 1971; it remained to be seen whether the model would ever actually reach production

22 hp unit, the Rapid a 1558 cc, 42 hp unit and the Superb a 3140 cc, 85 hp unit. Ironically enough, in 1939 Skoda were to reach their highest pre-war car production figure of 6371 cars in the year.

Following the German invasion of Czechoslovakia, the factory was taken over to contribute to the German war effort. Two days after the German forces surrendered on 7 May 1945, the Skoda factory was damaged by bombs. By the end of 1945, however, production of small passenger cars had resumed and the factory had been nationalised. First cars to come off the production line were a descendant of the Popular, the Skoda 1100 and the big Superb.

The S1101 was introduced in 1946 with an 1100 cc engine and gradually the range was extended to incorporate estate, convertible, van, ambulance and patrol car versions. Before the discontinuation of production in 1950, 67,000 cars of this type were manufactured at a daily rate of sixty vehicles. Within three years of the war ending, Skoda 1100s were being exported, mainly to East European countries, but also to Scandinavia, South America, Africa, Australia and New Zealand.

In the 1948 Francorchamps 24 Hour Race, they were beaten only by a British HRG. With special bodywork, Skoda cars have also raced at Le Mans.

In 1950 the company took over the manufacture of Tatraplan cars from the Tatra Works at Koprivnice as part of the Government's nationalisation programme and proceeded to produce one model, the 2-litre, rear-engined Tatraplan, which had been derived from the pre-war Type 97 Tatra. In the years up to 1954 when the model was discontinued some 5000 units were produced.

The Skoda 1200 was introduced in 1952 with a roomy, all metal, four door body on the S1101 type chassis and with a larger capacity engine. In the 1953 to 1955 period this type was in production together with the T805 lorry which had been developed in the Tatra Works in 1950.

In 1955 the manufacture of Skoda 1200 cars was transferred to the subsidiary works of the Automobile Works National Corporation in Vrchlabi and Kvasiny, where it continued until 1970. The same year saw the introduction of the two door Skoda 440-Spartak which was powered by a 1100 cc engine developing 40 hp and was the predecessor of the later S445 1200 cc model, the S450 and the Octavia and Octavia Combi. Up to the discontinuation of these models, 382,000 cars were built by Skoda.

A year later saw the beginning of an extensive modernisation programme for the factory which included the installation of over 100 production lines. A team of workers in the Automobile Works National Corporation at Mlada Boleslav designed and built the first automatic machining line for cylinder heads in Czechoslovakia.

Three years later work began on the construction of a new plant in compliance with a government ruling aimed at increasing production of passenger cars. On an area of 80 hectares, some forty buildings were erected within a period of $4\frac{1}{2}$ years, of which the mechanical workshops (60,000 square metres) and coachbuilding shops (75,000 square metres) represented the largest constructions of their kind in Czechoslovakia. The new metallurgical plant which was built at the same time included a forging shop, a foundry for cast iron and a foundry for aluminium alloys. The plant has the capacity to build some 120,000 automobiles a year.

Production began with the Skoda 1000 MB (MB for Mlada Boleslav), a roomy four-door saloon of chassis-less design with a rear mounted 988 cc, 40 bhp engine. The adoption of this design, the first of its type in the history of the factory, resulted in a reduction in the gross vehicle weight and an increase in performance. From this basic type were derived first the Skoda 1100MB and, after a restyling of the body, the Skoda 100, 110 and 110R Coupé models.

Four years later new tool shops and ancillary plants were built but in 1969 a fire destroyed the largest building of the old factory, the mechanical assembly shop. By that time Skoda had produced over 500,000 1000 and 1100MB models, and a year later a new building to replace the burnt one was constructed. Daily output exceeded 630 cars a day in 1973 and on 29th August the millionth Skoda 1000MB was assembled. For the first time in its history the factory exported over 10,000 cars which represented some 70 per cent of its production.

In 1974 the Skoda range consisted of two versions of the 100 saloon both powered by a four-cylinder, in-line, 988 cc, 42 hp engine; two saloon versions of the 110 and a coupé version of the 110, all powered by a 1107 cc, 48 hp (52 hp in the 110LS and Coupé versions) under the bonnet.

Work on increasing the production capacity of the factory has been underway for some time now in preparation for the promised introduction of a new model in the 1240 cc to 1500 cc range. BJ

1100R

Škoda Automobilové Závody Nárdoni Podnik of Trídá Rude armady, Mladá Boleslav, Czechoslovakia builds low-price rear-engined cars.

The top of the company's range in late 1975 was the 1100R coupé, two-door sports version of the popular 1100 four-door saloon.

The coupé uses an 1107 cc four-cylinder engine that produces 52 bhp at 4650 rpm and 64 lb ft at 3500 rpm. These give the car a top speed of 90 mph and enable it to accelerate to 50 mph from rest in 13.5 secs. A fuel consumption of over 33 mpg can quite easily be returned.

But it is in the suspension department that this Skoda falls short. With an independent front by wishbones, an anti-roll bar, coil springs and telescopic dampers, and an independent rear by swinging semi-axles, swinging longitudinal leading arms,

an anti-roll bar, coil springs and telescopic dampers, the handling has distinct tendency to oversteer. The fact that the engine is in the rear also contributes to the problem and is no help for the road-holding which generally is poor.

Despite seeming an unsporting car in practice, if not in looks, the coupé has done remarkably well in its class in various rallies.

One interesting point on the car is the gear lever. Skoda market the 1100R as a 'sports car', despite the lack of sports-car performance. Well, the gear lever is cross-drilled and looks like a long thin piece of gruyère. Whether this is in the interests of weight saving or just for looks is up to the driver to decide!

ENGINE Rear-mounted, water-cooled straight-four. 72 mm (2.83 in) bore × 68 mm (2.68

in) stroke = 1107 cc (67.54 cu in). Maximum power (DIN) 52 bhp at 4650 rpm; maximum torque (DIN) 64 lb ft at 3500 rpm. Light-alloy cylinder block and cast-iron head. Compression ratio 9.5:1. 3 main bearings. 2 valves per cylinder operated, via pushrods and rockers, by a single camshaft, side. 1 Jikov 32 DDSR downdraught twin-barrel carburettor.

TRANSMISSION Single-dry-plate clutch and four-speed manual gearbox. Ratios, 1st 3.800, 2nd 2.120, 3rd 1.410, 4th 0.960, rev 3.270:1. Spiral-bevel final drive. Ratio 4.444.

CHASSIS Integral.

SUSPENSION Front—independent by wishbones, coil springs, an anti-roll bar and telescopic dampers, rear—independent by swinging semi-axles, swinging longitudinal leading arms, coil

springs and dampers.

STEERING Screw and nut. Turns from lock to lock 2.50.

BRAKES Discs front, drums rear.

WHEELS 4.5 in × 14 in steel.

TYRES 155SR × 14.

DIMENSIONS AND WEIGHT Wheelbase 94.49 in; track—front 50.39 in, rear—49.21 in; length 163.39 in; width 63.78 in; height 68.90 in; ground clearance 6.89 in; dry weight 1841 lb; turning circle between walls 33.5 ft; fuel tank capacity 7 gals.

BODY Sports coupé. 2-door, 4–5-seater.

PERFORMANCE Maximum speed 90 mph. Acceleration 0–50 mph 13.5 secs. Fuel consumption approximately 33 mpg.

Raymond the Lionheart

THE RACING DRIVER RAYMOND SOMMER was the son of Roger Sommer, a wealthy manufacturer of felt, who from 1909 to 1912 had been one of France's best-known pioneer aviators and manufacturers of aircraft, but had sold his aviation business to MM Bathiat and Sanchez-Besa in 1913 and 'returned from aviation to the less exciting but more remunerative business of making felt slippers and such things'.

Thus young Raymond, born in 1906, was brought up in an atmosphere of 'mechanical sport and progress'; he first started motor racing with a 4.6-litre Chrysler straight-eight, which had a carburettor for each cylinder, and, though he retired at Le Mans in 1931, he and his co-driver Delemer won the sports car class in the Belgian 24 hours' race at Spa.

In March 1932, still driving the Chrysler, he was first in the general classification of the Paris–Nice Trial, and also set a new class record in the La Turbie hillclimb. Soon afterwards, he bought an 8C2300 Alfa Romeo and, by way of a try-out, won the Torvilliers race at Troyes. With Luigi Chinetti as co-driver, he entered the Alfa for the 24 Heures du Mans, and drove for 18 hours out of the 24 as his partner was unwell; the result was a victory for the equipe, with the Alfa covering 2954 km. A month later, Sommer came second in the Nice Grand Prix, while in September he won the Nice Grand Prix with his 2.6 litre P3 Alfa, defeating Nuvolari with spectacular ease and style.

Nuvolari shared the Monza with Sommer in that year's Le Mans 24 hours, and despite frequent halts for fuel caused by a leaking petrol tank, the Alfa notched up Sommer's second victory in this event.

Sommer's verve and courage at the wheel earned him the nickname of *Raymond Coeur de Lion*; he drove like a devil, it was said, and would never retire from a race while there was still hope, even when a breakdown had lost him all chance of winning.

Driving a Maserati, he was third in the 1935 Belgian Grand Prix; with a new 3.2 litre Alfa P3 he won the Comminges Grand Prix and was third in the Marne GP, while 1936 saw him take fourth place in the Vanderbilt Cup on the Roosevelt Raceway.

Just before World War II, in 1937 and 1939, Sommer earned himself the title of Champion of France. When war broke out, he was refused a commission in the French Army, preferring to fight as an ordinary *poilu*: even so, he still managed to shoot down a low-flying German aeroplane with his rifle.

After the war, backed by veteran motoring journalist Charles Faroux, Sommer was at the head of the unpopular—but eventually successful—campaign to free Doctor Persche from Dijon prison, and was soon back in motor racing, coming second in the very first post-war event, organised in the Bois de Boulogne in 1945. The following season saw victories in the Marseille

Raymond Sommer at the wheel of an Alfa Romeo in 1933 at the Belgian Grand Prix, *above,* and *below,* on his way to victory in his Maserati in the 1946 Bois de Boulogne

Grand Prix, the Circuit de Trois Villes and the St Cloud GP, a second in the Turin Grand Prix and the Brussels Meeting, a list of successes which were enough earned him his third French championship.

In 1947, Sommer crashed at Pau, nearly biting off his tongue in the impact, and was eliminated from both the Grand Prix d'Europe at Spa and the Prix de la Marne at Reims after his Maserati chassis frame broke on both occasions. He then tried the CTA-Arsenal at Lyon—it broke its back axle on the starting line.

His luck seemed to have changed at Turin, at the wheel of one of the new V12 2-litre Ferraris, and led all the way from the start, running away from the rest of the field with consummate ease and making the fastest lap of 69.88 mph and

recording an average of 67.5 mph over the 312.5 mile distance.

He raced a Talbot in 1948 and 1949, and drove the unlucky 16-cylinder BRM in its *début* at Silverstone but, recalling the CTA-Arsenal, its transmission broke on the starting line.

Then, while taking part in the unimportant Haute Garonne Grand Prix on the Gardours circuit on 10 September 1950, Sommer crashed fatally in his 1100 cc Cooper, apparently the victim of a seized wheel bearing.

'Drive your hardest, take the lead early and frighten off the opposition—if possible,' had been Raymond Sommer's credo. Not long before his death, France had awarded him the Cross of the Legion of Honour as 'the greatest driver in the country.'   DBW

TURNING THE VOLUME DOWN

Preventing unwanted sounds from reaching the occupants of a motor car involves a great deal of planning and thought

METHODS OF PREVENTING 'unwanted sounds' from reaching the occupants of a car have long been a subject for research. The engine, exhaust system and tyre/road combination form a built-in sound-producing apparatus for every car, while the airflow round the body gives rise to a variety of aerodynamic noises.

It has been determined that most noises reaching the interior of the car lie in the lower frequency ranges, below 1000 Hz, those above about 16 Hz being audible. Below 16 Hz, vibrations are felt rather than heard; it is of interest to note that the lowest frequencies, between 0.5 Hz and 3 Hz, are believed to be responsible for car sickness in children.

Another factor that arises is sound feedback and frequency mixing. For example, the road wheels may cause the chassis to vibrate at a certain frequency; this may 'beat' with a regular engine noise, thus generating a third frequency that will set up oscillations in a panel. The vibrations felt in a car occur mostly in a vertical plane, but there is a small transverse component due to lateral flexing of the tyres.

An empty car shell is like a drum, and in such a shell the occupants would suffer intolerable 'booming' or, in engineering terms, structural or body cavity resonances, as sounds reverberate from one panel to another.

The car designer first tries to 'design out' as many noises as possible by putting vibration calculations and many related factors through a computer. The results obtained are verified or modified by practical experience, the designer locating the various sound and vibration sources, and, step by step, trying to eliminate them, isolate them, or by some means muffle them so that they are not audible or cannot be felt within the vehicle.

A difference must be noted between radiated noise and transmitted noise: Radiated noise is carried by air waves, transmitted noise by vibrations through the structure. In general, it is relatively easy to cut out radiated noise, simply by closing the windows tightly and ensuring that the door seals are doing their job;

Below: although anti-vibration panels are fitted to most cars made since the 1960s, special felt material is still affixed to the panels in strategic places, such as along the dash, on the bulkhead between the passenger compartment and the engine and underneath the bonnet lid

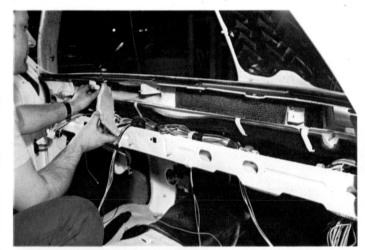

but the suppression of transmitted noise is more difficult and much of the work cannot be finalised until numerous tests on a variety of road surfaces have been carried out.

Having eliminated as many primary sources as possible—by partly isolating the engine by flexible mountings; by fitting an expansion chamber and silencer to the exhaust; by suspending the exhaust system from flexible hangers, by eliminating rattles and closing in the body by means of effective seals—the designer's next step is to prevent vibration in the various body panels.

There are two general methods of stopping this 'drumming'; one method is to stiffen the panels mechanically, either by means of 'swage lines' or 'crowns' produced at the pressing stage, or by welding or bonding metal channels across large panels, such as the bonnet or boot lids. A reasonably uniform degree of rigidity must be applied throughout the vehicle, otherwise the vibration or resonance may merely be shifted to another area.

The second method is the application of sound-insulating materials to the panels themselves—inside the outer door skins, the floor wells and rear quarter panels, for example. When this is done, the bonding of the insulating material to the metal must be perfect; special adhesives, usually requiring heat curing, have been evolved for this purpose. If the bonding fails, then further vibration is set up between the metal and the insulating material and the final result may be worse than it was originally.

Under the floor pan and wheel arches a bitumenized underseal material is sprayed on—the thicker the better, if weight considerations are not important. This underseal serves the dual purpose of protecting the metal as well as deadening sound. The underside of the bonnet is sometimes sprayed with the same material.

The one large unbroken area, the roof, receives more elaborate treatment. One leading manufacturer fits a double skin, with insulating panels bonded to the inside. A sound-absorbing material, usually of foamed plastics, is bonded to the headlining.

Other sound-absorbing materials complete the interior furnishings—felt, then carpet, on the floor; well-padded seats; padded interior door trim; thick felt or fibreglass against the firewall, and a resilient padded dashboard.

In a vehicle so treated, it should be possible to carry on a normal, quiet conversation without difficulty, even with the interior heater—itself 'noise con-ditioned'—in full operation.   AGH

Below: a 1975 Pontiac Catalina, showing the sound deadening material fitted as standard at the top of the range and as an optional extra lower down; every part of the passenger compartment, except for the windows, is treated

IN-CAR ENTERTAINMENT

To the uninitiated, the world of in-car entertainment can be thoroughly confusing

TO THE UNINITIATED, the world of in-car entertainment can be most bewildering. Equipment falls into a number of categories and prices range from about £15 for a simple manually tuned radio, to more than £400 for the most sophisticated device. Because the whole field is still a closed book to many in spite of its rapid increase in popularity in recent years it is necessary to go back to basics to explain what it is all about.

The term 'in-car entertainment' or ICE as it is sometimes known boils down to equipping a car with a machine that provides its driver and passengers with some form of audible diversion by way of music, talks, plays and news bulletins, although the latter can seldom be regarded as entertainment in these days of economic gloom. In mentioning diversion one does not wish to imply that the equipment will distract the attention of a driver. Used properly it may soothe an impatient driver and help while away a long journey; used improperly it could have the opposite effect and annoy other road users.

Under the collective heading of ICE there are radios, tape players and units combining these facilities in a single steel box. Radios come in two basic forms and have either manual tuning only or manual tuning plus push-button selection of predetermined stations.

Almost every car radio has frontal dimensions of 7 in wide × 2 in high with front to rear depth varying between about $3\frac{1}{2}$ in to $6\frac{1}{2}$ in so that it can either be fitted into the slot for radio provided by the car manufacturer, or suspended beneath the facia or parcel shelf. In addition to a manual tuning knob, low-priced sets have the volume control combined with an on/off switch and push-button or slider to select either of its wavebands, usually the medium and long wavebands.

Although there is no definite division by price between manual-only tuning sets and push-button units, the latter are generally more expensive due to the additional cost of the tuner mechanism. All push-button sets also have a manual tuner and this is used to set-up the push-buttons. Procedure is simple. The manual tuner is used to select five stations, four buttons of which are allocated to the medium waveband and one to long waves, although the combination is sometimes varied. Having found, say, Radio One in London on 247 metres or 1214 kHz if the dial is calibrated in kilohertz. When tuning it is wise not to rely on the scale for accuracy but to make final adjustment by ear until unwanted noises are eliminated and maximum bass response is obtained. The first medium wave button is pulled fully outwards towards the user and then pushed fully home again. That is all there is to it and all the other buttons can be set in like manner, except that the long wave button must first be pressed inwards to select that waveband before it too can be set. Manual tuning can be employed at any time without changing the button settings.

A fully variable tone control is another feature of most push-button sets and it is certainly a standard fitting on all the middle and upper price models. This permits finer adjustment of tonal balance to suit the more critical listener. Movement up the price scale also introduces a wider choice of, or combination of wavebands. While the medium and long wavebands feature on the majority of car receivers, additional possibilities now include coverage of short wavebands and the VHF/GM band leading ultimately to a set offering stereo reproduction from many BBC and all commercial radio transmissions.

Choice of waveband coverage deserves some thought. For general usage in the UK the medium and long wavebands should be regarded as essentials, the latter, particularly for the traveller, as Radio Two on

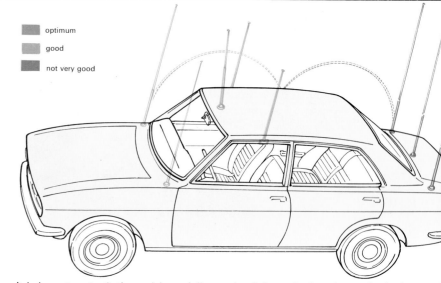

optimum

good

not very good

It is important to fit the aerial carefully, so that it is earthed to the car body, has as s[...] wire as possible, is as far away from the engine as possible and is not obscured by body[...] usually a compromise is the only practical solution

1,500 metres can be heard almost anywhere while moving about this island. FM is essential despite its limited range of transmissions, because of the fine quality of reproduction. For even better quality the next move is to stereo FM but as this demands twin amplifier stages, few car radios are offered with this facility. Stereo FM, however, becomes more common among combined radio/tape units.

That is a summary of car radios treated as individual items. It is time to move to tape players before bringing it all together as combined units which constitute the third phase in in-car entertainment units.

Tape players fall under two basic headings, each with their own variations. First to enter the UK market via America in about 1966 was the cartridge or 8-track machine, so called because its tape is wound in a continuous loop inside a plastic case or cartridge.

All tapes are recorded in stereo using eight tracks,

Opposite page, top: one of the earliest car-radio installations, seen in 1931; the roof-mounted aerial resembles a fence rather than the modern antenna

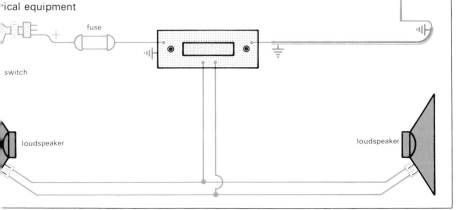

g and connecting a radio is usually simple, although some equire special brackets; the only connections needed are e ignition switch, the aerial and the speaker(s). The est complication is usually in fitting supressors to other ical equipment

aerial

fuse

switch

loudspeaker

loudspeaker

Left: the dashboard of the Dual Ghia of 1957, showing a special console in which a radio and record-player are mounted; tapes soon ousted disc recordings from the car

Below left: the Autovox Melody combined radio and cassette-tape recorder; this medium and long-wave unit has the advantage of being able to record direct from the radio

making four pairs of stereo tracks. To get an overall playing time of, say, 60 minutes on a tape of given length and moving at a speed of $3\frac{3}{4}$ inches per second, the playback head has to 'read' a different pair of tracks every 15 minutes. It takes this time for the reel of

tape to complete a circuit and as the piece of foil joining the ends of the tape momentarily bridges a pair of contacts, a solenoid is actuated. The solenoid is linked to a cam arrangement and as this is rotated pulls the playback head downwards, in relation to the tape, in four successive stages. Thus each pair of stereo tracks comprising one of the four programmes, is 'read' in turn. When the bottom stage is completed, the head springs back to its top position. The sequence now restarts and will continue until the cartridge is extracted from the machine.

The course of the tape inside 8-track cartridge is nearly as complicated as the process itself. The $\frac{1}{4}$ in wide tape is wound on a single reel at the centre of the cartridge case with one end coming from the centre of the reel and the other the outside. The tape passes over a pinch wheel, pressure pads and guide rollers. The ends of the tape are joined by a short piece of foil to create a continuous loop. When the cartridge is pushed into the player, the pinch wheel presses against a capstan driven at constant speed by a small motor inside the player. Movement from the capstan is transferred to the tape so that it is pulled across the face of the replay head, while, inside the case, tape is paid out from the centre of the reel and wound back on the outside circumference.

Because of the circumferential differences between the inner and outer layers of the reeled tape, students of physics may be excused if they exclaim that this system cannot work. What they may not know is that the tape is lubricated so that one layer slips against the next throughout the reel so automatically making allowance for the seemingly impossible physical properties of the system.

Basic 8-track players have three controls, sound volume, another to adjust stereo balance between the left and right speakers and a third to vary the tone. As prices rise so sophistication increases with the addition of fast forward wind. This is a bit of a misnomer because, for mechanical reasons, the tape cannot be moved at more than three times normal speed without risk of tangling. Other refinements include a repeat switch which, while in operation, cancels the unit's automatic switching mechanism, so that any given programme will repeat as long as required. However, fast wind used in conjunction with the manual track changing switch fitted to all units, can help to speed up the location of a particular passage in one of the four programmes, but this is inclined to be a hit-and-miss operation because there is no visible indication of tape position.

The 8-track player, of course, is the father of the quadraphonic player. The two types of units are basically similar and in some cases are compatible in that some will play standard 8-track cartridges as well as the special quad variety. However, because recordings now occupy four tracks at a time (quad) instead of two as in stereo, the tape contains two programmes only. To correspond with the recorded tracks, the playback head now has four magnetic gaps, signals from which pass to four amplifiers and then to four speakers placed at the front and rear of a car. Quad players have controls similar to an 8-track unit except for the addition of a front/rear balance control. Just to make choice even more difficult there are variations in the form of 8-track units which will produce simulated quad through four speakers from standard stereo tapes and quad units that will do this in addition to handling proper quad tapes. The artificial quad system is called 'Matrix' while the true method is named 'Discrete'. Quadrophony is known also as the 'surround sound', a pretty apt description.

While the 8-track system was designed especially for in-car use and is ideal for providing background music where the starting point of a recording is not critical, its rival, the cassette, is advancing rapidly. As a portable, battery-operated recording system used both seriously and for amusement, the history of the cassette probably extends as far back in this country as 8-track does in America.

People had been playing with cassette recorders and making their own recordings on blank tape for some time before Philips launched the first commercially recorded cassettes, called Musicassettes, in 1966. Shortly afterwards that company modified an existing portable recorder so that it could be used with some of their car radios in a car. Radiomobile did likewise and the swing to cassette becoming an adjunct to driving, began and it has been gaining ground ever since.

The system is termed 'cassette' because it is based on the Philips pioneered method of enclosing two miniature tape reels within a slim, compact, plastic box, christened a cassette. Among the reasons for its quick popularity in size, which is about half that of an 8-track cartridge, and that it can be wound or re-wound at 30 times its normal playing speed of $1\frac{7}{8}$ inches per second. As it is possible to wind tapes back, recordings can always be started from the beginning. This is an important factor for those who enjoy serious music.

Initially, reproduction quality from cassette players was poor compared with good 8-track but so many advances have been made in tape manufacture and improvement in replay heads, plus the adoption of the Dolby noise reduction system, that quality differences, if any, are no longer a significant problem.

Until recently, however, cassette systems did suffer one major disadvantage compared with 8-track. Because cassettes use only two pairs of recorded tracks, it is necessary to extract the cassette from the player at the end of each side, turn it over and replace in the machine, to play the other half. Now, with the advent of auto-reverse mechanism on some players rendering manual intervention unnecessary, the remaining defensive bastion of 8-track is crumbling.

There is one other plus-point for cassette: cost. There are many costing less than £20 and it is possible to make one's own recordings which can be played back on an in-car unit. It must be pointed out, that it is illegal, even for one's own personal use, to make a copy of any commercial recording or most broadcast material.

Having given a brief outline of the types of car radio and tape players available it is now possible to discuss them together in the form of combination units, which is the area where most growth and development is taking place.

Combination units, as the name implies, means a radio combined with either a cartridge or cassette tape player and enclosed in the same steel box. Much ingenuity has been put into their design to keep the frontal dimensions of units to the 7 in × 2 in size, so permitting in-dash fitting. Front-to-rear depth may exceed the $6\frac{1}{2}$ in mentioned earlier so, when selecting a set for fitting in this manner, this dimension should be noted because different cars and models vary in the amount of behind facia space available.

However, getting the two parts together is like pouring a quart into a pint pot. This scramble for space has squeezed out the push-button radio tuner, except for two cartridge combination units where their inclusion has made the units very slightly oversize for conventional in-dash fitting. At the moment there are no cassette machines with a push-button tuning system such as described earlier, but models with this

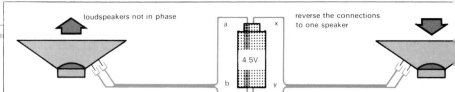

If two speakers are to be fitted to a radio or tape player, be it monaural or stereophonic must be in phase (in other words the cones must move in the same direction. To check battery should be connected as shown

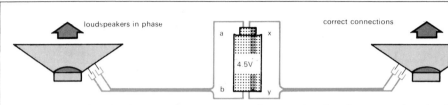

If on connecting the battery, the cones move in opposite directions, x and y shoul transposed to correct this

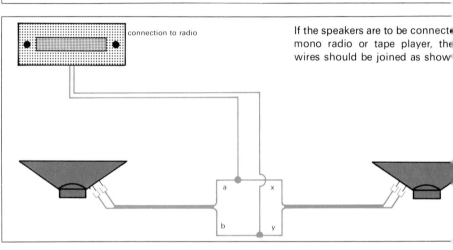

If the speakers are to be connect mono radio or tape player, the wires should be joined as show

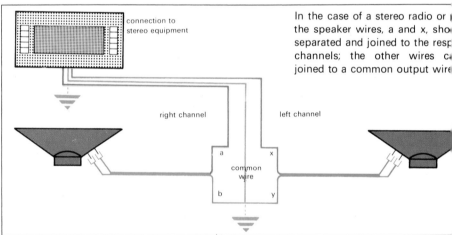

In the case of a stereo radio or the speaker wires, a and x, sho separated and joined to the resp channels; the other wires c joined to a common output wire

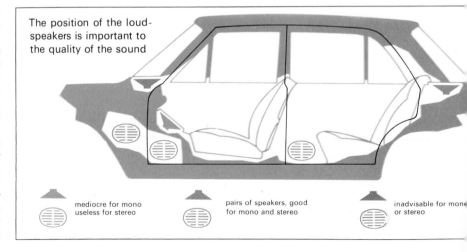

The position of the loudspeakers is important to the quality of the sound

mediocre for mono useless for stereo

pairs of speakers, good for mono and stereo

inadvisable for mon or stereo

Top: a Philips RN712 radio/cassette recorder, with medium, long and VHF or FM wavebands; the unit is shown fitted to a Jaguar coupé

Above: a six-valve radio of 1947, fitted with medium wave only

Above right: a modern, pushbutton-tuning, all-transistor radio, capable of receiving medium, long and FM programmes

facility are expected from two or three British manufacturers next spring. An alternative method has been adopted by Philips for their top-price combination tape and radio models as well as one of their radio only units.

This is the Turnolock system which is actuated by successional pushes on a button or knob. Six stations can be pre-set simply by tuning the set manually and then pushing the button for the next station. The button also changes wavebands. Although the system may seem easy to use it does have snags, chief among them being that manual tuning will always change at least one pre-set station and this can be annoying, particularly if the displaced station happens to be a popular one.

Since all tape players, with only one or two exceptions, reproduce in stereo means that when their mechanism is combined with radio, the two-channel amplifiers are available for stereo radio reproduction if the radio covers the FM waveband and incorporates a decoder circuit. This is why more stereo FM radios are to be found among combination units than among plain radios which normally only have a mono output.

Thanks to the interest in stereo FM broadcasting shown by the commercial radio stations, and to a lesser extent by the BBC, more and more listeners are coming to enjoy the enhanced quality of musical broadcasts which are at their best when transmissions are 'live'. Unfortunately, good reception requires greater attention to the suppression of noises generated by the engine and certain components of a car. Such sets must be installed with greater care than is the case with a medium or long waveband radio to get the best results.

Sets designers have done much to filter out unwanted noises and the most successful manufacturer so far is probably Philips who use a patented interference absorbtion circuit (known as I.A.C.) on FM to achieve this end—and with a remarkable degree of success too.

Finally, one must mention that there is yet another method of tuning, available only on a few top-price radios. This is the signal-seeker system operated by pressing a bar. This action starts the receiver on an electronically-driven search for stations of suitable power. When one is encountered, the tuner stops. If the station programme is not to one's liking, the actuating bar is pressed again and the signal-seeker makes another attempt to satisfy.

EGC

SPEED IN THE SUN

The South African Grand Prix has become a regular and popular feature of the World Championship series

THE SOUTH AFRICAN GRAND PRIX became an international fixture in the mid-1930s. Although several Europeans made the trek, it was more for the adventure than the racing. A handicap event, the result often depended on luck with the fastest entries standing no hope of victory. In the 1960s, however, the South African Grand Prix became firmly established in the World Championship series. First, with an end-of-December date, it was the last round of the World Championship. Later a move to January, and then to March, pushed it to the head of the list until the advent of the Argentine and Brazilian GPs. Until 1966 the race was run at circuits at East London, while from 1967 onwards the home of the South African Grand Prix has been the popular Kyalami, near Johannesburg.

The first South African Grand Prix was held on 17 December 1934 at the Prince George road circuit five miles south-west of East London. A 15.2-mile affair, it was comprised of public roads and included the notorious West Bank section through the outskirts of a village. The race was run on an individual handicap basis over six laps, a total of 91.2 miles. Whitney Straight, an American who had just become a British citizen, had flown from London with his younger brother Michael and British star Dick Seaman to compete in his last event. Driving his 2.9-litre Maserati 8CM from the scratch mark, Straight won at an average speed of 85.68 mph. J. H. Case's Ford was

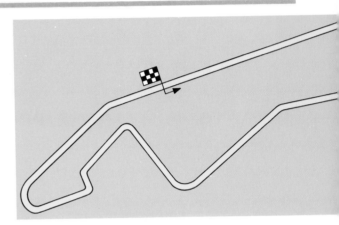

Right: outline of the 2.55-mile Kyalami circuit near Johannesburg, South Africa; it was built in 1961 and in 1967 became the home of the South African Grand Prix.

Below right: the East London circuit, venue for the SAGP from 1960 until 1966

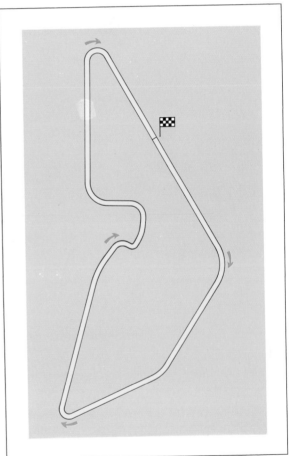

second and Michael Straight's Railton-Terraplane third. Seaman, racing a works MG K3, was fifth following three pit stops that were necessary to deal with a faulty hand fuel pump.

The first Grand Prix was originally known as the South African Border 100, but when another race was planned for January 1936 it was termed the second

Above: Clay Regazzoni's Ferrari undergoes a routine check during practice for the 1975 South African Grand Prix at Kyalami

Grand Prix. A shortened, 11.03-mile circuit was used which by-passed the village, the link road being given the name Potter's Pass after the person who constructed it. Race distance was eighteen laps. The handicaps were sent to Britain for checking by A. V. Ebblewhite, the famous pre-war timekeeper who arranged the handicapping at Brooklands. Entries included everything from local Ford specials to Richard Shuttleworth and T. P. Cholmondeley Tapper in Alfa Romeos (a P3 and a Monza respectively), two 3.3-litre Bugatti T59s for Jean-Pierre Wimille and Earl Howe and Arthur Dobson's 1½-litre Riley from overseas. The Riley led into the closing stages, only to blow up and hand victory to 'Mario' Massacurati's Bugatti T35B from Wimille and South African Pat Fairfield's ERA A-type. Shuttleworth crashed seriously after his car was caught by the wind; he was unconscious for several days and it was some months before he could return home to Britain.

In 1937 two works Auto Union B-types for Bernd

Below right: Denny Hulme of New Zealand hurls his McLaren-Ford through Leeukop Bend, on his way to third place in the 1969 South African Grand Prix at Kyalami

handicap was too severe and in trying to make up time he first wore out a tyre and later lost a wheel when a hub broke. South Africans dominated in 1938, Buller Meyer's 1500 cc Riley conquering D. C. Richardson's 1100 cc version. Foreign competitors included Italians Giovanni Lurani, Piero Taruffi, Luigi Villoresi, Lazlo Hartmann, Lord Howe and Raymond Mays, all over-handicapped. Last pre-war South African Grand Prix, a straight 1500 cc race in 1939, saw victory go to Luigi Villoresi in his Scuderia Ambrosiana-entered Maserati 4CM from team-mate Franco Cortese.

The South African Grand Prix series was not revived until 1960, but several important races were

run in the immediate post-war years. Peter Whitehead and Tony Gaze ran their Ferraris, Bill Holt and Mike Young their Connaughts and Dick Gibson his Cooper in South African internationals. Racing at East London had to be abandoned after a series of fatal accidents, so a new, permanent venue was sought. At first a circuit utilising a long straight on the original Prince George layout was planned, but building developments prevented this. Instead a new 2.4356-mile track was built in the shape of a rather flat triangle alongside the Indian Ocean overlooked by a hillside which formed a natural grandstand.

On 1 January 1960, 50,000 spectators flocked to the new East London track to watch several top European entries in Formula Two machinery take on South Africa's best drivers. Stirling Moss's Cooper T45-Borgward led initially, to be overtaken by team-mate Chris Bristow. Then Bristow spun and was eventually eliminated with gearbox failure leaving Moss comfortably ahead of Belgian Paul Frère's T45-Climax. Into the closing laps fuel-injection problems slowed Moss considerably and Frère took a lead he was never to lose with six of the 60 laps to complete. Confusingly perhaps, a second Grand Prix was run that year, in December. Over 80 laps, it provided an easy victory for Moss in the Rob Walker-entered Porsche from Jo Bonnier's works machine. A year later Jim Clark's works-entered Lotus 21-Climax beat the UDT-Laystall Lotus 18/21-Climax of Stirling Moss with Jo Bonnier's works Porsche second and top South African Tony Maggs fourth in a Yeoman Credit-entered Cooper T55-Climax.

The success of the three post-war Grands Prix at East London led to the granting of World Championship status to the 1962 race. And what a cliff-hanger it was! Since the previous championship race at Watkins Glen in October, over two-and-a-half months before, the title had been in the balance. Either Graham Hill or Jim Clark could be World Champion, but mathematics decreed that in order for Clark to take all, he had to win the race. Clark shot ahead in his Lotus 25-Climax and as the race approached three-quarters

Rosemeyer and Ernst von Delius were enticed to South Africa, but the monster cars were heavily handicapped and Rosemeyer could only manage third place. Fairfield's ERA won from a Riley. Richard Seaman participated in his famous revamped Delage, his last appearance in the French car before he joined the Mercedes-Benz Grand Prix team; however, his

Above: Clay Regazzoni's Ferrari leads the McLaren M23 of Emerson Fittipaldi during the 1975 South African GP

distance he was securely in front. Then a wisp of smoke appeared from the engine. A small bolt had contrived to unscrew itself, and oil was escaping. Eventually, with 63 of the 82 laps run, Clark was forced to retire and Hill's BRM P57 won both the race and the World Championship. Cooper works drivers Bruce McLaren and Tony Maggs were second and third and Jack Brabham's Brabham BT3-Climax arrived in fourth position.

The 1963 Grand Prix did not settle the championship, but it helped new World Champion Jim Clark set a record. It was the Scotsman's seventh Grand Prix win of the season, a record total for a year. Clark was never headed throughout the 85 laps and only second man Dan Gurney (Brabham BT7-Climax) remained unlapped at the finish. There was no race in 1964—by running the event a week later the South African Grand Prix became the opening round of the 1965 World Championship series. It was Jim Clark in devastating mood once more, no one being able to challenge the Scot's Lotus 33-Climax during the 85-lap race. John Surtees (Ferrari 158) and Graham Hill (BRM P261) were second and third.

The new 3-litre Formula One was introduced in 1966 and as many top teams were unready in January the Grand Prix lost its championship status. Mike Spence's 2-litre Lotus 33-Climax held out over sixty laps to place in first position in front of Jo Siffert's 1¾-litre Brabham BT11-BRM.

A new chapter in the story of the South African Grand Prix began in 1967. The venue was changed to Kyalami, a 2.55-mile circuit near Johannesburg and the first Grand Prix circuit in the Transvaal, which was opened in November, 1961. The hilly countryside provided excellent vantage points and the track, comprising a long straight and a series of twists and turns, proved to be very popular with the drivers. One problem, however, was its altitude: at 5400 ft above sea level overheating and loss of power had to be counteracted. The 1967 Grand Prix over 80 laps was watched by a record 90,000 crowd, reportedly the biggest crowd ever at a South African sporting event, and with the favourites falling by the wayside it looked as if John Love of Rhodesia, a multi-South African Champion, would grab victory in his misfiring four-cylinder Cooper T79-Climax. But he had to stop for fuel and give best to the V12 Cooper T81-Maserati driven by Pedro Rodriguez.

In 1968 the advent of the Cosworth-Ford DFV engine had changed Formula One racing. Jim Clark and Graham Hill led a Lotus 49-Ford 1-2 victory and in doing so Clark scored his 25th (and sadly last) Grand Prix win, breaking Juan Manuel Fangio's record. This potential was realised the following year when Stewart led the 80-lap race from beginning to end in the Tyrrell-prepared Matra MS10-Ford. Ford-engined cars took the first six places. The race was run in March, ensuring more new-season cars and a very helpful drop in temperature.

The 1970 South African Grand Prix marked the *début* of a completely new Formula One manufacturer, March. Five March 701-Fords were entered for works drivers Chris Amon and Jo Siffert, STP's Mario Andretti and Ken Tyrrell's pair, Jackie Stewart and Johnny Servoz-Gavin. Tongues were set wagging when Stewart and Amon recorded the two best practice times, but the best March could achieve in the race was Stewart's third behind winner Jack Brabham's new monocoque Brabham BT33-Ford and Denny Hulme's McLaren M14A-Ford. Hulme seemed the likely winner in 1971 in the new McLaren M19A-Ford, but a bolt dropped out of the suspension in the

closing minutes, allowing Mario Andretti (Ferrari 312B-1/71) to snatch a 20.9s victory from Jackie Stewart's Tyrrell 001-Ford.

Hulme made up for his heartbreak the following year, his Yardley-sponsored McLaren M19A triumphing over Emerson Fittipaldi's John Player Special/ Lotus 72-Ford and team-mate Peter Revson's McLaren. Pole position man Jackie Stewart had led from laps 2 to 44 before the gearbox of his Tyrrell 003-Ford seized. Stewart won the 1973 race after a brilliant performance. A crash in practice forced him to start from the seventh row of the starting grid in team-mate François Cevert's Tyrrell 006-Ford but could not keep him from slicing through the field to take the lead on lap seven. An early-race crash involving Clay Regazzoni's BRM P160D could have had fearful consequences had the Swiss driver not been promptly aided from the blazing wreck by Mike Hailwood, whose own Surtees TS14-Ford had been eliminated in the same accident.

In pre-race testing for the 1974 Grand Prix Peter Revson crashed his UOP Shadow DN3A-Ford at speed into the guard-rail after its front suspension failed; the bottom rail broke and the car went under the top rail which inflicted fatal head and chest injuries. This accident took the edge off Carlos Reutemann's win in a Brabham BT44-Ford, the first victory for the Argentinian in Grand Prix racing. A surprise second was Jean-Pierre Beltoise in the new BRM P201. In 1975 the crowd went delirious as local favourite Jody Scheckter in a Tyrrell 007-Ford became the first South African in the thirty-seven years of the race to win his home Grand Prix. MK

Above: the crowds at Clubhouse corner, Kyalami, must be pleased as local hero Jody Scheckter sweeps through to victory, with Tyrrell-Ford 007, in the 1975 race

EARLY ITALIAN CLASSIC CARS

The SPA company was founded by a member of the famous Ceirano family and later became a part of the giant Fiat empire

Left: victor of the 1909 Targa Florio was Baron Ciuppa; he is shown here on the winning car, the SPA 28/40 hp

THE NAME OF CEIRANO RECURS insistently throughout the early years of Italian motoring history: it was Giovanni Ceirano's factory which was taken over by the Fiat company in 1899 to build motor cars; Matteo Ceirano was behind Itala; Giovanni was later responsible for SCAT and Rapid cars before World War I and for Ceirano and Newton-Ceirano after it, while in 1906 Matteo had founded the Societa Piemontese Automobili in Turin, aided by Michele Ansaldi.

The first SPA cars were little different from the contemporary Italas—big, rugged machines of 24 and 60 hp with, unusually, shaft drive: by 1907 the range had grown to include a 60 hp six, and a 30/35 hp six, and a light 15/24 hp four, as well as the 40 hp four. They were imported into England by H. E. Hall & Co, of Riding House Street, London W, who showed all four as polished chassis at the Olympia Motor Show in November 1907.

The following year another of the Fratelli Ceirano, Ernesto, took third place in the Targa Florio in a SPA, while Frencesco Ciuppa was equally successful two years later in another in 1909.

In 1910 the British agency for SPA was taken over by Thomas Green & Son, Limited, an old-established firm of ironfounders and engineers of Smithfield Ironworks, Leeds, Green & Son were better-known as manufacturers of lawnmowers.

At first they offered the 15/20 hp SPA, which *The*

Autocar described: 'The frame is, as usual, of channel section steel, well cambered, and most generously flared as to the flanges of the side members in rear of the insweep by the dashboard. The longitudinals are smartly upswept over the back axle, and the rear member has its flanges produced to form clip brackets, taking the butt ends of the three-quarter elliptical rear springs.

'The engine, which is supported directly from the frame proper, is of the *mono bloc* order, and makes a very neat appearance beneath the bonnet . . . the carburettor, which has two jets, and is water-jacketed, is placed on the right of the engine, with the gas leads formed in the casting and passing between the pairs of cylinders. It has a vertically-acting throttle pedal, and is also lever operated with a vacuum damped automatic air valve over. The exhaust lead is also cast with the cylinders, so that the engine has no outside pipes whatever, and makes a very clean job . . . no radiator fan is provided, but in lieu thereof the large flywheel is cast with vaned arms, which serve to induce a strong draught through the radiator and engine space.

'A multi-disc clutch of good design serves to convey the drive from the engine to the gear box, a neat, flexible and easily-detached joint intervening.'

Price of the 15/20 with side-entrance coachwork was £385: also available were a twin-cylinder 10 hp (£295 in chassis form) offered only during the 1910 season, a

Below: the 1912 25/30 hp four-cylinder of 4398 cc

Centre: a 23S 20 hp 2724 cc of 1922

Bottom: this Torpedo of 1924 was based on a 24S chassis

16/20 which seemed to be identical to the 15/20 in everything save price (£395 in chassis form against £335), a 20/25 hp (£485) a 25/30 hp (£555), a 40/50 hp (£685) and two big sixes, a 30/40 hp (£685) and 60/70 hp (£975).

The SPAs, claimed Greens, with no little pride, were 'The admittedly best cars embodying the present automobile mechanism sent out of Italy'.

At the 1911 Olympia Show they exhibited only 16/20 hp SPAs, which seemed to be woefully over-bodied: 'Seven seater Cabriolet, five seats inside and one next to driver. Price £550. Seven seater Cabriolette, five seats alongside driver, one special let-down seat made concealed in door when not in use. All-enclosed dickey seat behind for two persons. Price £550'.

The six-cylinder models were dropped for the model year 1913, and the range was of the 12/15 hp, 16/20 hp, 25/30 hp and an all-new 50 hp with a long-stroke 7.6-litre engine.

The long-suffering 16/20 was endowed for Olympia with an All-Enclosed Limousine which reached new heights of cumbersomeness: 'To carry five or seven passengers; front can be shut off when owner wishes his chauffeur to drive, and two removable chairs inside.'

A sporting version of the 25 hp chassis, which had a 4398 cc power unit, was available, with a top speed of just under 70 mph; one of these cars, with pointed-tail skiff coachwork and RAF detachable wire wheels instead of the standard wooden-spoked items, survives in elegant surroundings at the Le Mans Museum in France.

An increase in stroke transformed the 16/20 into the 18/25 for 1914, but otherwise the range was unchanged: the last of the old model were exhibited at the 1913 Olympia Show, where the public were treated to the annual spectacle of three 16/20s groaning under the various heavy coupé, saloon and landaulette coachwork placed on the chassis.

After the war, two models were offered, the 2.3 litre Tipo 23, which seemed to be little more than an updated version of the old 16/20, and the Tipo 24, of similar design but having six cylinders and 4.4 litres. There was a sporting variant of the four, the Tipo 23S, with a 75 mph top speed, but the most exciting post-war model appeared in 1922, in the shape of the 30/40 hp Super Sports.

This had the same cylinder dimensions as the six, but was equipped with twin overhead camshafts and four valves per cylinder; tubular connecting rods, light alloy pistons and steel cylinder liners completed the internal specification of the engine, which was endowed with twin carburettors. Front wheel brakes were standard, and a Teutonically vee-shaped radiator was normal wear. Driving one of these fine six-cylinder SPAs, Beria D'Argentina won the Aosta-Grand St Bernard hillclimb, and the model was also able to take the first two places in its class in the 1924 3000 km Alpine Cup contest, an extremely competitive race.

In 1925, SPA became a component of the mighty Fiat empire. Car production ceased almost immediately, but the marque has steadily continued to gain new fame in the commercial vehicle and engineering fields, into the 1970s.   DBW

Top left: the SPA type 25 of 1927, with cabriolet coachwork by Farina

Centre left: the large and luxurious SPA type 23 tourer was produced from 1920 until 1925

Below left: the six-seater SPA type 25 open tourer of 1922. Production of this model continued until 1926

Below right: the SPA type 24S of 1921 was powered by this six-cylinder, 4426 cc engine; it was fitted with twin-overhead-camshafts and four valves per cylinder

Bottom: the sporty SPA type 23S of 1922; it was powered by a four-cylinder, mono-block engine of 2724 cc

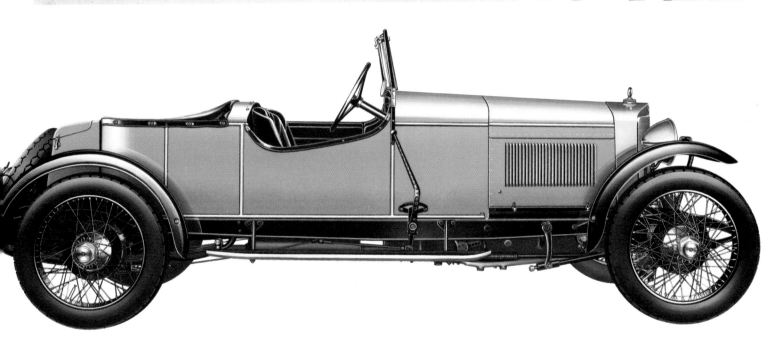

Top: a 1909 two-seater SPA tourer; with no windscreen and no overhead covering, the car offered its occupants little protection against the elements

Above left: a SPA type 24S in action during a motor race in 1926

Above right: the luxury SPA type 24S four-door saloon of 1920

Right: another SPA type 24S; this is the attractive coupé-de-ville version. The 24S model remained in production from 1920 until 1926

A COURSE FOR COURAGE

Success at the famous Belgian Spa circuit requires a lot of skill and a great deal of daring and courage

THE STORY OF the *Circuit National de Francorchamps*, a road circuit situated near the town of Spa in the Ardennes, spans half a century. Francorchamps is a circuit that demands courage and daring from the drivers, a circuit where spectators can see men working hard at terrific speeds. But it is a sad story because many of the world's top drivers have been killed there, including British drivers Dick Seaman, Archie Scott-Brown, Alan Stacey and Chris Bristow. Even worse, it is a story of irresponsible and even stupid attempts, chiefly in the 1950s, to make the circuit ever faster.

The circuit was conceived by Jules de Thier, from Spa. A motor racing enthusiast, de Thier evolved a triangular 9.24-mile course using public roads set in a valley and lined by a dense pine forest, farm cottages and fields. From the start, shortly after a sharp hairpin bend at La Source near the village of Francorchamps (which itself is five miles from the town of Spa), the road plunged downhill, went left to the Old Frontier hairpin (before World War I the German/Belgian border) and then climbed up and over a wooded crest. Then the trees stopped, the road twisted left, right and then ventured towards Burnenville, a fast right-hander bordered by farm-buildings. Malmédy in its

Below: Beltoise's BRM P160 leads a gaggle of cars in the 1972 Belgian Grand Prix

Bottom: Peter Arundell takes time to look at the scenery in his Lotus-BRM H16 at a deserted track

early days was a right-angle bend which led to the Masta Straight, a 'straight' of almost two miles past farms and through Masta village with its notorious, flat-out kink. Then came Stavelot, originally a hairpin bend, and the road began to rise again, twisting and turning through full-throttle curves towards the La Source hairpin and the start/finish line.

Resurfacing before World War II made the track smoother, but in 1947 the Old Frontier hairpin was removed, being replaced by an uphill sweep at Eau Rouge which reduced circuit length to 9 miles. More modifications followed: the circuit was widened in places, corners eased slightly. Lap speeds rose. The right-angle turn at Malmédy was replaced by a long sweep, which increased cars' entry speed on to the long Masta Straight, at the end of which a slightly banked sweep replaced the Stavelot hairpin. The inside of La Source was also banked. This reduced the lap distance to 8.77 miles and speeds rose even faster. In 1957 more resurfacing and corner-easing, bringing the length down to 8.76 miles, resulting in yet higher speeds.

First race, in 1924, was a 24-hour event for *voitures à chássis catalogués* designed to rival the similar race at Le Mans. Henri Springuel and Becquet, driving a two litre Bignan, covered 1168.2 miles at an average speed of 48.98 mph. Francorchamps' fame spread quickly, for in 1925 the Royal Automobile Club de Belgique were asked to organise the European Grand Prix (also the first Belgian Grand Prix). With the withdrawal of the Sunbeams and Guyots, there were but seven starters, four Delages and three Alfa Romeos. Antonio

Ascari led the 502-mile race from start to finish in his Alfa Romeo P2, averaging 74.44 mph. Team-mate Giuseppe Campari was second—22 m behind.

The 24-hour race was held each year until 1933 and then again in 1938 before war intervened. The Grand Prix was held from 1930–35 and then in 1937 and 1939. Fastest race was in 1937, when the powerful German Mercedes-Benz and Auto Union teams ruled Grand Prix racing. Rudolf Hasse, driving a supercharged 6-litre Auto Union C-type, averaged 104.11 mph. Two years later speeds were reduced by heavy rain. Hermann Lang's supercharged 3-litre Mercedes-Benz W163 averaged 94.43 mph, but it was a sad victory. Dick Seaman, the British driver, was leading when he lost control of his Mercedes at the fast left-hand curve before La Source, crashed into the trees and died of burns received when the car caught alight.

The 24-hour race gained prestige as the years wore on. In 1928 the supercharged $1\frac{1}{2}$-litre Alfa Romeo crewed by Boris Ivanowski/Attilio Marinoni became the first car to exceed 100 km/h for the 24 hours, their official average being 102.60 km/h (63.75 mph). Apart from 1931, when a massive, supercharged 7.1-litre Mercedes-Benz shared by Prince Djordjadze/Freddy Zehender won, Alfa Romeo dominated the race. Marinoni scored a personal hat-trick by driving the winning car three years in succession, his co-drivers for 1929 and 1930 being Robert Benoist and Pietro Ghersi respectively. Alfa Romeo's 2.3-litre 8C models won in 1932 (Antonio Brivio/Eugenio Siena) and 1933 (Louis Chiron/Luigi Chinetti), while a 2.9-litre sports car set a record average of 77.58 mph in 1938 (Carlo Pintacuda/Francesco Severi). There was a fatal accident in 1929 when Bugatti driver Freddy Charlier overturned between Masta Village and Stavelot.

Francorchamps was back in action in 1947 (now without the Old Frontier hairpin) for the second post-war Belgian Grand Prix. There was an extremely good entry headed by four works Alfa Romeo 158s. Jean Pierre Wimille's Alfa won beating team-mate Achille Varzi against team orders. Carlo Trossi was third after having been relieved for four laps by Alfa manager Battista Guidotti while Trossi was having his nose, which had been cut by a flying stone, bandaged.

The 24-hour race was revived briefly in 1948 and 1949. British drivers St John Horsfall and Leslie Johnson took their 2-litre Aston Martins to victory in 1948, although their joy was tempered with the death of British driver Richard Stallebrass at Malmédy. The following year Luigi Chinetti followed-up his Le Mans win with victory in the Francorchamps 24-hours, sharing his 2-litre Ferrari 166 Mille Miglia with Jean Lucas. Fourth overall came Horsfall after a single-handed run in his pre-war Aston Martin. Fuel consumption decided the 1949 Belgian Grand Prix: Louis Rosier's $4\frac{1}{2}$-litre Talbot-Lago was able to come through to win after a non-stop drive.

Into the 1950s the Belgian Grand Prix became firmly established in the World Championship calendar, being cancelled only in 1957 and 1959 owing to financial problems. Alfa Romeos dominated in 1950 and 1951, winners being Juan Manuel Fangio and Giuseppe Farina respectively, and it was no surprise when Alberto Ascari's 2-litre Ferrari 500 scooped the honours in 1952 and 1953. It was Fangio again in 1954 and 1955, with Maserati 250F and Mercedes-Benz W196 respectively, but the great Argentinian ran into trouble in 1956 and the young British driver Peter Collins (Ferrari D50) won his first-ever Grand Prix. With the modifications to Stavelot and Malmédy speeds had risen, Fangio's 1955 average being 118.83 mph for the 315.85 miles.

Resurfacing and widening meant a much faster circuit in 1957. Even though the Grand Prix had to be cancelled, the RAC Belgique Grand Prix for sports cars saw records smashed. Tony Brooks' 3-litre Aston Martin DBR1/300 won the race at 118.55 mph, while Olivier Gendebien's 4.1-litre Ferrari 335 Sport made fastest lap, breaking the 200 km/h mark with 203.202 km/h, (126.26 mph). When the Grand Prix cars returned in 1958 the circuit was 10 mph faster than when they last appeared in 1956. The organisers were waging a war with Reims and Monza for the title of the fastest Grand Prix circuit in Europe, but at some cost. . . . Even before the race Britain's Archie Scott-

Above: two Matras lead on the opening lap of the Spa 1000 km race in 1973; the race was won by Derek Bell and Mike Hailwood's Mirage. Although the circuit is picturesque, the speed differential between the winning cars and also rans in this class of racing at Spa makes lapping somewhat dangerous

Brown had lost his life in a sports car race when his Lister-Jaguar spun and crashed on a damp track. In practice for the Grand Prix Jean Behra's BRM P25 had oil spray on to its rear tyres at 150 mph along the Masta Straight. It spun wildly for a long distance. In the race itself Luigi Musso's Ferrari Dino 246 crashed at 160 mph at Stavelot, ran off the road into a field, struck a house and some concrete posts. Miraculously both drivers escaped unhurt. Tony Brooks (Vanwall) was the victor in a peculiar race. Brooks, whose average speed of 129.93 mph made this the fastest road-race yet run in Europe, had his gearbox seize on the run to the line and finished jammed in third; second man Mike Hawthorn's Ferrari Dino 246 blew-up as it crossed the line; third finisher Stuart Lewis-Evans limped home with his Vanwall's front suspension broken. Another lap and Cliff Allison's tiny 2.2-litre Lotus 12-Climax might have won!

Jack Brabham's 133.63 mph victory in his Cooper

Above: the cars await the start of the 1970 Belgian Grand Prix at Spa; the race was won by Pedro Rodriquez in his P153 BRM. Grand Prix drivers were of the opinion that the track was too dangerous, and the last Belgian GP was held there in 1972

T53-Climax in the 1960 Belgian Grand Prix was overshadowed by four accidents. Both Stirling Moss and Mike Taylor crashed and were seriously hurt when their Lotus 18-Climaxes failed in practice; Moss lost a wheel at 140 mph, Taylor's steering went at 100 mph. Worse was to come in the race. Alan Stacey crashed his Lotus 18-Climax without apparent reason—possibly he was struck in the face by a bird—and was killed instantly. Chris Bristow, at twenty-two one of Britain's brightest hopes, lost control, crashed through a fence and was decapitated.

A reduction in engine size from $2\frac{1}{2}$ to $1\frac{1}{2}$ litres lowered speeds slightly, but in the 1961 event British driver Cliff Allison broke his legs in a practice accident. Phil Hill (Ferrari Dino 156) won the race. In 1962 Trevor Taylor's Lotus 24-Climax collided with Willy Mairesse's Ferrari Dino at 120 mph; the Lotus demolished a telegraph pole which landed inches from Taylor's head, while Mairesse's car caught alight. Taylor was unhurt, Mairesse suffered slight burns. Jim Clark scored his first-ever Grand Prix win that year in a Lotus 25-Climax; Clark, who admitted he hated the circuit, was to win the Belgian Grand Prix for the next three years.

In 1963 a new obstacle presented itself. The Ardennes were prone to sudden rainstorms and one came in the closing laps of the Grand Prix. Five drivers crashed and the rain fell so hard team managers asked the organisers to stop the race. They refused. In 1956 another driver was badly hurt. Dickie Attwood's Lotus 25-BRM hit a puddle, spun, hit a telegraph pole and caught fire. Attwood suffered burns.

Worse was to come in 1966. It was announced seconds before the start of the Grand Prix that rain was falling on the back sections of the circuit, but no one informed the drivers. Two miles from the start the field suddenly ran into a wall of rain on the fast Burnenville Corner. Jo Bonnier (Cooper T81-Maserati) spun and finished up balanced half over a sheer drop; Mike Spence (Lotus 24-BRM) spun in avoidance. Denny Hulme (Brabham BT22-Climax) and Jo Siffert (Cooper T81-Maserati) collided. On the Masta Straight the three BRM P261s of Jackie Stewart, Graham Hill and Bob Bondurant crashed in separate incidents; Stewart's went into a ditch and was wrecked, trapping Stewart in the fuel-soaked wreck with a broken shoulder. John Surtees (Ferrari 312/66) eventually won the race after a tremendous duel with Jochen Rindt (Cooper T81-Maserati), who had contrived to spin round seven times without hitting anything on that eventful first lap.

In 1967 Mike Parkes (Ferrari 312/67) crashed on the opening lap of the Grand Prix and suffered serious leg injuries. The race was won by Dan Gurney's Weslake-engined Eagle, while in 1968 Bruce McLaren's McLaren M7A-Ford won another incident-spoilt race. Brian Redman suffered a badly broken arm when the front suspension of his Cooper T86B-BRM broke at high speed, causing it to leap a concrete barrier and crash into a parked car. Seat-belts saved Redman's life. The lap record, held by John Surtees 3-litre Honda RA301, was now a staggering 149.83 mph.

Finally, in 1969, the Formula One Constructors' Association issued an ultimatum to the organisers of the Grand Prix. Eventually it was agreed to erect barriers and a procedure for racing in the wet was hammered out, but the race was not held after all. The Belgian Government's insistence on unlimited insurance cover caused the Grand Prix' cancellation.

A safer Francorchamps was presented to competitors in the 1970 Belgian Grand Prix. In addition to guard-rails a chicane had been incorporated at Malmédy. Most drivers still disliked the track, but Pedro Rodriguez loved it and took his BRM P153 to a record 149.94 mph victory. Second man Chris Amon (March 701B-Ford) made fastest lap of 152.07 mph. The 1971 race was cancelled as the CSI declared Francorchamps unsafe for single-seater racing cars. Subsequent Belgian Grands Prix have been held at Zolder and Nivelles-Baulers.

Meanwhile, the Francorchamps 24-hours had been revived briefly in 1953 when, as a sports car race, Giuseppe Farina/Mike Hawthorn (Ferrari 375 Mille Miglia) had won at 94.84 mph. In 1964 the race was revived again for touring cars and in this format it has been run every year since. But in the twelve events nine drivers have died, as well as spectators and track marshals and after the 1975 race—when one driver, a marshal and a marshal's spectating son were killed—a searching inquiry began not only into the future of the race but the future of the circuit itself.

Many critics of Francorchamps thought it ironic that when the CIS banned Formula One cars from the circuit they permitted the Spa 1000-km sports car race to continue, this event catering for even more powerful cars. The Grand Prix Drivers' Association advised their members not to compete in this race, but some lovers of the 8.76-mile circuit continued to do so. In 1971 the fastest road-race in history was run there. Pedro Rodriguez/Jackie Oliver in their 5-litre Porsche 917K averaged 154.77 mph, while Jo Siffert—who shared a similar car with Derek Bell and finished second—made fastest lap of 162.09 mph. The Porsches were reported to have attained over 220 mph.   MK

FIRST RUN IN 1913, the *Gran Premio de España* has a somewhat patchy history. It was held four times in both the 1920s and 1930s, resurrected twice in the 1950s and placed back firmly in the motor racing calendar in 1967. Since 1968 it has been a qualifying round of the World Championship and has alternated between two venues, the slow, artificial track at Jarama near Madrid and the hilly road circuit through Montjuich Park in Barcelona.

The first Spanish Grand Prix of 1913 was a 191-mile touring car event won by Spaniard Carlos de Salamanca's 7.4-litre Rolls-Royce at an average speed of 54.00 mph. Admittedly not run to Grand Prix-type regulations, it provided Rolls-Royce with its only national Grand Prix win. The race was held in the Guadarrama mountains.

Spain was not new territory for the infant sport of motor racing, however. Indeed, the country was involved in the development of the race circuit as opposed to the city-to-city events so popular at the turn of the century. It was the ill-fated Paris–Madrid race of 1903, stopped at Bordeaux before it even got to Spain, which brought about the end of this type of event. In 1909 and 1910 the Catalan Cup was run at Sitges for *voiturette* machines, important events both won by Peugeot driver Jules Goux. Sitges was the scene of the 1923 Spanish Grand Prix, a poorly-supported event run under the 2-litre formula. Alberto Divo's Sunbeam battled with Count Louis Zborowski's Miller. Divo won after Zborowski (of Chitty-Chitty-Bang-Bang fame) had to change a tyre in the closing stages, while a youthful Tazio Nuvolari was third in his Chiribi.

Lasarte, a 11.03-mile circuit in the hills outside San Sebastian, became a popular venue for Spanish motor racing. In 1926 the European Grand Prix was run one week, followed by a *formule libre* Spanish Grand Prix the next. Henry Segrave's 4-litre V12 Sunbeam was an obvious favourite, but sadly had to retire early with a

HIGH SPEED IN SPAIN

The history of the Spanish Grand Prix is crowded with controversial events many of which were political

fractured front axle and left Meo Costantini an easy winner in his works-entered 2.3-litre Bugatti T35 ahead of team-mate Jules Goux.

In 1927 it was Delage *v* Talbot. Albert Divo's Talbot led briefly, but was overhauled quickly by Delage's Robert Benoist, who remained ahead until the finish. Delages driven by Edmond Bourlier and André Morel were second and third, completing a clean-sweep for the *marque*. The following year's race was run the day after the *formule libre* San Sebastian Grand Prix won by Louis Chiron's 2-litre Bugatti T35C. It was a handicap affair for sports cars, won by Chiron who nonchalantly fitted cycle wings and a windscreen to his 'Bug'. It was Chiron and Bugatti the following year when a fuel limit was imposed.

The Spanish Grand Prix came out of the doldrums in 1930 when Italian Achille Varzi's 2.5-litre Maserati 8C triumphed after a battle with Bugatti drivers Marcel Lehoux, Philippe Etancelin and René Dreyfus. In fact, such was the pace Dreyfus crashed and his team-mates succumbed to mechanical disorders. The next race was not until 1933. Still at Lasarte, at the end of a hectic if sad season, it promised to be a fine race with the first appearance of the new 2.8-litre Bugatti T59s for Achille Varzi and René Dreyfus. However, they

Below: left: Jochen Rindt's Lotus 49 at Barcelona in 1969; he and team mate Graham Hill were both eliminated in accidents at the same spot, caused by the collapse of their rear wings. As a result Lotus stopped using the wings following the race.

Below: Jean-Pierre Jarier, Tom Pryce and Carlos Pace start off on their quest to win the 1975 race

were humbled by Tazio Nuvolari's 3-litre Maserati 8CM, which led until Nuvolari tried a shade too hard and ended his race against a tree. The 2.6-litre Alfa Romeo P3s of Louis Chiron and Luigi Fagioli which claimed first and second places.

The new 750 kg Grand Prix formula was implemented in 1934 and both Mercedes-Benz and Auto Union entered October's Spanish Grand Prix. Luigi Fagioli and Rudi Caracciola scored a 1–2 for Mercedes, but the works Bugatti T59s put up a surprisingly strong challenge, Nuvolari's finishing third ahead of the best-placed Auto Union. Next year the leading positions were reversed, Caracciola heading Fagioli to the finish by over $1\frac{1}{2}$ minutes with a third Mercedes-Benz W25 driven by Manfred von Brauchitsch third. Hans Stuck had made his usual meteoric start to lead the field in his Auto Union, but the rear-engined car's transmission wilted at half-distance.

The Spanish Civil War and World War II put a stop to international motor racing in Spain until 1946 when the Peñya Rhin Grand Prix was run on the Pedralbes street circuit at Barcelona. It was repeated in 1948 and 1950 and the following year the Spanish Grand Prix was revived at the same venue. Run on 20 October 1951, it was the end-of-season decider in the World Championship. Either Alfa Romeo's Juan Manuel Fangio or Alberto Ascari of Ferrari (who had cheekily defeated Alfa on their home track at Monza a month before) could take the title. In practice Ascari had taken pole position, taking his powerful, $4\frac{1}{2}$-litre Ferrari 375 round the 3.925-mile circuit in a time of 2 m 10.59 s. Fangio's supercharged $1\frac{1}{2}$-litre Alfa Romeo 159M— developing over 400 bhp but consuming its methanol-based fuel at the astonishing rate of 1.6 mpg—screamed around in 2 m 12.27 s. Froilán González (2 m 14.01 s), Luigi Villoresi (2 m 16.38 s) and Piero Taruffi (2 m 16.80 s) backed-up Ascari, while Fangio's Alfa Romeo team-mates were Giuseppe Farina (2 m 14.94 s), Emmanuel de Graffenried (2 m 16.40 s) and Felice Bonetto (2 m 21.80 s). Ascari snatched the initial lead, but Fangio soon got to within striking distance and on lap four went ahead. Ascari slowed and on lap nine entered the pits to change a wheel. A tread had come off his tyre. Before one-fifth distance his three team-mates had also stopped for similar reasons. It transpired that in the interests of speed Ferrari had fitted smaller (16 instead of 17 in) diameter wheels. The gamble failed and Fangio became World Champion.

The Grand Prix was not run again until 1954. This time the World Championship had been settled in favour of Mercedes driver Juan Manuel Fangio, but a top-line entry was attracted to Pedralbes, including the new Lancia D50s of Alberto Ascari and Luigi Villoresi which were making their *début*. Indeed, Ascari showed tremendous speed as he led the first nine laps before retiring with clutch failure. Mike Hawthorn's $2\frac{1}{2}$-litre Ferrari 553 came through to win, conquering Luigi Musso's Maserati 250F and Fangio's very sick Mercedes-Benz W196. Repercussions following the disastrous Le Mans accident caused the cancellation of the 1956 Spanish Grand Prix and although the date appeared tentatively in calendars for some years the race was not revived until 1967.

By now Spain had joined the age of the clinical autodromes and Dutch circuit designer John Hugenholtz created a tight, 2.115-mile circuit at Jarama, 18 miles north of Madrid. After a preliminary Formula Two race in July a non-championship Formula One event was planned for November. Only four full 3-litre cars were entered and the two works Lotus 49-Fords of Jim Clark and Graham Hill took first and second.

But the circuit was unsatisfactory. The edges of the track were lined with loose gravel which soon got on to the track and made it impossibly slippery for the wide-tyred machines. Additionally marker cones which defined the corners were hard and damaged suspensions. Worse still, the guard-rail was mounted too high and when Jackie Stewart's Formula Two Matra MS7-Ford slid on the gravel and flew off-course it went straight under the barrier. Writing in *Autocourse*,

Below: Jacky Ickx in his Ferrari 312B had a fine battle with Jackie Stewart in 1971, but he could not stop the Scotsman from gaining his third successive win

Above: the rains came to Spain's plains in 1974, and it gave Ronnie Peterson a chance to match his driving skills and car's handling over the otherwise too powerful Ferraris; his Lotus 76 is seen here ahead of Lauda, Reggazoni, Ickx, Fittipaldi and Scheckter

Stewart said, 'It got to the point where the barrier came right up to my crash helmet and knocked the peak off. My head was wedged so tightly between the barrier and the roll-over bar that I couldn't even turn it; another six inches forward and that would have been the end of me.'

A May date was given to the 1968 Spanish Grand Prix which was granted World Championship status. However, a month before there was a Formula Two race and when top drivers discovered that safety modifications had not been carried out as promised they threatened to boycott the race. At the last minute the required work was done and Graham Hill (Lotus 49-Ford) won the race. In 1969 the Grand Prix reverted to Barcelona, this time the resurfaced and modified 2.355-mile Montjuich Park circuit which had been used for motor racing since the mid-1930s. Jackie Stewart stroked his Matra MS80-Ford to an easy win, covering 90 laps to the 88 of second man Bruce McLaren (McLaren M7C-Ford). Politically the race was of great importance. Both Lotus 49B-Fords of Graham Hill and Jochen Rindt were eliminated in alarming, but separate, incidents at the same place. The high-speed accidents were both caused by the high-mounted aerofoils on the cars and it was just the excuse the CSI wanted to restrict such devices, which they did five weeks later. Both drivers' lives—and, indeed, many spectators'—were saved by the guard-rails which had been installed shortly before the race.

In 1970 it was back to Jarama and more politics, this time over the Spanish organisers' interpretation of qualifying rules. An argument over whether sixteen or twenty cars could start raged until the cars were sitting on the starting grid; ultimately the four unlucky ones were wheeled off with police assistance. Stewart won again, this time giving the new March *marque* its first (and only until 1975) World Championship race victory. Of more significance, perhaps, was the fact this race saw the first appearance of the Lotus 72, a car of advanced design which had a 'career' lasting six seasons and helped provide Lotus with the 1970 and

1972 World Championships.

Montjuich in 1971 saw Stewart win again, this time in Ken Tyrrell's new Tyrrell 003-Ford after a duel with Jacky Ickx' Ferrari 312B-2/71. Then Emerson Fittipaldi scored two popular wins, at Jarama in 1972 and Montjuich in 1973, finishing the latter race on a flat rear tyre. In 1974, at Jarama, superior pitwork by Ferrari helped give Niki Lauda and Clay Regazzoni a one-lap advantage over third man Emerson Fittipaldi (McLaren M23-Ford) as they took their fleet, computer-developed 312B-3/74s to an easy 1–2 result.

The 1975 Spanish Grand Prix was one many people would prefer to forget. As the drivers arrived in Montjuich Park it became apparent that the guard-rails had not been fastened properly—if at all. The vast majority refused to practise and arguments raged. Eventually team crews helped secure some of the barriers and when the CSI refused to intervene in the dispute and the organisers blackmailed the teams into taking part, threatening to impound the cars for some weeks, practice began. Emerson Fittipaldi took a firm stand, covering the three mandatory qualifying laps at slow speed and then refusing to race. In the actual race two other drivers retired in protest after but one lap, but the others participated in a hectic motor race. There were spins and collisions galore and finally disaster occurred when Rolf Stommelen's Hill GH1-Ford lost its rear wing and went out of control. The barriers *did* take the impact, but the car ricocheted off them and leapt over the barriers killing five people and injuring ten more. Stommelen himself suffered severe leg injuries plus a broken wrist and broken ribs. The race was stopped midway through the 29th of the 55 laps and Jochen Mass declared winner.

A new, permanent circuit to replace Montjuich Park has been discussed for some years. It is unlikely that a Formula One race would be run in Barcelona until it is built, which means that Jarama, a dull circuit which never seems to be able to entice spectators away from the Madrid bull-fights, is likely to host the Spanish Grand Prix annually instead of every two years. MK

The first plug:
Lenoir, 1860

Bosch racing plug
with mica insulator

THE SPARK OF LIFE

Without the correct type of spark plug it is impossible to expect the modern motor car to function properly

Champion of 1901
with several parts

Beru of 1905 with
brass segments

plug with cooling fins
and mica insulator

GT with three
ss electrodes

Way-Assauto of 1904
with two electrodes

RMV of 1910 with
several parts

Champion of 1910 with
priming tap

Above: a selection of early spark plugs of vastly differing types and sizes

DURING WORLD WAR II the major British spark plug manufacturers, like most other companies with names to preserve and frozen profits to disperse, continued to advertise their wares. The insulators of the sparking plugs that kept our fighters in the sky, they told us, were made of a material that would be a true ruby if suitably pigmented—but of course, they assured us, no such impurity as colouring matter would be allowed in their precious ceramics.

Precious materials were already familiar in some spark plugs, and they continue to find a place therein from time to time. Gold and silver, platinum and iridium have all found uses, admittedly in very small quantities. Those albino ruby insulators were merely chemical siblings of the ruby, just as coal is to a diamond; and while Lodge christened their *Corundite*, KLG called theirs *Sintox*, which was more honest and down-to-earth. The stuff was merely sintered aluminium oxide.

Very good stuff it was, and remained. Sintered alumina creates a material of surprising mechanical strength, excellent electrical insulation characteristics, astonishing heat resistance, and a heaven-sent suitability for mass production methods.

All these properties are of great importance, for the spark plug leads an extremely hard life, enjoying very little attention (indeed, if it demands a lot it is the wrong sparking plug for the job) and expected to be sold at knock-down prices. It may vary in proportions but not in principles, whether it has to do duty in such extreme services as a water-cooled four-stroke hearse or an air-cooled two-stroke racing motorcycle. In either case, or in any between these extremes, the spark plug is just a little thing that can be screwed into the wall of an engine's combustion chamber, and there

offer a gap across which a high-tension spark may be prompted to leap in order to ignite the mixture.

Thus the construction is fundamentally simple. There is a steel body which screws into the engine and has convenient hexagon flats formed on it for spanners, and into the bore of this body is an insulating mass through the centre of which passes a metal electrode. To the outer end of this electrode a suitable high-voltage pulse is brought by the high-tension lead from the engine's distributor; at the other end, where the electrode protrudes into the combustion chamber, it is kept company at a distance of 20 or 30 thousandths of an inch by an earthing electrode protruding from the metal body of the plug.

The central electrode has an arduous task, and this is where the fancy metals often feature. Because heat resistance and electrical conductivity are necessary attributes, alloys of nickel are commonplace, sometimes sheathed in copper or fused silica for a better bond with the insulator material. This bonding and sealing is important for a number of practical reasons of which some are very simple and fundamental: a leak would be deleterious, looseness could be disastrous. In the quite recent past it was common for special-purpose plugs—notably for racing—expected to have a long life or to endure particularly severe heat, to have points made of platinum alloy in which iridium or tungsten would also be present. Platinum being very costly, these points were made of thin wire welded into position; but they have been known to loosen and fall out of the plug into the engine cylinder. The result can be a wrecked engine, and for peace of mind it is worth taking the trouble to select plugs so constructed that the electrode points cannot fall out of it.

Manufacturing techniques are better nowadays, and for the past three or four years certain racing two-stroke engines have been relying upon a new centre electrode material known as Gold Palladium: a fine wire of this alloy, which has a gold content of about

50 per cent, is fixed to a stub of the nickel alloy that is otherwise regarded as conventional nowadays in all plugs, even in racing. This special tip extends the heat range of the spark plug and makes it less susceptible to fouling.

Heat value is the most important factor determining the suitability of a plug for a given engine. The difference in operating temperatures between a mild-mannered touring engine doing a lot of idling and a highly-tuned racing engine run at high loads and speeds for protracted periods, is considerable. In the former, it is necessary for the plug to run fairly hot so that any depositions of oil or other contaminants will be burned away. If they are not, the oil will accumulate and turn to carbon, forming an encrustation over the walls of the insulator body around which the spark can track to earth without jumping its appointed gap, and therefore without igniting the compressed charge in the combustion chamber. At the other extreme, if a

Right: the plug on the left has a gold palladium central electrode, which lowers the minimum voltage required for a spark and, due to its small nature, facilitates the elimination of deposits

Far right: a diagram showing the temperature gradients present in an average spark plug

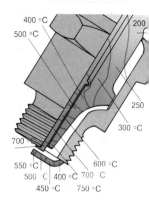

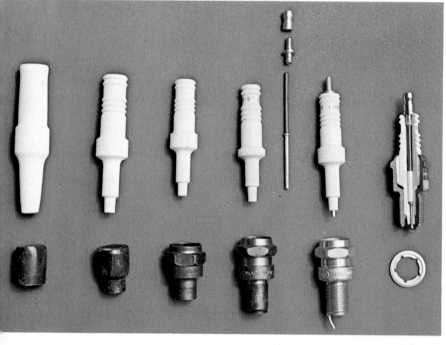

Above: the components of a spark plug at various stages of manufacture; in the top row, the insulator starts off as a raw piece of ceramic material and is turned until the shape is correct —the central electrode is inserted down the centre; in the bottom row, the metal body is formed by extrusion— the second electrode is welded on; to the right is a cutaway view of a complete plug

Above right: a transverse section through a spark plug with an internal air gap

hot-running plug were fitted in a high-performance engine driven hard, its tip would soon become incandescent, causing pre-ignition that would probably wreck the engine—starting by burning a hole in the piston crown—before the plug itself failed.

Plugs that run cool are also known as 'hard' plugs, hot-running ones as 'soft'. It does not matter which terminology is employed, so long as the correct principles are remembered: a soft plug for a soft engine, a cool plug for a hot engine, and vice versa. Clearly it is vital to use the type of plug specified by the engine manufacturer: it might be permissible to choose one grade softer when doing a lot of gentle driving (such as in urban traffic) if fouling and eventual misfiring is a problem, as it might be if the condition of the engine were such as to allow more than the usual amount of lubricating oil to get past piston rings or valve guides into the combustion chamber. If this course is adopted, care must be taken not to use full throttle for long, nor high revs at all. Conversely, if some very hard driving is anticipated, especially on motorways or tracks that allow high speeds and loads to be sustained for long periods, and most especially if the engine is suspected of running on a mixture slightly weaker than is correct, then a harder grade of plug would be recommended. Again, if the engine has

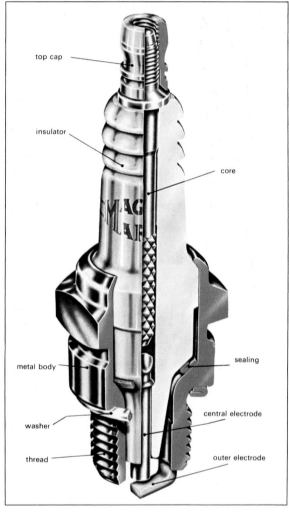

been fitted with a capacitor discharge ignition system, a harder grade could be adopted because the characteristics of these systems include a very rapid voltage rise, encouraging the spark to jump the gap regardless of fouling conditions.

Only inside the walls of the plug body can any significant difference be seen between a hard plug and a soft one. A cool hard plug has very little of its central electrode protruding from the tip of the insulator, and not much area of the insulator itself will be exposed to the heat of combustion, for the insulator will be seated in the metal body of the plug quite close to the nose. The object of this is to shorten the path whereby heat may escape from the plug tip to the body and thence, through the contact area of its threaded portion, to the material of the engine cylinder head and thus away. A soft hot-running plug provides a longer path for the

engine fault diagnosis; but the art is by no means as simple as is commonly supposed, for the various additives present in fuels and oils sometimes play tricks with the deposition processes, creating a plug

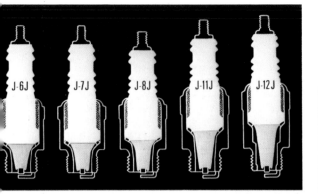

Far left: a series of spark plugs with differing heat ranges; from left to right they vary from cold to hot types, the heat having to travel further through the insulator to escape in the latter sort
Left: some modern plugs have projecting electrodes, which are cooled by the incoming charge of petrol and air

heat to travel: the insulator material leaves more of the central electrode exposed, and is seated high up in the plug body, from which it follows that it exposes more of its surface to combustion heat. This greater exposure ensures that the tip remains hot, encouraging the immediate burning off of any potential deposits: even if they do not burn immediately, they have to extend over a greater surface before eventually creating an effective short circuit, or tracking path whereby the spark might be earthed, and thus fail.

The formation of deposits on the plug tip is clearly a constant problem, for it is implicit in the nature of the internal combustion engine that it should continually produce carbon so long as it is running. The art of spark plug design and selection is to ensure that the plug runs hot enough to burn up deposits, without running too hot. It is very sensitive to carburation: if the mixture be too rich, the latent heat of evaporation of the excessive fuel will cause it to run cooler, leaving a tell-tale coating of black soot on the plug. An excessively weak mixture will conversely make it run hotter, in which case the usual signs of overheating are a bleached or pale brown colouration of the metal surfaces of the plug exposed to combustion. These and numerous other signs may be interpreted by a skilled and experienced eye to constitute a valuable means of

appearance that could be wrongly interpreted. Amongst these spurious deposits the most easily recognisable are little beads of lead salts, which form on the insulator in certain high-temperature conditions: these originate in the lead compounds added to petrol to suppress detonation or knock, and it was the introduction of these compounds (tetraethyl lead being the most famous) that forced the spark plug industry to develop its present type of insulating materials. Previously the best spark plug insulators were made of mica, which had superseded the simple porcelain of the earliest plugs; but mica could not stand the chemical attack of the lead compounds, and modern ceramics took its place.

For some years after this it remained the practice to make plug bodies in two parts that could be unscrewed for cleaning purposes. This practice has been abandoned because the seating and sealing of the insulator, upon the washers which provide its only thermal contact with the plug body, could not be reliable. Modern sealed plugs can be cleaned by careful scraping with a thin-bladed knife, though that will not get very far, or by sand blasting, which creates danger of residual abrasive particles remaining embedded inside the walls of the plug body where they can grow incandescent in the heat of combustion. In any case, if a

Above: from left to right in the top row, the pictures show a normal spark plug and ones fouled by carbon and damaged by overheating and pre-ignition; in the bottom row from left to right, the pictures show oil fouling, heavy deposits due, perhaps, to excessive use of upper-cylinder lubricant, impact damage to the insulator and abrasive erosion caused by excessive cleaning

set of plugs needs to be cleaned more than once during its useful life, which is limited by the prudent to about 10,000 miles, either the plugs are the wrong grade for the engine, or the engine itself is at fault.

There is still some useful cleaning that can be done: the outside of the plug, in particular the surface of the insulator body, must be kept clean by regular wiping (with a rag or tissue dampened with petrol or alcohol) lest accretions of dirt provide a tracking path whereby the spark can escape to earth from the top of the central electrode. The only other desirable maintenance is the checking and correct setting of the spark gap. This used to be as little as 0.018 inch in the old days of magnetos and inefficient coil ignition systems, but on modern high-compression engines the gap is commonly 0.03 inch or even more. Gauges are marketed

with which the gap can conveniently be measured, but they are not always accurate: a pitted or bent electrode will offer a bigger gap than conventional gauges will indicate. Use of a round wire of known diameter is preferable, and with some of the less common types of earthing electrode such as the once-popular multiple-point, and the racing side-electrode, the wire is often easier to use.

Variations in spark gap design are amongst the most notable, even notorious, of departures from spark plug convention. There have been numerous so-called 'fuel igniters' marketed in or by American manufacturers, all claiming better performance, greater economy and longer life, without needing any attention. Some of the claims are undoubtedly excessive, but the working principle of these igniters (which can still be called spark plugs) is valid in certain circumstances. These exist within the combustion chambers of the flat-12 Formula One Ferrari engine, and also in the Formula Two BMW motor sometimes employed by March; and for these applications the most reputable and responsible of American plug makers, Champion, furnish what they more accurately describe as surface discharge plugs. In these the fairly large-diameter tip of the central electrode is surrounded by a constant gap, the earthing electrode being a concentric ring or annulus, and the entire nose of the plug is given a flush surface because the gap is filled by a semi-conductor material. The spark jumps across this surface from the central electrode to the annulus, usually taking the shortest route: as this causes microscopic erosion, the next spark moves to the next point on the annulus, so the effect is for the spark to travel round in circles. The erosion is barely more than theoretical, plugs of this type having an extremely long life. What is far more important is that they have a virtually infinite heat range, so fouling is emphatically not a problem. In fact the surface discharge plug does not really work properly until it is dirty! Nor does it work properly unless the spark pulse has the requisite characteristics, which again are supplied by a capacitor discharge system. Even that is not enough, for the plug annulus must be in the right position relative to the

combustion chamber, and engines that are not designed to use plugs of this type are seldom able to exploit them effectively.

The sensitivity of engines to these niceties of construction are often surprising. Some engines, but by no means at all, may be well served by plugs of the extended-nose variety, in which the electrodes and the tip of the insulator protrude into the combustion chamber, relying on the high velocity draught of cool fresh mixture during each induction phase to carry away the excess of the heat absorbed during the previous combustion and exhaust phases. Otherwise most of the constructional differences in modern plugs are invisible, consisting of spark-intensifying gaps in the central electrode, resistors, and other inclusions to improve ignition performance or suppress radio-

Below, far left: a Champion surface discharge plug, as used in certain racing applications, and a double-electrode variety common in Wankel engines

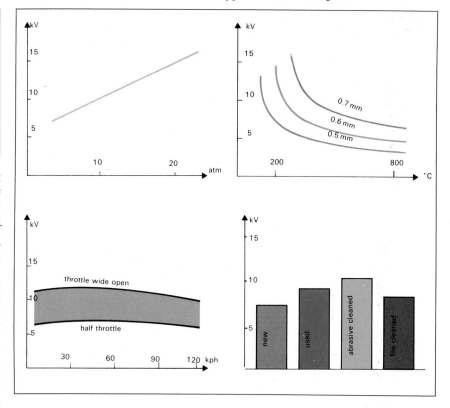

Above: a series of graphs showing the variation of spark-plug efficiency as a function of compression, temperature and gap, speed and electrode condition (the lines or blocks show the voltages required to produce a spark)

frequency interference. Elsewhere, plug construction is remarkably uniform and almost as standardised as tyre valves: there are only three standard diameters for the threaded portion of the body (10, 14 and 18 mm), the smallest being welcomed for the space it saves, and the largest being enjoyed for its greater heat range, while the 14 mm plug is standard for most road-going cars. The length of the threaded portion also varies, and is a dimension that is too easily overlooked: a short-reach plug in a medium or long-reach hole will be too shrouded to work effectively, and is likely to become fouled rapidly—although some engines are designed so that the plug tip is deliberately shrouded—while a plug that is too long may either protrude into the combustion chamber and there overheat or even cause mechanical damage by contact with the piston or valves, or alternatively if the head construction prevents this it will not be able to seat properly on its flange, in which case it will not be able to shed its heat properly nor be gas tight. This flange is usually flat, and seats on a sealing washer that should be replaced by a new one whenever the plug is removed; but some plugs, notably those employed by Vauxhall and certain other GM cars, have an angled seat which is stronger and provides a better heat path.   LJKS

STANDING APART FROM THE CROWD

There have been many small manufacturers catering for people looking for something a little different

Above left: one of the better-built 'replicars' was the Albany

Above right: cashing in on the Lotus Seven's success many years earlier was the Jeffrey; based on a tubular spaceframe chassis, the car could be used with a variety of engines

THERE HAVE BEEN MANY companies and back-garden concerns in all parts of the world producing brands of specialist cars. These have been mainly small production run cars directed at the enthusiast, usually with little money, but with a desire to set himself apart from the crowd.

However many companies there have been, it is generally accepted that the roots of specialist cars are deep in British soil, having been planted just after World War II. There are many reasons why Britain was in the fore-front of the garden shed car-production business, not least being that any enthusiast who could handle a spanner could see no reason why he could not emulate the larger manufacturers; indeed, he was probably right. Other factors were the distinct lack of cheap sporting machinery after the war: the larger companies were getting back on their feet by producing more generally acceptable saloons. The sports cars that were available were usually well out of the young enthusiasts pocket; for instance, Jaguar were bringing out their quick but pricey XK120. So, it was up to the man in the street to build his own car. And, with cars like the Austin Seven and the Ford 10 to work on, it was not a hard task. The Austin Seven, available for next to nothing after the war, is generally accepted as having been the basis of UK specialist cars. This was mainly due to its body which could easily be removed from the chassis, giving the prospective car maker a good rolling-chassis base to clothe.

One of the first companies to start serious production of what was to be termed 'kit cars' was Buckler of Reading, Berkshire. Nineteen forty-seven was the year that the company started building their own 'complete' cars, as opposed to merely manufacturing bodies (in fact, there was hardly a company that became known for just building bodies alone). The Buckler, in its original Mk V form, utilised a space-frame chassis and Ford 10 engine, gearbox and running gear. The company modified many parts like suspension and gears to make the cars accelerate and handle better than their Ford 10 saloon fathers. A smart two-seater body clothed the early Bucklers, and the marque was quite successful in the heyday of the specialist car. An interesting point on these cars: the chassis was of such proportions that when the door was opened, one had to then climb over the space frame to reach the driving seat!

Later Bucklers produced could be used in conjunction with BMC and Coventry Climax engines; some had de Dion rear axles and a few were built on backbone chassis. The cars proved quite popular in competition and when production ceased in 1962, over 500 had been built.

The Birmingham company of Dellow took the opposite route by first building competition cars and then going on to make road cars. Again Ford 10 based, the Dellows proved to be quite successful in trials and rallies; some vehicles were offered in supercharged form. The road cars that the company produced were all based on the trial-car concept. That was up until the advent of the Mk VI in 1957 which was a sports car proper. Unfortunately, this car did not catch on, and it marked the end of the firm.

Competition seemed to be the ideal base for the small manufacturer to advertise his wares, as Dellow had shown. Another concern to prosper from racing was Arnott cars of North London. Mainly builders of

Below: the massive tubular frame of a Buckler DD2, this car's engine is a Ford of 1500 cc; note, in this picture, the absence of coil springs and dampers

ful of the British breed of small-car builders, and it was his Lotus Seven that killed off many of the other concerns. It was a car with the same engine as many of its competitors, the immortal 1172 cc side-valve Ford, but which seemed just that bit more sophisticated. Perhaps it was the same breeding in the Seven that Lotus' racing cars were beginning to evidence on the international racing scene, while other mere mortal's cars could only find success in small 'clubbie' type events. Fairthorpe of Denham carried on, though, and are still in production at the time of writing; seemingly oblivious to the Lotus presence.

The Biggleswade company of Berkeley started in 1956 producing specialist cars of a different kind. These were small devices powered by a variety of motorcycle engines, usually Excelsior or Royal Enfields. The glassfibre cars could be purchased as either three or four-wheelers, and soft or hard-top. In 1961, Berkeley announced a car using the Ford 997 cc engine. Only one car of this type was built, and the company became but another memory for a great deal of enthusiasts.

While many cars were being produced in Britain only to fall by the wayside and turn up later under damp tarpaulins in garden sheds all over the country, the rest of the world had its share of designs, too. For instance, the USA had the Arnolt which was produced between 1953 and 1964. The Chicago-based company used MG chassis and Bertone bodies on cars that could hardly be put into the same league as the British vehicles. The most popular of these machines were the Bristol-engined devices that scored quite a few racing successes. The Woodhill Fiberglass Body Corporation of Tustin California also built cars to a slightly more sophisticated standard than their British counterparts. From 1952 to 1958 they manufactured cars based on Willys running gear and with engines up to Cadillac 300 bhp units. And the rest of Europe also had specialist cars. The Enzmann concern, of Schupfheim Switzerland, in 1957, were one of the first companies to use the Volkswagen platform chassis and engine as a basis for their sports cars. In all, a hundred or so of these little doorless glassfibre cars were made in the firm's nine-year existence. France contributed to the small sports-car field with many companies producing bodies and chassis to take Dyna-pangard engines, including the odd little REAC, with a submarine-type body. The body itself of the REAC was actually built in Casablanca.

Back in England, the specialist cars were becoming more specialised, with cars like the Ashley and Falcon. Ashley, who were later to make more of a

Above: a Dellow, which gained much success in trials and rallies

Formula Three cars and long-distance racers, they did make a few vehicles for road use in their six-year life-span. Turner of Wolverhampton started on the same lines as Arnott but took things to a greater extent. Their first car in 1951 could be powered by any number of engines from Lea Francis to Vauxhall. Throughout the 1950s and the early 1960s, several Turners were produced, mostly with BMC engines and running gear. The later cars were quite sophisticated machines and even rivalled the large combine companies' cars in execution of design. If one mentions competition starting a company on a successful career in road-car production, one cannot omit the efforts of Colin Chapman who started himself building trials cars in 1947. Chapman was, without doubt, the most success-

name with their glassfibre roofs for a variety of sports cars, initially made shells to clothe old Fords. Later on, they marketed complete kits basically designed for BMC parts before concentrating on the hard-top business in 1961.

Falcon too, started by building glassfibre bodies. Their first production car used a chassis based on well-known designer, Len Terry's ideas. Again, the engine used was a certain Ford unit of 1172 cc. Later, several versions were marketed, the two-seater Caribbean and the two-plus-two Bermuda. Just before this firm folded, a two seater aptly named the Peregrine was marketed. In all, 2000 or so Falcon body and body/chassis units were sold. Encompassing roughly the same time span as Falcon, the Tornado company of

Top: the car which was the base of the Lotus Seven, one of the most famous specialist cars ever; this is the Six
Above left: the immaculate interior of the Dri-Sleeve Moonraker; the Mark II Cortina instruments give the game away, though
Above right: the Triumph-engined Peerless

Rickmansworth first built the Typhoon, a device that looked like an early Marcos and one that obviously had the same aerodynamic qualities. Four hundred of the space-frame-chassis Ford-engined cars were built, and later models, like the Tempest and Talisman, proved almost as popular. One Typhoon had used a Triumph TR2 engine, a power unit that was seen in several other cars. Swallow Dorettis a few years previous had top speeds of 100 mph courtesy of the TR2 engine, and Peerless were about to go off on the same TR trip in 1957. The Peerless was an aggressive-looking car that took its name from the American car of the early part of the century, by way of the company's sponsor renovating old Peerless lorries after World War I. The TR3 engine gave the car a top speed of

Specialist cars in competition

Left: Len Terry has been responsible for many specialist chassis for road and race cars; this is his Terrier of 1961, at Silverstone

Below left: Lola have made a few specialist road cars, but have concentrated on race machines; this is their 1961 1098 cc car

Right: Jem Marsh, founder of Marcos, is seen here in his prototype in 1961

Below right: an 1100 cc Turner

about 110 mph. It proved remarkably popular, over two hundred being produced in three years. A slightly modified version, built under the Warwick name, was produced from 1960 to 1962.

GSM started up in Capetown, South Africa, building cars named Deltas. In 1960, the project was transferred to Kent where production got under way on the Ford 105E-engined ladder-frame chassis car. The car, available in open or closed form, sold as a kit at the staggering price of £1250. The whole project was less successful in England, and the owners returned to South Africa to build 1500 cc two-plus-twos.

The Rochdale company of Rochdale began in the early days of the specialist cars, 1948, by building bodies for racing cars. Throughout the 1950s, the company concentrated on producing glassfibre bodies for customers to fit on their own chassis. Immensely successful at this they produced over eight hundred shells—the decision was made to build complete cars, or at least whole cars in various pieces for the buyer to fix together.

The Rochdale Olympic was introduced in 1960, a true monocoque glassfibre car, which utilised a Riley 1.5-litre engine. As Lotus had found with their Elite, the monocoque design made the car extremely taut and gave the bulbous little vehicle fine handling. A Phase II Olympic was built in 1963 with the addition of an opening rear door. The power unit for the later car was a Ford Cortina GT which gave the car a respectable top speed of 115 mph. In all, about four hundred and fifty Rochdales had been built by the time production stopped in 1968. As the Ford and Austin had proved sound bases for kit cars in the

1950s, the arrival of the Mini on the scene sounded the advent of a new breed of car. With an engine and front sub-frame that could be unbolted with little trouble, people thought it would be easy to put it on the front or back of a different chassis. Chris Lawrence, who was later to build the early Monicas, produced some cars known as Deep Sandersons through the early part of the 1960s. His 301 had a Mini engine mounted in the rear of a low glassfibre-bodied car. Although only a few actual road cars were built, the machines fared well in competition, reaching enormous speeds from their tuned Cooper S engines: at Le Mans in 1964, one car reached a speed of 146 mph on a mere 1275 cc.

Other Mini-based sports cars to appear were the similar Mini Marcos and Mini Jem, small closed two-seaters with the engine sub-frame bolted to the front of the chassis. The height of the engine did not help in making the cars very pretty but, nevertheless, they were successful, the Jem being the neater of the two. The Ogle company produced the SX1000 which used the Mini engine in conjunction with the standard BMC floorpan. Because it was an Ogle, the finished product was made to a very high standard. The Ogle sparked off many other similar designs like the Camber GT, the Irish Timeire and the Viking Minisport.

The best Mini way to go, though, was obviously by way of mounting the engine in the rear. Unipower

Above: the LMX Sirex, built in Turin, featured a Ford 2.3-litre V6 engine

Below: one of the many cars to spring from the fertile mind of Neville Trickett is this Siva V8; power was provided by a V8 Chrysler engine of 7.2 litres

Below right: one of the Adams-designed Probe series, this featured a Volkswagen engine

Above: claimed by many to be one of the best-looking specialist cars of all time, the Add Nova

Below: this Imp-engined Centaur was based on a Probe body

produced the best of the breed in their small and svelte GT, while Cox built the larger but no less lovable GTM. In the early 1970s there were two Lotus Seven-like mid-engined Mini-based cars, the Nota Fang and the Status Minipower. Nota had started building cars in New South Wales, Australia with some success, although in England the car failed to catch on. Strikingly similar in shape, the Minipower, built by an ex-Lotus employee, seemed to be a better proposition. Like the Unipower, the Status had a right-hand gearchange, *a la* racing cars.

The Mini's sparring partner, the Hillman Imp, also provided a cheap yet easily tuneable power unit for rear-engined sports cars. Paul Emery, who tuned Imp engines with great success, built his own GT, a full space-frame car with a glassfibre body and a neat anti-squat anti-dive suspension system. Emery used the Coventry Climax-based Imp engine in the centre of his car, which helped it to handle and corner beautifully. It was due to this that the car was so quick on the track.

Dennis Adams, who produced many of the Marcos designs, built the amazing Probe series, originally Imp powered, that were so low they seemed ready to overtake other vehicles by passing underneath! Standing 29 ins high from the ground, the car had to be entered from the roof. Later Adams' designs on the same lines called for the utilisation of BMC 1800 and American V8 power units.

Other Imp-based vehicles available included the Ginetta G15, the Davrian and the oddly-named Sheen Imperator, of which no more than two examples were built. Bruce Meyers, on the other side of the Atlantic, was about to give the specialist-car industry a boost that would add at least ten years to its history. In 1966, he brought out the Manx, the first of a line of countless 'Beach Buggies'. The open top, open-wheeled car was just a basic body dropped straight onto a Volkswagen floorpan. The Volks engine was used and all that was needed was a set of fat wheels and tyres, not only to make it practical on beaches, but to give the car a certain aggressive look.

There were probably more vehicles built on this theme than on any other, and, when the idea of the buggy fizzled out, there were the Volks-based sports cars to take their place. These were of all shapes and sizes ranging from plain, ordinary coupés to ones that resembled 917 Porsches, right down to the familiar

light-blue finish, and of course, without forgetting the orange lower stripes.

In England, the GP Speedshop, which produced one of England's first buggies, looking very much like the Meyers Manx, produced the first British Volkswagen sports car, the Centron. Cars like the Silhouette followed, and on the 'race-car' theme there were vehicles like the Group Six, based on a Group Five-style car, and the self-explanatory Beaujangle Can-Am. Various beach buggies were built on a Mini base in England, while Mini-Moke-based vehicles like the Scamp, the Yak and the three-wheeled Ranger sprang up from nowhere, seemingly. In Britain, there was a new peak in industry during the late 1960s and early 1970s, as magazines like *Hot Car* and *Custom Car* would give space to any new concept or idea. For the man who wanted to do it all himself, Geoff Jago's Rodding Scene would supply bare bodies and chassis to the Englishman with more enthusiasm than money so he could emulate his counterparts with their thousands of chromium-plated dollars on the far side of the 'pond'. Opus, at one time run by motor-racing entrepreneur Rob Walker, did the same sort of thing, albeit on a smaller basis. Meanwhile, the Lotus Seven was still going strong, and other kit-car builders took the 'if you can't beat 'em . . .' attitude and built cars on the exact same lines, albeit some ten years later. However, there was still a market for that sort of car as Jeffrey and Dutton found out to their pleasant surprise. On a different theme, there were a few companies building 'replicars', the pioneer being Excalibur with their Mercedes Benz and Buggatti cars. In America, too, there were variations on the Auburn, Cord and Duesenberg triangle and the Classic, which followed the 1931 Ford Model A style.

In England, Siva, who also built weird and wonder-

Above: there were many odd but practical devices under the banner of specialist cars built in the 1970s; this is the cheap-to-run, three-wheeled, Mini-based Ranger Cub of 1974

ful sports cars with engines from Beetles to V8 Astons, produced odd Ford-based 'Roadsters' of no particular style. However, they looked old and were definitely fun. SP, of Battle near Hastings, built the Highwayman. This followed no particular fashion either, but this car which cost £6000 was perhaps directed at an entirely different market.

The SS Jaguar gave birth to a succession of replicas on both sides of the Atlantic, as did the D-type Jaguar in England. The Albany was as precise and neat as any, again in no particular (except old) style, while pride of place must be given to the immaculate Dri-Sleeve Moonraker. Exactly like a 35 'Bug' except for fat wheels, the Moonraker was expertly finished in every detail, from the wiring that criss-crossed the bonnet to the machined-aluminium dashboard. In all there have been countless builders of specialist cars. Some were unsophisticated and crude while some were examples for many larger manufacturers. The only common denominator with them all is that they were different and fun—and quite often, cheap. The mere fact that they were different from the majority set them and their owners, apart from the masses in their comfy, crash-proof boxes. The knowledge that his home-made sellotaped female attracter could collapse at any second gave the owner a certain affinity with his machine. There have been many trends and styles in design, there have been ups and downs. VAT killed them and expensive petrol gave them an extra life (lightweight sports cars are not only quicker, but are more frugal!). Perhaps, though, while large manufacturers build saloons, there will always be people somewhere trying to build something different, if only for the sheer hell of it. And that in a time when most of us are being automated into obscurity can be no bad thing. LJC

MEASURING THE RATE OF PROGRESS

A speedometer in working order has become a legal requirement for cars in almost every country in the world

Left: a speedometer and odometer assembly built during the 1910s; equipped with what for those times was a luxury in the form of a trip-meter, at the right of the unit

Below: the internal parts of the odometer assembly built into a speedometer of the 1920s; the wheels record up to 99,999.9 km, while the hair-spring in the centre controls the speedometer needle when it is fitted

A SPEEDOMETER IN WORKING ORDER is a legal requirement on road vehicles in virtually all countries of the world; fortunately, most of the instruments in use today are of a well-tried and proven design and rarely give any trouble.

Nowadays, the speedometer usually forms part of a fascia unit including indicator lights, temperature and fuel gauges, and sometimes other instruments. Illumination is provided by one or two low-wattage lamps, giving glare-free lighting.

The oldest speedometer, introduced about the turn of the century, was of the centrifugal governor (automatic regulator) type—a scaled-down edition of the governors still to be seen on old steam engines. Later came the chronometric speedometer, based on a constant time period measured against the speed of rotation of a road wheel (i.e., distance travelled), thus obtaining the speed. The chronometric model was relatively unaffected by vibration and for this reason was favoured on motor bicycles until quite recently.

The drive on these older models was usually by a gear on the inside of the front wheel, meshing with a pinion turning a flexible cable.

The instrument in almost universal use today, however, is the magnetic speedometer, a relatively cheap and reliable magnetic device, operated by a rotating flexible drive cable housed in a flexible tube. The cable is formed from stranded wire, with square endpieces, driven by worm and pinion from the drive (propeller shaft) end of the gearbox.

The cable spins a circular permanent magnet, producing a rotating magnetic flux that induces eddy currents in a spindle-mounted aluminium disc. A stationary field plate completes the magnetic circuit. An electric field is set up in the disc by the eddy currents and reacts on the rotating magnetic flux. This results in a torque, linear with the speed of rotation of the drive shaft, being set up in the disc (Foucault effect). A pointer, moving over an mph (kph) scale, is attached to the disc; a light coil spring returns the pointer to zero. Occasionally, a soft iron rotor, spun within a stationary magnet, produces the field.

Variations include a cylinder, concentric with the aluminium disc, marked with a speed scale on its edge, moving past a cursor; or a speed scale tape, sometimes with the addition of coloured segments, driven by a cord and pulleys from the disc.

Calibration can be effected by varying the magnetic flux, either by partial demagnetization or by altering the air gap between the magnet and the return circuit. Calibration marks—very small white dots—can usually be seen on the scale. The instrument is usually set to read slightly high so that the driver does not inadvertently exceed the speed limit.

An odometer (distance recorder), comprising a series of small drums bearing the figures zero to nine, is usually located inside the speedometer case. The tenth of a mile drum is driven by a small worm and pinion drive from the speedometer drive cable; as this drum completes its turn, a pin on its side engages a slot in a gear driving the unit drum; as the unit drum passes nine and approaches zero, the 'tens' drum is engaged, and so on. Sometimes, a 'trip' meter is added—this has fewer drums, driven in a similar manner, but is capable of being manually reset to zero.

Because of its cheapness and reliability, the magnetic speedometer is likely to remain standard equipment in private cars and small vans for some time to come. However, this type of speedometer has a limitation imposed by the drive cable, which can only be run straight or in a gentle bend. For this reason, larger commercial vehicles normally use a remotely operated electric speedometer, usually a moving coil instrument driven by the rectified output of a speed-proportional ac generator. The odometer is operated from the vehicle dc battery, interrupted by a speed-proportional contractor.

A later, electronic type of remotely operated speedometer uses a road-speed dependent, pulse generator to provide a signal source. Newer developments include a digital voltmeter that will display either the road speed or the average speed of a vehicle at the touch of a switch. As electronic components cheapen, there is little doubt that the speedometer of the future will be a 'solid state' package, with an LED (light-emitting diode) display.

The magnetic speedometer itself rarely gives any trouble and normally can be replaced only as a complete unit. The drive cable, however, should be lubricated every 12,000 miles, using an SAE 140 oil or an appropriate grease. Jerky operation of the speedometer pointer is a fairly certain indication that the cable needs lubricating, although a damaged cable may produce the same symptom.

To lubricate, it is necessary to remove the cable complete with tube, which is usually secured by a knurled screw cap, bolt or circlip at both the gearbox and the back of the speedometer. The cable can then be slid out of the tube and examined; if there are any broken strands, the cable should be replaced, otherwise it should be lubricated and refitted to the vehicle.

If the square cable end does not fully engage in the gearbox housing, rotate the cable slightly, maintaining slight pressure. When the square cable end is engaged, tighten the screw cap or other holding device. If the squared end will not enter the speedometer, push the vehicle in gear to and fro to bring the cable into align-

ment, then secure the speedometer end.

The speedometer unit itself can be replaced; if no workshop manual is available, examine carefully the fixing method before removing the old unit. It may be necessary, on some vehicles, to remove some other part, or all, of the fascia unit to gain access.

Remember that, if a car is modified in such a way (e.g., by changing the differential ratio, or fitting wheels or tyres of different diameter) as to change any of the design features related to the original calibration of the speedometer, the speedometer and odometer will then be inaccurate and should be re-calibrated.   AGH

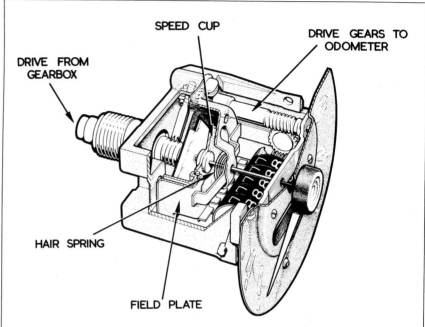

Above: a cutaway speedometer, showing the components of an AC-Delco unit, which is typical of the breed

Far left: an Italian Veglia unit, with built-in warning lights

Left: two groups of figures for recording distance; the lower ones constitute the trip-meter

Below: the working parts of an odometer; the white gear links the two drums when the two yellow teeth pass over it

'YER PAYS
YER MONEY...'

By using racing cars as an advertising medium, sponsors have helped to continue the growth of the motor-racing industry

Above: Willi Kauhsen's Porsche 917/10 leaves the viewer in no doubt as to the name of his sponsor; by 1975, the escalating cost of motor racing meant that sponsorship was vital— only the wealthiest could operate without a sponsor; it also meant that many talented drivers who could not obtain sponsorship were forced to drop out of the sport

IN THE UNITED STATES motor sport sponsorship has been a highly organised affair for many years. In his autobiography, race driver Eddie Rickenbacker wrote, 'That year, 1916, the Maxwell Special teams won seven of the thirteen major races we entered. Exhibitions and sponsors' fees brought in several thousand dollars more. At the end of the season we had a kitty of $78,000 to split among the personnel of the team, over what we had already drawn. I personally made $60,000 that year . . .' Rickenbacker, of course, went on to become the famous American fighter ace of World War I and later in his career actually owned the Indianapolis Speedway, the international Mecca of commercialised motor sport. Advertisements began to appear on racing cars in the States just a few years before World War II, but that inevitable development was still a long way off in Europe.

It was not until 1967 that the RAC in Britain permitted racing teams to carry the names of their entrants and drivers on their cars. The following year they were allowed to advertise products, provided that the "decals" did not exceed 55 sq in in size. A new regulation in 1972 permitted holders of an "Open Trade RAC Entrants' Licence" to advertise whatever they liked with stickers and signwriting of any size, the only proviso being one of 'good taste'. The international governing body of motor racing, the FIA, took a passive attitude to these developments and thus the way was open for a totally unprecedented expansion of motor sport sponsorship.

Of course, sponsorship does not necessarily entail commercial activities of any kind. Literally, a sponsor is a 'person who makes himself responsible for another,' and sponsors of this kind, individual enthusiasts who simply enjoy backing a car or a driver, are probably as old as the sport itself. Lord Hesketh, the fabulously wealthy young aristocrat who backs James Hunt in Formula One racing, is the best-known current sponsor to follow this tradition.

The sudden injection of large sums of advertising money has had a dramatic effect on motor sport, and cars can no longer be identified with their country of origin by their colour. Many dyed-in-the-wool enthusiasts were horrified when Team Lotus abandoned British Racing Green in favour of Gold Leaf Team Lotus red, white and gold. And they were stunned when the British Grand Prix became the John Player Grand Prix . . .

Some of these self-styled commentators feel that motor sport has lost its purity, prostituted itself in fact, by allowing the cars to become nothing more than moving billboards. Engineering ingenuity has been stifled by the need to promote unrelated products such as cigarettes, aperitifs, toys, cosmetics and the like. They feel that pure single-seater racing cars have degenerated into near-identical kit cars with an engine made here, a gearbox there, and a standard chassis built to hold all the parts together. They argue that because advertising and marketing executives hold the sponsorship purse-strings, an element of conservatism has crept into the designers' drawing boards. Other people argue that motor racing, like any other spectator sport today, is part of the vast entertainment industry and must adapt itself accordingly.

The truth lies somewhere in between these two attitudes. Whatever the effect on the sport, the fact remains that whenever a company is seen to be involved in the sport as a sponsor there is probably someone within that company who prefers motor sport to other forms of competition, and who is sufficiently influential to direct part of the company's promotional and advertising budgets in that direction. If a company backs golf or cricket, it is a fair bet that the chairman or managing director is a golf or cricket fanatic. In other words, companies involved in the sponsorship of sports of any kind usually have the best interests of those sports at heart.

But it would be naive to suggest that companies sponsor motor sport purely because the chairman happens to like the idea. The tobacco companies moved into motor racing and, later on, rallying when the government banned television advertising of cigarettes. Similarly they moved into cricket, golf, tennis, and many other branches of sport, building up a great deal of goodwill amongst enthusiasts in each field of activity. Certain politicians find even this form of advertising offensive but they are finding that, unlike the banning of television advertising, it is not easy to prohibit the tobacco companies from supporting sport. Large sections of the public feel a certain loyalty to any sponsor of their favourite sports, and their opinion is eloquently voiced in hundreds of specialist sporting publications. The fact that only one Grand Prix racing driver smokes cigarettes regularly, and even then not in large quantities, is irrelevant. It is amusing to note that, even though he does not race for a tobacco company, that particular driver is constantly being presented with large quantities of free cigarettes!

Sponsors and team managers seldom disclose the actual sums of money involved, but Ken Tyrrell, who was Jackie Stewart's team manager and part sponsor throughout Stewart's victorious years in Formula One racing, stated that it cost £600,000 to run a two-car

Formula One team through the 1974 season. It must, obviously enough, cost more than that today. A great deal of this money, for many of the Grand Prix teams, comes from tobacco companies such as John Player and Marlboro. Until they appeared on the motor racing scene the major sponsors of the sport were motoring-orientated concerns such as oil companies and tyre companies. They backed down on the grounds of cost towards the end of the 1960s. If the tobacco companies are forced to withdraw from sports sponsorship it will be interesting to see who steps into their shoes in Formula One racing.

It is the budding race driver's first duty to understand these complexities of modern life. In the past, many top drivers were simply rich individuals who preferred to spend their weekends in racing cars instead of, say, on a golf course. These days, almost anybody can make the grade in motor sport provided that he has the talent behind the wheel and, naturally, the ability to find sponsors. How does a promising beginner climb the ladder to Grand Prix stardom?

First of all, he has to find enough cash to get going. The lucky ones get a start in the relatively cheap world of kart racing, with their fathers paying the bills. Before they are old enough to hold a proper driving licence they are learning the tricks of car control and close competition. In their late teens they can make the move to proper motor racing, ideally in Formula Ford single seaters which provide excellent training for hoped-for futures in Grand Prix races. Unless they are very lucky and they have £5,000 or more to spend on a season of FF racing, it is here that they will have to find their first sponsor. This is where previous experience in kart racing will prove invaluable. The notion of a sponsor backing a completely inexperienced driver is a myth, but anybody with promise and some experience and with sufficient determination can scrape together enough money to get going.

In their quest for sponsors they will also find that

Below left: a Tyrrell Ford with sponsorship by courtesy of the giant French Elf oil company; during the mid 1970s, Elf supported numerous teams in various formulae

Below right: another major sponsor during the mid 1970s was the John Player cigarette company; such was their influence that the Lotus team, whom Players sponsored, even called their cars John Player Specials instead of Lotuses

Bottom: the helmets of Niki Lauda and Jackie Ickx, both bearing the insignia of their various sponsors

although many of the other drivers *appear* to be generously sponsored by disinterested companies, in many cases these are simply the names of those drivers' private businesses. Those drivers who do have proper sponsors at this level of the sport are seldom the recipients of full backing. More often, these sponsors are providing as little as ten per cent of the cash that is actually spent. Furthermore, sponsors are found not by writing begging letters to dozens of uninterested company directors but by personal contact—a lucky introduction or a chance meeting—in virtually every case. It's a tough world for the innocent beginner! But those who are determined to make the grade usually do so at least for as far as their driving talent can take them.

A very small number of drivers with the 'gift of the gab' have managed to talk their way right up the scale, scoring reasonable results on the way thanks to having the best equipment. Their one mistake has been their failure to realise that they do not quite have the talent to justify a career in Formula One—they are public relations experts and not Grand Prix drivers! Once in Grand Prix racing they endure a few humiliating races before fading rapidly from the scene. Whatever you think about the effects of massive sponsorship in top class motor racing, the standard of driving required from the men who succeed is simply incomprehensible to the average motorist. And so long as it stays that way the sport must be in good health.

Some of the world's best drivers are quite incapable of talking their way into a good drive, but racing team managers have noted their talents and sponsors have been found for them. Other drivers have been determined enough to find the money they need to buy the best 'works' drives at each stage in the development of their careers, and they have produced the results to justify their sponsors' faith in them. At current prices this means that for a season in Formula Three or Formula Atlantic racing they will have persuaded a sponsor to provide some £25,000. A season in Formula 5000 costs about £70,000.

Saloon car racing can be expensive, too, and it can cost £25,000 to race a Group One saloon in the RAC Touring Car Championship. Here, most of the successful cars are supported by car manufacturers or importers, while sponsors provide some cash or other services to help pay the bills in some cases. A girlie magazine, for example, might sponsor a car that is being run by a manufacturer or importer in this class of racing. Part of the 'sponsorship' might be in the form of advertising of that make of car in the magazine.

Companies do not necessarily have to sponsor individual drivers or teams to be involved in motor sport. They can sponsor a complete race meeting or rally or a series of events that makes up a championship. Every car in those events will carry their company name and good publicity can be obtained at the event itself and in the Press afterwards.

Some companies offer bonus payments to drivers who carry stickers advertising their products, and drivers who opt for such agreements can claim a cash reward of around £25 to £40 each time they win. Similar agreements exist in the very top levels of motor sport and there the competitors' rewards are far greater. Sponsors can back an individual driver but not his car. Ronnie Peterson, the JPS-Lotus star driver from Sweden, is personally contracted to 'Vick' and he carries that company name on his helmet. Britain's top rally driver, Roger Clark, always drives for Ford but is personally contracted to Cossack hair spray. These companies use these drivers in their advertising campaigns to try to capture a particular image and identification for their products.

Sponsorship deals can become quite complicated, of course, and readers, I hope, will refrain from a cynical smile if I mention one of my own deals! Wishing to tackle the Avon Motor Tour of Britain, a three-day event that combines rally type special

Below left: the Formula One March team is famous for its many varied and involved sponsorship deals to which the decals on this machine bear witness

Below right: one of the most interesting sponsors to appear in Formula One racing was the Yardley cosmetic company; it originally financed the BRM team cars, but later transferred its allegiance to the more successful McLaren team

ALEX DIAS RIBEIRO

Right: mixing drinking with driving—the F1 Brabham team is sponsored by the Martini and Rossi drinks company

Far right: the ultimate sponsor; Alex Dias Ribeiro, a devout Baptist, carries the message 'Jesus saves' on his helmet

Below: another unusual sponsor—this is the Durex Lola T400 Formula 5000 machine of Richard Scott

stages and races at five different circuits, I first approached Penthouse magazine and asked whether one of their Penthouse Pets would like to be a co-driver in the Tour. An excellent lady by the name of Madeleine 'volunteered' for the job and it was only then that I started looking for the money to run a car. About £3,000 was needed, but with a Penthouse Pet on the event a great deal of publicity was virtually guaranteed and Strand Glass became the principal sponsors. Then we chose the car and organised half a dozen bonus contracts with companies such as Dunlop, Duckhams, Simoniz, and Champion. With all that work and the preparation of the car to attend to, the actual driving becomes a mere fraction of the job, but I hasten to add that we did win our class as planned and the lovely Madeleine made us jolly famous for a few weeks. Even though they may not have been the sponsors it should be mentioned that the car was a Fiat.

Drivers from this level right to the top of the sport have to become involved in sponsorship deals rather in this manner and it has been suggested that the race drivers' schools should not bother with showing the pupils how to drive fast—they should teach politics, economics, and salesmanship! That's perhaps too cynical a view, for as we have seen, a driver who can not produce the goods will not last long. The nature of motor sport means that he will be left behind.

One unfortunate aspect of commercial sponsorship of motor sport is that television companies have sometimes argued that they cannot put major events on the air because the vehicles carry advertising. But the races, on those rare occasions when they are televised, are often so badly presented that it is almost impossible to read anything on the cars anyway. The BBC refused to televise a Formula 5000 race early in 1975 until one of the cars, sponsored by Durex, covered up that company name. It would not be proper to expose the viewing public to advertising for such a product, they argued. The team manager and the sponsors agreed to cover the name, the car won the race, and the resultant publicity in the press was of course far greater than it would have been had no fuss been made over the ethics of exposing the public to birth control advertising. Motor sport, because of its modern commercialised nature, seems to confuse the television companies, who have no compunction whatsoever in letting their cameramen dwell lovingly over sponsors' banners around the boundaries of cricket fields, by the greens at golf matches, and at horse race finishing posts . . .

Motor sport would continue without spectators and without sponsors simply because there are thousands of people who enjoy driving cars to their limits. The presence of large crowds and major sponsors, however, enables motor sport to raise itself above that amateur level, and so it will remain for as long as the many major sponsors continue to find that their money has been well spent. TD

FUN ON FOUR WHEELS

Recognising a sports car is relatively easy. Trying to establish an exact definition of the term 'sports cars' is very difficult

Above: the Frazer Nash Standard three-seater of 1925 which was powered by a side-valve Anzani engine of 1500 cc

ACCORDING TO A BRITISH DEFINITION of about 1910, a sports car is any that a gentleman cannot enter without stooping or removing his top hat. According to an American definition of 1960, a sports car is any in which the front seats fold down to form beds.

Speed and acceleration are not suitable criteria for judging whether a car is a sports car. Most of the popular sports cars of the 1930s could be out-accelerated by most of the popular American saloons of the same period, which were emphatically not sports cars. An MG Midget, which *is*, can be passed with 25 mph in hand by a Rolls-Royce Silver Shadow, which is *not*—and it is no use asking how we can be so certain that a car qualifies for the title or fails to, for though definition may be so elusive, recognition is usually easy.

That does not mean that the criteria have anything to do with the appearance of the car. The question cannot be determined by the size and shape of the wheels, the presence or absence of applied decoration, of bonnet straps, or even of a roof. The Morgan Plus 4 of the middle 1950s was very open and very

clearly a sports car, but the equally open Paramount 10 of the same time was not.

This suggests that handling and roadholding, crispness of response and sensuality of controls—notably the gearchange—might be what distinguishes the sports car; but it is not so. All these properties may be found developed to a very high degree in the Bristol 406, but it was a good deal less sporting than the contemporary Sunbeam Alpine which was positively soggy.

It was just as unsatisfactory to justify use of the expression by reference to a car's suitability for competition, otherwise we would have to admit as sports cars such past winners of the Monte Carlo Rally as the Ford Zephyr and the Jaguar Mk. 7, which would never do. In fact it seems unsatisfactory to attempt to define sports cars at all: they are so infinite in their variety that the only effective definition is by example—which, by definition, is no definition at all. Yet there remains a germ of validity in the idea of suitability for competition, if only because motoring sport is almost as limitless in its variety as the sports

car itself. Well before the expression first came into use (it began to appear in catalogues after World War I), the Apperson Jackrabbit was advertised in 1907 as being intended to 'cater to that limited class of owners who want a car that can be put to any service—racing or touring.' The Apperson came out in 1904, but a year earlier Daimler proved that when necessary their production tourers could fill the racing bill. The team of three 90 horsepower Mercédès racing cars specially prepared for the Gordon Bennett race in Ireland was destroyed in a fire at the Daimler factory a few days before the event. Some privately owned 60 horsepower Mercédès tourers were then hastily stripped of their lamps and mudguards and substituted in the race, which one of them won.

It was in 1912 that the design of the racing car began to be significantly different from that of the production tourer. The sudden ef-floration of the high-speed engine of relatively small capacity and newly aggrandized volumetric efficiency, resulting from the twin-overhead-camshaft valve gear devised by Birkigt of Hispano-Suiza and exploited by Henry for Peugeot, started a new fashion in racing engines that has persisted to the present day; and the demands it made in transmission engineering and in driving skills effected a rapid change in the character of the racing car, while the design and behaviour of the tourer continued almost unchanged.

Since 1922, by which time this divarication had become so clear cut that the representative Grand Prix racer was a two-litre car with an engine made by jewellers—while the typical tourer was a clumsy banger apparently built by blacksmiths—it has been clear that the ultimate in sports cars must be a road-going version of the Grand Prix racer, with lights, mudguards, and seats for two. In the mid-1920s this was by no means difficult to arrange, for racing cars were still two-seaters until 1927, even though the riding mechanic was no longer carried in Grands Prix after 1923.

The first to make a thorough-going conversion of this type was Bugatti, whose divine type 35 needed no more than some skimpy mudguards, some elegant electrics, and *perhaps* a flimsy hood and full-width windscreen (though two aero-screens looked much better) to make it the most covetable that the true, the wealthy and the capable enthusiast could imagine. Maserati were soon to follow this example, for in the years of anarchy beginning in 1928, when race organisers and entrants ignored the strictures of the official regulations, it soon became clear that with a reversion to the spirit of the two-litre Formula prevailing in 1922–25, with bodies and chassis suitable for the carriage of two people, it would be possible to use the cars not only for the classic races, but also for sports-car events or even ordinary use on the road. Indeed it was during this period that the *Grand Prix de l'Automobile Club de France*, once the only race of the season really to matter, was run for the first time as a sports car event; and in the years that followed, when generally hard times reduced participation by factories, who become more dependent upon the abilities and zeal of private owners and drivers to maintain their reputations, racing cars were designed under the influence of sports car requirements. This could be seen in the appearance of the 1931 Monza Alfa Romeo, a 2.3 litre straight-eight racing car which was in due course to become the basis of a catalogued sports model, but in the meantime was one of the two dominant cars in Grand Prix racing. The other was the type 51 Bugatti, very similar in all but its cylinder head to the type 35.

The Monza Alfa Romeo was easily made into a two-seater too, but its successor the P3 Monoposto, with its bifurcated propeller shaft designed around the concept of a single centrally-seated driver, could not be so adapted. As late as 1934 it was still the Monza model that Varzi and Nuvolari drove to come first and second in the Mille Miglia; but it was clear that the P3 Monoposto was a very much faster car, still capable of winning Grands Prix against the formidable new German opposition, and in 1935 a two-seater version was somehow cobbled up with lamps and mudguards to win the Mille Miglia. It was a stopgap design, for in 1935 Alfa Romeo fielded a new straight 8 GP car with independent suspension all round, the central drive shaft running straight back to a gearbox integral with the final drive. This made possible a super-sports car in the best Alfa Romeo tradition: the 8C 2900A of 1936 was simply the new GP car with a two-seater body, cycle-type mudguards, and two aero screens, albeit with a 2.9 litre engine instead of the 3.8 of the single-seater. By that time the only cars that mattered in GP racing were the Auto-Union and Mercedes-Benz: the fantastic power and speed—not to mention the thirst—of these much more advanced machines made it quite inconceivable that any sports car versions of them could be envisaged.

Thus, for a while, the sports-racing two-seater began to lag noticeably behind the pure racer in performance. A new line of development had to be tried if progress was to be maintained: if sports car regulations demanded mudguards and provision for passengers, then these liabilities would have to be converted into assets. For the first time since the brilliantly successful Chenard Walcker carried the colours of France in the sports car races of 1925, streamlined bodywork began to appear. The all-enveloping open car was best exemplified by the special Bugattis that succeeded at Le Mans in 1937 and 1939; the streamlined saloon, with a teardrop canopy on a pontoon-like hull, made its most significant appearance in the Alfa Romeo that very nearly won that race in 1938, a car with most interesting Pininfarina bodywork that constituted a link between the pioneering work of Jaray and the post-war generation of sporting coupés that appeared to take their inspiration from the Cisitalia. Whatever the niceties of its engine and chassis, the toprank sports car would never again look like a Grand Prix racer with knobs on.

Recollection of the $4\frac{1}{2}$ litre Lago Talbots that ran so convincingly at Le Mans in the early post-war years might appear to give the lie to this, but it was always unjust that these cars should have been accused of being thinly disguised GP racers: the truth was that the Talbot single-seater, which remained competitive in Grands Prix until 1951, was merely an adaptation of what had originally been a sports car. As for the pretty little slipper-bodied type 125 and 166 Ferraris of 1948 and 1949, these were short lived: although mechanically they had so much in common with their stark-bodied single-seater counterparts, they were soon uniformly dressed in full-width pannelling whenever two seats were necessary. In this memorably pretty *barchetta* form they were very successful, displaying stamina that seemed curiously at variance with the racing record of their single-seater brethren, but which nevertheless demonstrated for all the world to see the virtues of long-distance sports car racing as a means of engineering development. In the years that followed Ferrari maintained the Alfa Romeo tradition of campaigning in sports car events with machines that were praised as thoroughbreds by those on his side, and sneered at

Right: the 1935 PB MG was one of the many sports cars built by that company which were simple yet sporting; they were not very fast, however

Below: Morgan's immortal three-wheeler Super Sports of 1933; the JAP engine was an 1100 cc unit

as thinly disguised racers by those who were not. The V12 $4\frac{1}{2}$ litre Ferrari, the V6 Dino in assorted sizes and shapes, and the Formula Two four-cylinder cars were all revamped as two-seaters, and the later P3 and P4 sports racers were quite clearly and directly derived from the firm's current Grand Prix practice, even though the engines were of larger capacity than Formula One rules admitted. Eventually, as the long-distance races counting for the manufacturers' championship became more and more lax in the rules governing the so-called 'prototypes' that were admissible, the sports-racing Ferrari became mechanically almost identical to the GP version: the type 312 B sports racer was a full-bodied and mildly de-tuned version of the flat 12 Formula One car, and its only effective rival was the Matra that was produced in precisely the same way.

The racing car with lights is an ideal that appeals to more people than could possibly buy or build one. The character is more accessible than the identity. The four-cylinder type 37 Bugatti was virtually a $1\frac{1}{2}$ litre economy version of the straight 8 type 35, and just as amenable to running either stripped or caparisoned. The six-cylinder 1100 cc Amilcar was a beautiful exercise in miniaturisation, its twin-camshaft supercharged engine nestling in a low little

chassis that confirmed it in every respect as a scaled-down racer. Alfa Romeo, whose two-seater versions of their Grand Prix cars were never intended for general sale, captured their shadow in the more expansive and less expensive substance of road cars which gradually grew from $1\frac{1}{2}$ to 2.3 litres, and transposed the style and feel, but not the speed, of their track cars to the roads of Europe. By the 1950s, when nearly all outright racers conformed to a general chassis layout based on that of the 1937 GP Mercedes-Benz, the sports racing Aston Martins had chassis that were cast in exactly the same mould, but carried engines that owed little to any of them. Pegaso did much the same, but their engine could have gone into a GP car, while their bodywork was clearly aimed at rich customers who preferred self indulgence to self immolation. Then when Cooper and Lotus brought about the morphological revolution that left a racing driver sitting in front of his engine instead of behind it, they likewise produced two-seater sports-racers devised on strictly similar lines but with engines of different capacity. The original Cooper Monaco was an outstanding example of the ingenuity with which designers sought to get around the more onerous rules governing passenger accommodation: others in the past have made the passengers seat a pretty notional one, wickedly cramped and impossibly uncomfortable, but Cooper virtually cut it in two and put half on each side of the centrally located driver's seat! They were soon called to order, but it was a wonderful example of the absurd impracticality of the two-seater racing car. A more convincing example was yet to come, and has only very recently departed; the CanAm sports car, an aerodynamically bodied Grand Prix racer with bigger brakes and tyres and an enormous engine, has two seats but no lights or other concessions to the conventions of the highway.

One of the oddest manifestations of sports car mania is that there are and always have been plenty of people willing, indeed eager, to endure all manner of such privations for the sake of owning (or being seen to own) what appeared to be a sports car, even though its performance in absolute terms might be mundane or even pathetic. Such cars were invariably little ones, stark and simple and light and easy to handle, more often than not powered by proprietary engines or engines derived from thoroughly ordinary and lack-lustre touring cars. Occasionally they had quite refined chassis and suspension, good brakes and delicious steering; generally they were unrefined contraptions put together from bits that might be detected elsewhere doing duty in utterly unremarkable cars. These little sportsters were essentially funcars, sizzle without steak: but they served a very useful

and gearboxes came from the big firms: the HRG had a Singer engine, the late Georges Irat was based on the mechanical elements of a front-wheel-drive Citroën. Since World War I precisely the same trends have been continued: funcars of quite respectable performance, yet by no means comparable to the true and costly sports-racers, have been made by the likes of Nardi and Stanguellini in Italy, by Honda (whose S800 engine was one of the brightest jewels in the sports-car heaven) in Japan, and most especially by Lotus in England. The stark Lotus 6, powered by an engine of Ford or BMC provenance and employing axles and transmission components that would have been beyond the abilities of the Lotus factory to make, was just as essentially the simple low-powered light-weight of youthful enthusiasts as the GN, Lombard or Senechal of the thirties. The rising standards of the

Above: BMW's beautiful 328, which, with a special body, won the 1940 Mille Miglia; this car was less of a compromise than many cars before

Right: this HRG 1500 cc of 1947 was more rugged

purpose in allowing the youthful and needy to taste the pleasures of what might be called enthusiastic motoring before the cares of this world and the fears of the next prompted a step down—or was it up?—into something more respectable. There were not many young men or women in the 1920s fortunate enough to be able to sally forth in a Bugatti 35 or even an Alfa 1750, but any of a host of spidery little French two-seaters would allow them to sublimate their thwarted desires. The Derby, the Salmson or the four-cylinder Amilcar filled the bill perfectly. They were ultra-light spindly things with scrawny tyres and sketchy bodies that were frequently not even two-seaters but more like the $1\frac{1}{2}$ seater developed by the true racing men, the idea being to get the riding mechanic out of the driver's way with no more room (and thus no more frontal area) than was absolutely necessary.

England too had its cheap little sporting funsters, but England had no road racing. Apart from leaping from bump to bump around the banked track at Brooklands—an occupation not calculated to do anything for the health or longevity of a lightly-built car—the only sporting activity available in Britain in the twenties and early thirties was the climbing of hills. The result was that British sports cars tended to have nothing much in the way of high-speed stability and even less in the way of brakes, but they were light and compact. They also had gearboxes that were more suited to the gradients and hairpins of one-day sport-ing trials than to the optimisation of performance on ordinary roads: first and second gears could be very low indeed. This made a mockery of cars such as the Singers and MGs that flourished in the thirties, for they were styled as though they were roadracers and geared as though they were mud-pluggers—for the simple reason that ordinary touring cars had wide-ratio gearboxes, and those same boxes could be cheaply used for what purported to be sports cars.

More and more frequently the small sports car could be related to a small touring car from the same manufacturer. Riley did it with the 9 hp chassis, the MG was a Morris, the Fiat Coppa d'Oro was a sporting two-seater variant in the Ballila range. Other low-price sports cars were built by specialists whose engines

1960s encouraged a different kind of Lotus, the Elan—much more refined, more comfortable, more present-able and more practical for every kind of everyday motoring, yet still very much a sports car of the kind that one owned and drove for the sheer pleasure of it rather than with any thoughts of competition in mind. Nor could the production-derived quantity-produced sporting two-seaters that became a British speciality—the Triumph TR series, the Austin-Healeys, the MG middleweights—hope to be competitive in anything other than strictly amateur club events, however much their manufacturers might delude the public into thinking otherwise with the aid of special team cars built at formidable expense and campaigned with the most professional organizing skill.

The simple and slightly uncomfortable truth of the 1960s was that many a so-called sports car was no faster nor more roadworthy than some of the high-performance four-seater saloons being turned out by the big firms. The Ford Cortina GT and the BMC Mini Cooper really set the cat among the pigeons, proving capable of tuning and general emendation that gave them on-the-road performance such as many a rakish-looking two-seater could not match. With better accommodation (and, often, lower insur-ance rates) than sports cars of comparable price could

offer, such lively saloons as these were a great success with the public, and the manufacturers were by no means slow to recognise the makings of a profitable new market. Galloping specialisation in sports-car racing, and profound changes in the character of rallying, gave them further encouragement. The traditional sporting two-seater had become a toy, and works teams began to neglect them and to concentrate on cars that had been conceived as family saloons. It was a much more profitable exercise, directly encouraging the sale of family saloons.

In a sense the sports car—for that is what the sprightly saloon had become—had come full circle. There was a time when the world of motor sport was yet young, when specialisation was as foreign as professionalism, when sports cars were at their best high-performance versions of the four-seater tourers that were the choice of ordinary unadventurous motorists. In fact the practical sports car, as distinct from the racer with mudguards, evolved from the ordinary tourer in the great sporting trials of performance and reliability that were features of the motoring movement in the fast-developing days before World War I.

Whenever the sports car was begotten, it was delivered in 1910 when the Prinz Heinrich trials (begun in 1908) reached their climax. The Austrian-Daimler (later to be called Austro-Daimler) cars designed for this event by Ferdinand Porsche were

by the standards of the time rather lightly-built tourers, slim of body and uncommonly lively in performance, and they dominated the event despite the claims to greater power and sometimes greater speed offered by rivals of more gigantic proportions and less efficiency and agility.

In that same year Vauxhall produced a memorable model that became recognised as Britain's first sports car, the Prince Henry four-seater designed for that same event by Laurence Pomeroy the elder. With a

Above: brutal yet elegant, the superb Alfa Romeo 8C 2600 of 1937; this car features independent front suspension

Above: the graceful lines of what to many is a sports car; the Talbot Lago T26 GS, which features coachwork by Saoutchick

(as was the Austrian-Daimler and the Prince Henry Vauxhall) four-seaters. They had hoods that could be erected and sustain the wind forces generated at full speed; they had lights that were adequate for fast driving in open country, brakes that stopped them surprisingly well, and steering that was a pleasure when travelling fast. If they also had a ride quality that was hard to the kidneys, and gearboxes that demanded more skill than some customers could muster, they could be excused by reference to the standards of the day; and indeed there was a vociferous class of customers who, anxious to employ their cars as verification of the hair on their chests or the sleight of their hands, sought esteem in the purchase of cars that were reputed to be hard to master.

Sheer performance was of course always a selling point, however little the customer might be prepared to exploit it after concluding the deal. In the 1920s the average tourer was only fit for 50 mph or so, but the Lambda was guaranteed to exceed 70 and the early 3-litre Bentley could reach 60 in second gear, and just exceed 90 in its high top gear—though Bentley only reached satisfactory sales with a castrated 'touring model' with a wide-ratio gearbox and a 75 mph maximum. By 1939 a decent touring car—a six-cylinder Hudson or Wolseley, say—could reach 80 and cruise at 55, but the yardstick for sports cars with real claims to speed was 100.

By the end of the 1930s, indeed, the degeneration of the sports car, its reclassification as a type different not only in style but also in function from the tourer, was well on its way. For a long time this change had been held at bay by those enthusiastic pragmatists who organised the race at Le Mans, and whom we have to thank for some of the greatest sports cars of the between-wars era. Their profuse and pernickety rules, which insisted on proper carrying capacity and reasonable range and practical reliability, virtually defined the 3- and 4½-litre Bentleys, the Aries and the Chenard and the Lorraine Dietrich and the SS Mercedes-Benz and the M45 Lagonda, which were hallowed by the first dozen or so years of the world's most purposeful and significant motor race. Others were cast in the Le Mans image: races such as the revived TT, cars such as the Type 43 Bugatti, all ratified what promised to be a lasting tradition.

Times were changing, however, and the tradition could not last. From customers and manufacturers alike, the pressure to make the sports car a more specialised machine altered the whole course of the type's development. Very few people expected to be able to buy a car that could be entered with any hope of success in a major competition without special preparation, and correspondingly few manufacturers offered one: Frazer-Nash, Bugatti and (if you had some influence) Alfa Romeo were about the only ones. Others accepted that some alterations would be necessary; but the ordinary Aston Martin did not look so different from the genuine Le Mans model that the neighbours would notice. More important still, very few people wanted to drive hard with a full complement of passengers aboard, and even fewer designers could create a long tourer that would handle and accelerate as well as a short two-seater. The shape of the sports car, and its size, were drastically and irremediably altered in the 1930s: firms like Invicta and SS and Frazer-Nash in England, Darracq and Delahaye in France, and even Auburn in America, all in their several ways exploited the change and produced some memorable cars as a result.

The most important change came from Germany. At a time when the sports car was popularly supposed

lighter body and an engine enlarged to 4½ litres (but still a very flexible side-valve design) the car was developed in haste for the Shelsley Walsh hill-climb in 1913, succeeding there so brilliantly that when the war was over a demand for replicas was immediately voiced. With better brakes and electrics it thus became the Vauxhall Velox, better known as the 30/98 and faster in full touring trim than almost anything else on the road. With a slender lightweight body that defined a style to be recognised as classical, the 30/98 looked as taut and responsive as indeed it was—and is, for even today one can climb Prescott's hairpins and gradients as fast as a DB2/4 Aston Martin thirty years its junior.

Those thirty years embraced a period during which the most famous, the most lasting, and perhaps the most worthwhile sports cars enjoyed popular patronage and critical approval. They stemmed not from the empty imitation or even mockery of the classical racing car. They were perhaps most easily described as roadsters, for they started out as open cars that were essentially suited to service on real roads, making high performance a practical realisation for real people.

The distinction between the sports car and the tourer was (and often is still) difficult to draw. The 2-litre Lagonda was a touring car masquerading as a sports car; the 3-litre Bentley was a sports car that looked like a tourer. The point to be made is that in their definitive and most memorable forms they were to be a stern and uncompromising means of sub-jugating engineering refinement and civilised depart-ment to the demands of sheer performance, the classical and unashamedly brutal sports car was thrown into shockingly antique perspective by a svelte and silken machine with a stiff tubular chassis and relatively soft suspension, with independent control and springing of the front wheels, with a small engine of high volumetric efficiency, excellent hydraulic brakes, light but impeccable steering, and a flowing semi-stream-lined body style that completely upset convention. This was the BMW 328, and it was outstandingly successful in competition and in the market place. Not the least important of its features was that its 2-litre engine was derived from an existing production engine, with only a new (and admittedly quite remark-able) cylinder head to account for the fine turn of speed the car could show. It was the outstanding roadworthiness of the 328 that made the most pro-found impression on customers and competitors; and after the decade of sport bowed out with a convincing victory for a special-bodied 328 in the 1940 Mille Miglia, the stage was set for a complete revaluation of sports car design after World War II.

This is not to say that nothing of the same sort was tried between the appearance of the 328 in 1936 and its disappearance four years later. The V12 Lagonda, despite owing much of its design to W. O. Bentley, was similarly modern in most respects and could have done even better at Le Mans in 1939 than in fact it did; Peugeot and Aston Martin, Alfa Romeo and Atalanta, were likewise occupied in applying up-to-date ideas to outworn concepts. But it was only with the appearance of the surprisingly fast and stable Riley-engined Healey after the war, and then of the Jaguar XK120 in 1949, that the age of the modern sports roadster could be seen to have begun.

The Jaguar was phenomenal, in performance and price and looks. Maybe it was no faster than a really good Type 57SC Bugatti ten years its senior; maybe it looked suspiciously like the Mille Miglia BMW; but it was not only beautiful, but also beautifully accessible. Anybody could have one: the sports car was no longer the preserve of the rich and skilful and physically fit. The sports-racing car was already a different matter: during the 1950s the gulf between what could be driven on the open road and what could be com-petitive in racing widened seriously. People did occasionally drive Mille Miglia Ferraris through the streets of Milan, or L3 Connaughts through those of Manchester, but these cars were not meant for such use and were not very good at it. For kindred reasons the XK120 could not last to the Le Mans finish—and if it were considered a very fast but deliberately civilised two-seater tourer it was not reasonable to expect anything better. Most people, convinced by its speed and its open two-seater body, unhesitatingly pronounced it a sports car.

In a few more years came a car that was to set new standards of performance, of refinement, of drive-ability and of dual-role ability, though it was never to be cheap. The Mercedes-Benz 300SL had the old wine of a 3-litre production saloon's engine in the new bottle of a multitubular space-frame chassis, whose latticework inspired a whole new set of conventions in outright racing cars but was concealed by stream-lined *closed* bodywork that accepted the new con-ventions of the latest high-performance roadsters. Very high speeds and quite prodigious acceleration were combined with a newly fantastic degree of engine flexibility. Here was a car that could win the Le Mans race, or the Carrera Pan Americana for that matter, and

yet be driven easily through the crowded streets of cities like Mainz.

It was only in degree rather than in definition that it differed from others of the same period and later years. The Porsche 365 was no less significant in the evolution of the modern high-performance aero-dynamic closed roadholder, even though its production-derived engine (from the Volkswagen) gave it a very modest straight-line speed. The significant thing about these, and about so many other develop-ments of that same fertile period (which was at its most productive between about 1954 and 1966), was that the sports car as a fun car, a toy, had become almost completely divorced from the practical high-performance road car which the sports car had originally set out to be. The rule now was a closed and more or less aerodynamic body accepting two people in real comfort (and possibly two little ones in relative discomfort) together with a moderate quantity of luggage and such mechanical aids as were appropriate

to the level of performance sought—which might be anything from ordinary to inordinate.

These were called grand touring cars, borrowing a term that was applied to cars in about 1930 by Alfa Romeo, whose 6c *Gran Turismo* 1750 four-seaters were all that the name was meant to imply. The term grew popular, and should have been applied to such things as the $3\frac{1}{2}$ and $4\frac{1}{2}$ litre Derby-built Bentleys that Rolls-Royce persisted in describing as 'silent sports cars'; but instead it came to denote lithe long-legged coupés by the likes of Ferrari, Maserati, Aston Martin, Pegaso, Bristol and Lamborghini. The GT car was always supposed to be a high-quality product, as the best respected of its predecessors were, but the motor trade has never wanted imitators and poseurs: cheaply finished and poorly furnished pseudo-GT cars soon appeared from factories large and small, cars that had nothing grand about them whatsoever but

Above: the Ferrari Daytona, which was the last of the Maranello company's large front-engined sports cars; the 4.4-litre machine had a top speed of 175 mph and could accelerate from 0–60 mph in well under six seconds

which bore about the same relation to the real Grand Touring types as the M-type MG or the 10 hp Maximag might bear to finely tuned and engineered fury of a Targa Florio Maserati.

As always in the past, appearances counted for more than they ought. The AC Ace-Bristol open two-seater was appreciably slower than the closed version known as the Aceca; but more people bought it, because it was obviously more sporting! Likewise there was a lot more difference than met the eye

between the roadgoing Lamborghini Miura and the sports-racing Ford GT40; and the real value of the latter car to its makers was in earning glamour that the customer hoped might rub off on his six-cylinder three-speed Mustang, a near-brakeless upstart that was a commercially successful cosmetic and was accepted as a 'sporty' car—a new term that has come to confuse the issue even further. What the GT40 also did (apart from securing the first American victory at Le Mans, something that the noble efforts of Chrysler and Stutz in the 1920s and Cunningham in the 1950s had never quite accomplished) was to confirm what Lotus and Cooper and Abarth and most of all Porsche had already suggested: that if successful racing cars had to be rear-engined, good sports cars should be too. Today's Countach or Dino, Esprit or 911, is undoubtedly a sports car even if it never infringes a speed limit.

Whether it has an open four-seater or a closed two-seater body, whether it can barely stagger beyond 70 mph like the TC MG or go a clear 100 mph faster like the Ferrari Boxer, the sports car must have about it a certain aura. It is useless to suggest, as has been attempted, that a sports car is one that can be driven in a sporting manner: the Mercedes-Benz 450 SEL and the Bristol 411, even the Bentley Continental or—if it be a matter of sheer *go* without need to steer or stop—a Pontiac GTO, can be driven sportingly, competitively, aggressively and very fast. They are not sports cars, as their manufacturers would be quick to agree; but neither are or were the Lotus 15, the Mercedes-Benz 300SLR, the Alfa Romeo 33TT12 or the Porsche 917, despite their titles and despite any amount of lights and seats. They could all be described as highly specialised racing cars, which is no longer what sports cars are meant to be—whatever that is. LJKS

Left: developed from the Elan sports was this Lotus Elan +2, first seen in 1967; although using the basic Elan's 1558 cc engine, the 110 mph sports car utilised a slightly longer chassis. This, along with wider tracks, improved the car's cornering power, which had already been in the racing-car class

Below: the sports car of the 1970s; this is the Porsche Turbo, loosely based on ideas the Stuttgart firm formalised in Can-Am and sports-car racing

ROOM FOR JUST ONE MORE PERSON

Sports cars were raced even before single-seaters yet today they are little more than fully clothed Grand Prix cars

THERE IS LITTLE DOUBT that Grand Prix racing has long been considered the premier form of motor racing. However, a sports car afficionado will, very likely, hotly dispute the point.

Sportscar racing was born many years before Grands Prix were first held, and the very mention of Le Mans, the Targa Florio and the Mille Miglia, conjour-up vivid memories of some of the most famous motor races ever run. Who will ever forget the classic drivers whose names form a compendium of talent and renown.

There was Mike Hawthorn, Peter Collins, Tony Brooks, the amazing Stirling Moss in his equally amazing Mercedes. The great Ferrari duo of the fifties, Phil Hill and Olivier Gendebien, the new breed of Italians like Bandini, Vacarella, Scarfiotti, McLaren, Foyt and Gurney in the late sixties. In later years Britain's Brian Redman, the Belgian Jacky Ickx, the diminutive Italian Arturo Merzario all become top sportscar drivers along with Derek Bell, the great French partnership of Gerard Larrousse/Henri Pescarolo, and perhaps the two finest of all time . . . Jo (Seppi) Siffert and Pedro Rodriguez.

The very roots of sports car racing can be traced back to 1903, when the famous Gordon Bennett race was run, in which Mercedes entered their 60 hp cars. There followed a period of twenty years of steady progress in Sports Car racing. The Herkemer and Prince Henry Trials in 1905 were probably the first races to promote cars of a 'sports' nature, rather than straightforward saloons.

In the same year, what was later to be Britain's oldest motor race was first run. The Tourist Trophy featured a four lap event held on a 52 mile circuit on the Isle of Man. The cars had to conform to various overall weight factors, a load stipulation, and fuel consumption figures of around 26 mpg.

Just one year later, Count Vincenzo Florio organised the first ever Targa Florio on his beloved Piccolo Madonie circuit, which ran through towns, villages and around the mountains of Sicily. For a further 70 odd years, the Targa Florio remained one of the most gruelling and demanding races.

That first race was won by an Itala, and during the following years, the race never failed to attract upwards of half a million spectators who lined the circuit, perilously close to the cars, enthralled by the sheer magnetism of the race.

Sports car racing long suffered at the hands of the rule makers, and although there were periods when the regulations remained stable, all too often the governing bodies deemed it necessary to completely rewrite the rules. Despite the rule-makers' interference the sport flourished and reached another significant landmark in 1923 in the south of France.

Les 24 Heures Du Mans, without doubt the best known motor race in the world was won in its inaugural year by French drivers driving a French made

Chenard-Walcker. The following year saw the birth of one of Britain's most famous racing cars, the Bentley. Much to the chagrin of the French, the British racing green model won the 24 hour event. The classic 3 litre Bentley returned to the Sarthe circuit three years later, to continue and prove its winning ways and tendencies with four consecutive wins.

The leading motor manufacturers of the time were quick to realise the importance and prestige to be attained from competition involvement, and soon all the leading marques were contesting the major races. From Italy came Alfa Romeo, Ferrari and Maserati; from France, Delahaye, Talbot and Gordini were winning races and from Germany, the giant Mercedes The famous Bentleys heralded an historic epoch for British racing cars, together with Lagonda, Aston Martin, and the all-conquering Jaguars.

Stirling Moss and Denis Jenkinson were but small boys when the first Mille Miglia was run in 1927, 28 years before, the British pair won the now defunct classic in a Mercedes Benz, covering almost 1000 miles at an average speed of some 98 mph. The Italian event together with Le Mans, the Targa Florio and the Spa 24 hour race, formed the backbone of the International sports car scene during its formative years, but it was not until the late 'forties that the formula really

settled down, and came into its own.

The World Championship for Grand Prix cars commenced in 1950, and then three years later the World Sports Car Championship was introduced. In its first year of infancy, the Championship comprised seven races, commencing at the Sebring circuit in America, followed by five European races, with the climax being the gruelling Carrera Panamerica race through the heat and dust in Mexico.

The airfield circuit in Florida hosted the first ever

Above: Stirling Moss in action in the 1958 Lister-Jaguar; this model proved very popular with British club racers during the late 1950s

World Championship sports car race, but only Aston Martin took the trouble to ship over a works team. The 12-hour race saw British hopes soar skywards as the Aston Martin DB3 of Peter Collins/Geoff Duke took an immediate lead.

Their moment of glory was short-lived, however, the final result and the unique occasion, when the wealthy American Briggs-Cunningham, saw one of his 5.4-litre Chrysler engined cars, win a championship event. His Cunningham C4 was driven to victory by Phil Walters and John Fitch, whilst the second of the works Aston Martins driven by Reg Parnell/George Abecassis finished second ahead of the Johnston/

but during the run-in to Brescia, a track-rod on the Alfa broke, and Marzotto scored a popular victory ahead of Fangio/Sala. The Turin based Lancia team finished third ahead of Ferrari.

Although it was the thirtieth running of the 24-hour event, it was the first time it was run under the new championship rules, and it proved a filip for British cars. The fabulous 3.4 Jaguar C Types with their revolutionary disc brakes, dominated the race to finish first and second, although the 4.5 Ferrari coupé of Villoresi/Ascari posed a threat until it retired late with clutch problems.

Ferrari's Prancing Horse broke into a gallop and carried-off the next two races at Spa and the Nürburgring. C type Jaguars finished second and third on the Francochamps circuit, and although Lancia fielded a strong five-car team in the first ever 1000 km race in the Eifel mountains, they allowed a Jaguar to take second place in the race.

The final two races in this first season saw Aston Martin win the TT in Ulster, and the new 3.3 Lancia D24s had a field day in Mexico, finishing in the first three places in the Carrera Panamerica. Although Ferrari could only manage to score three points in Mexico, it was enough to win the championship from Jaguar, with Aston Martin third.

Ferrari had won the very first World Sports Car Championship, and the Maranello manufacturers embarked upon a trail of success which took them to an astounding eleven Championships out of twenty-two.

The famous marque trampled over opposition with almost total dominance, and won their class handsomely when in 1962–63, the FIA decided to re-write the rules yet again in favour of Appendix J Grand Touring Cars, with no limit on engine capacity.

It was Ferrari all the way again in 1954, with the Italian 4.5 and 4.9-litre cars winning four of the six Championship races. Lancia had mounted a concerted attack on the title, but despite their victories on the Mille Miglia, and the last ever Carrera Panamerica, they contented themselves with runner-up position. One of the shocks of the season was Stirling Moss/Lloyd, who took their tiny Italian 1.5 Osca to victory in the Sebring 12-hours despite some very stern opposition from Lancia.

Jaguar announced their new aerodynamic bodied semi-monocoque 3.4 D Type at Le Mans, and although Duncan Hamilton/Tony Rolt were able to stay on terms with the 4.9 Ferraris, they lost the 24-hour event by a mere two minutes.

Overshadowed by the terrible Le Mans accident which cost the life of Pierre Levegh and eighty spectators in 1955, the might of Stuttgart came to the

Top: the 2-litre Maserati Tipo 60; it was known as the Birdcage

Above right: the immortal D-type Jaguar of 1957

Above: the Chaparrals at Le Mans in 1967

Wilder 3.4 Jaguar C Type.

Close-on 1000 miles of rough, tough Italian road faced competitors in the second race in the Championship, the epic Mille Miglia. The ever-fervent Italians were praying for one of their 'rosso' machines to win, and to their unbridled delight Italian cars swept the board finishing 1–2–3–4. The race featured a tremendous dice for the lead between the 4.1 litre Ferrari of privateer Giannino Marzotto, and the 3.6 Alfa Romeo of the legendary Juan-Manuel Fangio,

fore with their brilliant fuel injected 300 SLR models. Mercedes Benz were determined to steal Enzo Ferrari's thunder, and at the end of the season, the 3-litre cars had won three of the six Championship events, including the Mille Miglia which provided Stirling Moss with yet another major victory, and Denis Jenkinson with one of the finest motor racing stories ever told.

Following the Le Mans disaster, the races at the Nürburgring and the Carrera Panamerica were cancelled. Jaguar scored a hollow victory at Le Mans with the D Type of Mike Hawthorn/Ivor Bueb.

Mercedes withdrew from racing in 1956, and in their place, Maserati mounted a strong challenge against Ferrari. The 'Grand Prix cars with bodies' of the previous season were outlawed in favour of an upper limit of 2.5 litres on 'pure' prototypes, and any over this figure would need to be accompanied by 100 replicas.

The 3 litre Maseratis tried in vain to secure the title, but it was Ferrari yet again who won three races to beat Maserati into second place.

The 2.5 litre prototype rules were rescinded for the fifth season in 1957, which meant the cars were conforming to the Le Mans rules.

Spurred-on by their impressive showing the previous year, Maserati unveiled their potent 4-cam V8 450S, and were within striking distance of Ferrari after wins at Sebring and in Sweden. The final race of the season in Venezuela proved a disaster for Maserati as all three cars crashed in fiery accidents, and Ferrari won the title for the fourth time.

Ron Flockhart/Ivor Bueb won Le Mans for the Ecurie Ecosse equipe in a D Type Jaguar, and then the FIA dropped their bombshell by announcing a 3-litre limit for the coming season. This, together with the complete decimation of the team in Venezuela, forced Maserati into virtual bankruptcy, and one of the most respected automotive names retired from motor racing.

In 1958, Ferrari went all the way again, this time in V 12 'Testa Rossa' machines. The Prancing Horse won four out of six races including Le Mans, but Porsche were beginning to make their presence felt with their small 1.6 RSKs, and the British company Aston Martin was showing a portent of things to come with the 3-litre DBR1.

Ferrari were saddened by the death of their drivers Peter Collins and Luigi Musso, and Jaguar's challenge had come to the end of the road, the six cylinder D types no longer competitive.

Had it not been for the insistence of Stirling Moss, Aston Martin might not have become the first British manufacturer to win the Championship, for David Brown, the head of Aston Martin, was intent on breaking the Ferrari stranglehold on Le Mans, but had little interest in the overall Championship.

Just five races constituted the series, and after Ferrari and Porsche won Sebring and the Targa Florio respectively, Moss begged Aston to contest the Nürburgring event in 1959. In fairy-story fashion Moss and Jack Brabham won the race, and Aston Martin clinched the Championship with victories by Gendebien/Hill at Le Mans, and Moss/Brooks at Goodwood in the Tourist Trophy.

The early 'sixties saw the regulations change and change again, as the demand for a more restricted GT championship became apparent after the years of Ferrari domination. A complex GT Championship was announced for the 1962 season, which virtually spelled the end of real 'sports racing' cars, and during 1962–63, the three different capacity classes saw Ferrari, Porsche and Abarth produce the champions.

Aston Martin had retired from motor racing as Ferrari won the title each year from 1960 to 1965. Maserati returned with the privately run spaceframe 'Birdcage' Tipos in 1960, but Maranello won the title narrowly from Porsche.

The front-engined 'Testa Rossa' enabled Ferrari to walk-off with the 1961 Championship, with Gendebien/Hill putting on brilliant performances to win Sebring, and Le Mans yet again, and the Frenchmen teamed-up with 'Taffy' Tripps to win the Targa Florio in one of the superb new rear engined 246 Dinos.

Although non-championship races at Sebring, Nürburgring, Le Mans and the Targa Florio were still run for experimental sports racing cars, it was Ferrari

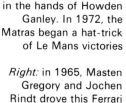

Top right: the Matra-Simca V12 at Le Mans in the hands of Howden Ganley. In 1972, the Matras began a hat-trick of Le Mans victories

Right: in 1965, Masten Gregory and Jochen Rindt drove this Ferrari 250LM coupé to victory at Le Mans; their victory was all the more prestigious because their Ferrari was a privately-entered machine, totally lacking in 'works' support

again clearing-up in 1962. This same year saw Jim Hall's 3.9 litre Corvette engined Chaparral make its debut at Sebring, and the amazing partnership of Gendebien/Hill won the French classic for the third and final time. Jim Clark frightened the opposition at the Nürburgring when he led the race for 11 laps in the tiny 1.5 twin cam Lotus 23, and Porsche introduced their new flat eight 2-litre cars.

Ferrari introduced his famous rear-engined 3 litre 250P, and again the red cars won everything of importance except the Targa Florio. However, the writing was already on the wall for Ferrari, as the shape of things to come had been unveiled at the London Racing Car Show in the form of Eric Broadley's Ford V8 engined Lola GT.

Nineteen sixty-four saw the resumption of the championship proper. Ford was intent on winning Le Mans with the GT40 which made its debut at the Nürburgring. There was simply no way of stopping Ferrari though, and they won eight of the nine Championship events, but Carroll Shelby's Ford V8 engined Cobra Coupés proved more than competitive against Ferrari in the GT class.

All eyes were on Le Mans in 1965, for Ford had installed a giant 7-litre engine in the GTs. Ford flopped dramatically at the Sarthe, where the 250LM driven by Masten Gregory/Jochen Rindt won for Ferrari. The American company did however win the opening event of the season at Daytona, and the AC Cobras under Alan Mann's management, won the GT class in the Championship.

At last it all came right for Ford in 1966 starting with wins at Daytona and Sebring, and then the culmination of their efforts at Le Mans as Fords crushed the opposition in a display of 7-litre power, and finished 1–2–3. The automatic transmission Chaparral won the Nürburgring event, and new Group 6 prototype, and Group 4 production (50 off) regulations were imposed. Ford had achieved their aim, and Ferrari were beaten for the first time in eight years.

The previous three years had seen the fortunes of that other great German manufacturer, Porsche take a turn for the better, and in 1968 with the introduction of their 2 litre 910 model, Porsche took the title for the first time. Annoyed by their defeat the previous year, Ferrari announced their new 4.4 litre 330P4V12s, which waged war against the 7 litre Ford Mk4s, and the John Wyer Gulf Oil GT40-based Mirage.

Carlo Chitti's Alfa Romeos in 2 litre form showed well at the beginning of the season, and Dan Gurney/A. J. Foyt won Le Mans for Ford, and thus Foyt became the first Indy winner to win the 24-hour classic. The Chaparral, now with wings won at Brands Hatch.

The regulations changed yet again in 1968, limiting the Group 6 cars to 3 litres, and Group 4 to 5 litres. Gone were the huge 7 litre machines, and in their place, 4.7 Gulf GT40s battled against the 2.2 907 Porsches, and the 3.0 908 model.

The CSIs decision on 3 litre Group 6 cars was enough for Ferrari to opt out of the Championship, and although the Fords were able to stay on terms with the Porsches, the title remained in Germany.

The new Ford Cosworth DFV powered F3L made its debut at Brands Hatch where it led the race for the first two hours. But after showing well at the Nürburgring, the car destroyed itself, and seriously injured Chris Irwin. The 2.5 T33 Alfa Romeo showed signs of promise, and the turbine engined Howmet scored championship points at Watkins Glen. Matra also arrived in 1961 with their F1 engined coupé, so things looked promising for the coming season.

A new era in sportscar racing was born in 1969 with the advent of the mighty 4.5 flat-12 Porsche 917. The beasts (upon which a cool £2,000,000 was reputedly spent on development), had a troubled early season, but won the last race at the Osterreichring.

Ferrari put his F1 engine into the 312P, but had little success, while a Lola T70 won the opening race. Le Mans saw one of the most exciting finishes ever, when the GT40 of Jacky Ickx beat the 908 coupé of Hans Hermann by a few feet after 24 hours racing; but Porsche retained the Championship.

A new European 2-litre sports car championship was run for the first time in 1970, and soon became

Below: Jacky Ickx of Belgium hurls his Ferrari around the treacherous Nürburgring circuit during the 1973 1000 km event; Ickx, and British co-driver Brian Redman, went on to win the event

popular with manufacturers and drivers alike. The series attracted some of the leading drivers, and was dominated in its early years by British built Chevrons and Lolas. Chevron took the title in the first year, and in subsequent series, Lola won twice, with the Osella Abarth concern winning in 1972. The first time a major car manufacturer took any interest was in 1974, when Alpine, backed by the resources and finance of Renault, smashed the opposition into the ground by winning every race, thanks to their superb machines and the ability of their drivers, Gerard Larrousse, Jean-Pierre Jabouille and Alain Serpaggi.

The works Porsche 917 effort was managed by JW Automotive, and sponsored by Gulf Oil for the 1970 season, and with drivers of the calibre of Brian Redman, Jo Siffert, Pedro Rodriguez and Leo Kinnunen, the Stuttgart cars steamrolled their way to victory, winning nine out of ten championship races. Specially lightened 908/3s won the Targa and Nürburgring, and a new 5 litre Porsche engine made its debut at Monza to combat the 512 V12 Ferrari.

Ferrari's 'race-testing' paid off in 1972, and they came in from the cold to re-claim 'their' title with the 312P. The Le Mans event was beginning to wane in popularity; only Matra sent along a works team.

Graham Hill/Henri Pecarolo guaranteed their investment, and the French convincingly won their own race for the first time in 22 years.

The following two years belonged to Matra as well with the French blue cars beating the Ferraris into second place in 1973, with Pescarolo again winning Le Mans, this time with Gerard Larrousse. This pair returned to the Sarthe the following year to repeat their success in one of the Gitanes backed Matra 670Cs.

Gulf Research Racing commenced the season with their new Mirages, later to become Gulf GR7s, and scored the first-ever win for the Cosworth DFV engine in an all-British sports car at Spa. Turbo-charging reared its head in the form of the RSR Carrera Porsches which began winning races, and the de Cadenet (nee Duckhams) flew the Union Jack high at Le Mans with Christ Craft/John Nicholson holding a strong third place, before leaving the race with suspension problems.

Having had two glorious years when they swept aside all before them, Matra ceased their operation, and with new regulations impending, the current season saw sports car racing decline to an all-time low ebb. Alpine Renault turbocharged their successful 2-litre model, and started winning immediately, but a curtailment of their programme has seen the works assisted Alfa Romeo come to the fore.

The future of international sports car racing is, at the time of writing, unsure. But whatever course the governing bodies decide to take, it is difficult to envisage a future as glorious as the past 22 years. HGW

Above: the French have traditionally been associated with sports-car racing since the very earliest days of motor sport; in fact, the Le Mans 24-hour endurance event is the most famous sports-car race in the world; seen here competing at Le Mans is the French-built Ligier JS3, brainchild of former French rugby international Guy Ligier

MOUNTAINS INTO MOLE HILLS

If it were not for springs, our ride would be far from smooth and much less than happy

A SPRING IS AN ELASTIC DEVICE that will compress or expand to an extent depending upon the force applied to it, and that will afterwards assume its original dimensions. Five types of spring are commonly used in motor vehicle suspension systems: leaf, torsion bar, coil, rubber and gas-filled devices are well known.

The extent to which a spring deflects under load is known as the 'spring rate'. Each of the above types of spring can be manufactured either with a linear spring rate (so that within its designed operating limits its deflection is directly proportional to the load) or with a non-linear spring rate (so that its deflection becomes less against a steadily increasing load).

A spring with a non-linear spring rate is desirable in motor vehicle suspension systems; the spring will be required to provide a comfortable ride when the motor vehicle is loaded with only the driver, and yet be firm enough to support full load.

The leaf spring is the most common form of spring used for suspension systems. It has the advantage of enabling a designer to produce a very simple and cheap suspension system; though it must be said that such a system has drawbacks.

A leaf spring consists of a number of leaves of chrome vanadium steel. These laminations are inter-leaved with an anti-friction material, or separated with pads of such material, to enable them to slide on one another as the spring flexes. A small bolt is usually fitted through the leaves at the centre of the spring to ensure that they remain in alignment. Clamps are fitted, to keep the laminations together, and a rubber bump stop is fitted between spring and chassis to prevent damage if the suspension 'bottoms'.

Most conventional leaf spring rear-suspension systems use the spring not only to cushion the vehicle from road shocks, but also to locate the wheels and axle relative to the chassis. In such a system, a solid rear axle is secured to the centres of two longitudinal springs by 'U' bolts and clamps. The front end of each spring is secured to the chassis via a rubber bush and the rear end is allowed the lateral movement caused by the bending of the spring, by a shackle, which is also mounted in rubber bushes.

Although the spring will absorb road shocks, it is sufficiently stiff to accept the torque reactions of acceleration and braking forces. It is possible to see the exposed leaf springs on some vehicles tending to 'wind up' as the driver accelerates from rest.

On high-performance cars, this wind-up can become excessive and interfere with the spring's ability to undertake its normal suspension duties, resulting in a loss of traction on uneven surfaces. To prevent this, an additional linkage may be fitted, which will absorb any tendency for the axle to rotate. This linkage may take the form of radius rods, rigidly fixed to the axle and attached to the chassis at points geometrically equivalent to the front spring attachments.

Torque from the drive shaft will cause a solid rear axle and leaf spring arrangement to tend to lift one wheel, which will produce loss of traction. Fast cornering will produce large lateral forces on the axle but transverse displacement can be prevented by transverse or diagonal tie-rods which will allow vertical movement while absorbing the cornering

Some examples of leaf springs in early motor-car suspension. *Below left* is the twin-leaf arrangement at the back of a 1913 Nazzaro; *bottom left* is the rear of a 1909 Model T Ford while, *below*, is an inverted leaf spring of a 1926 Diatto 20

forces. Eventually, the number and complexity of the linkages required for satisfactory roadholding raises the cost of this basically sensible, cheap system to near that of independent suspension systems, which can give greater performance.

Beam axles are no longer generally fitted to motor cars, as the high unsprung weight and sensitivity to wheel wobble are undesirable. Most commercial vehicles, however, still use a beam axle at the front. The lower operating speeds of these vehicles eliminates the disadvantages and the leaf spring and beam axle arrangement provides a simple and robust suspension system perfectly suitable for commercial use.

Leaf springs are fitted transversely to some vehicles, with the centre attached to the chassis and the two ends of the axle. Fiat have refined this idea by using two chassis mountings at points well outside the centre of the spring. This produces an anti-roll effect; as one wheel rises, a simple lever effect through the spring tends to raise the opposite wheel.

Quarter elliptic forms of leaf spring are also used. They are mainly limited to lightweight applications, such as baggage trailers, because the load at the point of attachment to the chassis is not well distributed. They are occasionally mounted transversely, with a stub axle welded to the outer end, to form an independent suspension system for small trailers.

A torsion bar is a spring that derives its elasticity from its ability to twist under load and return to its original state. For a given load, the deflection of a torsion bar increases with its length.

Torsion-bar suspension systems are used in a number of modern vehicles. Renault used torsion-bar suspension systems on their R16 series. The exceptionally large rear-wheel movements on these cars requires a transverse spring as wide as the car. One end is fixed and the working end is attached to a swinging arm. To fit two torsion bars right across the car, Renault had to step one wheel slightly ahead of the other. Either a solid or a laminated torsion bar spring may be used. The laminated type has the advantage that the spring rate may be adjusted simply by adding or removing laminations. If a solid torsion bar were to

break, the vehicle would probably be immobilized but in the laminated type, failure of one lamination is not serious and the vehicle will remain mobile.

An anti-roll bar is often a form of torsion bar, arranged to transmit the movement of one wheel to the wheel on the opposite side of the vehicle. In some suspension systems, such as the Mcpherson strut arrangement on some UK Fords, the anti-roll bar locates the front wheels in a fore and aft direction in addition to performing its duties as a spring.

Many modern cars use independent suspension systems employing coil springs. In such systems, the spring only absorbs wheel movement; the axle and wheels are located by linkages. A coil spring can be considered to be a torsion bar which has been coiled. An increase in length (by increasing the number of turns) will provide a greater deflection for a given load. Removing a turn or two from a coil spring in order to improve roadholding will both lower the vehicle's centre of gravity and produce a firmer ride.

Rubber is used as a spring material, notably on the BLMC Minis, in a suspension system which provides a limited degree of comfort but a degree of stability that enables the little car to hurtle round corners at apparently impossible speeds.

There are distinct advantages to be obtained from

Below: the popular coil spring as seen in one of the larger Ford cars; this is a front suspension mounting

Bottom: the suspension layout of a popular and cheap family car (Ford Escort); *left,* is a coil spring front unit (in conjunction with MacPherson struts), while at the rear, *right,* is a live axle and semi-elliptic leaf springs

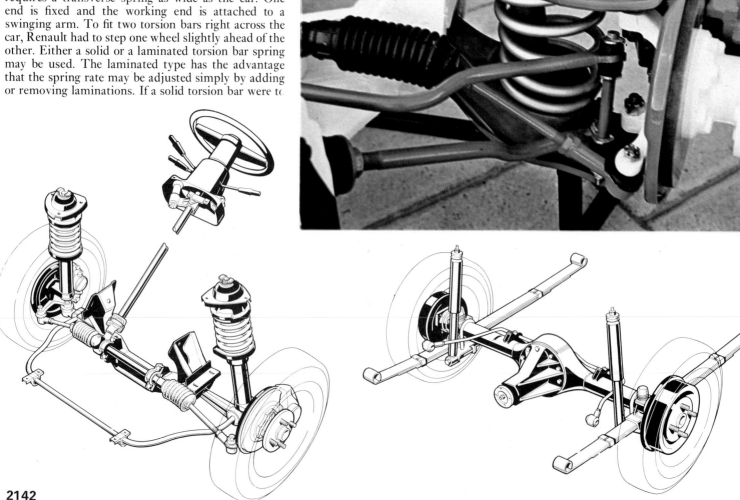

using rubber as a spring material. A suspension system of this material can be designed to occupy a very small space and the spring itself can be designed with a non-linear deflection.

After five years' production of rubber-sprung Minis, BLMC fitted the Hydrolastic system that had been so successful on the 1100 series. Unfortunately, the short wheelbase on the Mini produced an unacceptable degree of pitching and BLMC eventually reverted to the simple rubber cones and telescopic dampers.

complexity and cost, very few cars use a system whereby all four wheels are interconnected.

On the simplest type of system, using a mechanical coupling in the form of a spring, wheel movement is transmitted via a bellcrank, through a tension spring to the other wheel. The effect is that if one wheel rises, the coupled wheel also tends to rise. This system reduces changes in attitude under varying load conditions and reduces pitching.

BLMC have developed a more refined form of coupled suspension in the form of the Hydrolastic system fitted to their 1100 and 1800 series. Springing is effected by a chamber's expansion within an enclosing rubber spring. When a wheel rises, it displaces fluid through a small orifice into the flexible chamber. Damping is obtained by virtue of the small orifice through which the displaced fluid has to flow. Coupling is obtained by a small-bore tube which connects the spring chambers of both wheels on one side of the automobile.

Thus, as one front wheel rises, fluid is displaced into the chamber of the rear wheel on the same side, reducing any tendency to pitch. The rear suspension is also in an extended condition, as it waits to absorb the bump.

This system has the advantage of being fairly soft at low speeds and harder at high speeds, when the damping orifice offers a greater restriction to an increased fluid flow.

Further development of the Hydrolastic system has produced the Hydragas system; in this, the springing medium is compressed gas. Although it is extremely comfortable in normal use, high-speed driving over poor road surfaces can become unpleasant.

A more sophisticated, and considerably more expensive, pressurized gas suspension system is to be found, for example, on the larger French Citröens. On this type of system, air is supplied to the suspension system from a compressor driven by the engine. Such a system may have a manual control to stiffen the suspension, according to the road conditions, by increasing the pressure. There may also be devices fitted which will reduce or increase the pressure in the system automatically, with changes in load.

Most car manufacturers specify little or no maintenance for springs but it is worthwhile making an occasional check to ensure that they continue to operate efficiently and quietly. Leaf springs should be scrubbed with a wire brush, to remove any dirt and rust. Examine each leaf to see that it is not cracked and check that any anti-friction inserts are not missing or broken. If the spring is greased and does not employ anti-friction inserts, examine the area where the leaves rub. If wear has occurred, the spring should be renewed. Check that the spring clamps, and the 'U' bolts securing the axle are tight. Examine the spring shackles carefully; their worn condition may not be immediately noticeable. Check that any rubber components have not deteriorated and, finally, grease the leaves well.

Torsion bars of the laminated type should be wire-brushed and examined for broken laminations, if accessible. Check that mounting bolts are tight and grease the laminations as recommended. Solid torsion bars and coil springs require virtually no attention, although there may be a rubber insert between the top of a coil spring and the chassis. This should be checked to ensure it has not deteriorated or slipped out of position.

Rubber springs require no maintenance and the pressurized air systems will be subject to specialized maintenance, specified by the manufacturer.   NPG

Above: the front suspension of the Austin Allegro clearly showing the Hydragas unit; this system is a development of the popular Hydrolastic type

Independently sprung wheels have a disadvantage in that the attitude of a vehicle will vary considerably according to its loading. This can upset the handling properties and the headlight alignment. In efforts to minimize this disadvantage, designers have devised systems that connect the springing medium of independent suspension units in such a way that movement of one wheel is transmitted to the other wheel on the same side, or to all three other wheels.

Three types of coupling may be used; mechanical, hydraulic or a pressurized gas system. Because of the

UNTIL THE ADVENT OF DAF, Holland was hardly noted as a motor manufacturing country: for the most part, the pioneer Dutch car makers quietly built a handful of cars and then vanished equally quietly from the scene. But there was one exception . . . Spyker, a marque which lasted for a quarter of a century, which built cars which were always technically interesting, and which achieved posthumous fame when one of its products was selected as a star of the film *Genevieve*.

The brothers Hendrik and Jacobus Spijker were building carriages at Hilversum as early as 1880; then, in 1895, they began to import Benz cars from Germany and, latterly, to modify them, until in 1900 the first Spyker car saw the light of day. It was a *voiturette* with a front-mounted 5 hp air-cooled flat-twin engine; and the Spijker brothers (who had Anglicised the name of their product to facilitate export sales) had equipped a new factory at Trompenburg to cope with the anticipated demand. Alas, it did not come, for the *voiturette* was a fairly undistinguished little machine with none of the snob-appeal of an imported model; nor were there many overseas takers.

Jacobus's next design was more promising. This was the 20 hp of 1902, which followed the lines of the contemporary Mercédès or Peugeot, with a 3770 cc T-headed engine, with the cylinders cast separately, carried in a sub-frame between armoured wood side frames; there was also a 1885 cc twin-cylinder version. The four had the unusual feature for the period of a five-bearing crankshaft: but Mijnheer Spijker had plenty more technical surprises in store for the public.

The first appeared at the end of 1903 in the shape of a 'circular engine' in which the cylinders were enclosed in a dustbin-like casting to ensure the maximum of cooling water around the combustion chambers: but water circulation was too sluggish, and the circular engine overheated furiously often during the course of the 1904 season.

More promising was what is generally accepted as being the world's first six-cylinder car, the design of a young Belgian named Joseph Laviolette. Spyker

THE QUEEN'S FIRST CAR

Queen Wilhelmina was a devout fan of Spyker throughout the company's history

Below: the racing Spyker of 1903 had a six-cylinder, 8.5-litre, 50 hp engine

Bottom: a 1904 Spyker open tourer

subsequently claimed that this car had been conceived as far back as 1901 and built in 1902, but not revealed until a comprehensive test programme had been completed. For, apart from its six cylinders, the big 8685 cc Spyker also featured four-wheel-drive (though it wasn't the first four-wheel-drive vehicle, that distinction belonging to the Burstall & Hill

steam coach of the 1820s, which also pioneered front wheel braking).

The six-cylinder Spyker also had rudimentary four-wheel-braking, as there were drum brakes on the rear wheels and a transmission brake which acted on the front wheels. The transmission was quite sophisticated: a cone clutch incorporated in the massive flywheel took the drive to a separate gearbox within which was a differential acting between the fore and aft drive shafts; these terminated in live axles also equipped with differentials, while the gearbox had two speed ranges, with three speeds in each, giving a total of six forward speeds and two reverse.

One suspects that Laviolette and the Spijkers did not realise what they had wrought, for it seems as though they only regarded this complex transmission set-up as a panacea for the 'dreaded side-slip'—skidding—which was an ever-present danger on the greasy roads of the period.

The car was revealed at the 1903 Paris Salon, and brought over to England a short while after for the Crystal Palace and Agricultural Hall exhibitions. An *Autocar* correspondent managed to get a ride on the car, and recorded his impressions for the journal: 'Before the car was staged we were afforded the opportunity of making a short trip upon it over the roads about the Palace. It was impossible, of course, that such a powerful car should be given its head in a suburban district, but its driver gave us a suggestion of what the car could do by the way in which it took the very respectable slope of Anerley Hill. The rise simply seemed to fall down before it, and the sensation the climb afforded was more like an ascent in a fast lift than a run up on wheels. By the light of our brief trial, we are inclined to the opinion that steering wheel driving may be considered with advantage.'

Though this car was an experiment, and really intended for publicity purposes, Jacobus Spijker obviously 'considered with advantage' the merits of translating its complexities into production terms, for the six-cylinder, four-wheel-drive model was the basis of a limited run of 60 hp machines of similar

Below: the twin-cylinder Spyker of 1906; Jacobus Spijker's first two-cylinder model appeared in 1902 and followed the lines of the contemporary Mercédès and Peugeot models

design marketed during the 1904–7 period.

Four-cylinder fwd touring cars were also built, and at least one came to Britain, competing in the Bexhill Speed Trials in either 1904 or 1905.

The prototype six-cylinder car was retained by the company, and often driven on the road with a four-seated touring body with detachable canopy top. It also appeared in the odd competition: in 1906, Jacobus Spijker entered the car for the Birmingham Automobile Club's hillclimb, and, as they were crossing the North Sea on the Harwich ferry, Spijker's five-man team offered up communal prayers for rain on the day of the contest. The night before the event, the heavens opened, heavy rain poured down, and the test hill became slippery. The Spyker was the only competing vehicle to reach the summit, all the others being defeated by the greasy road surface.

The six-cylinder Spyker outlived the company: when the factory was sold up in 1925, the car was discovered, in an incomplete state, on an upper floor, and was acquired by an expatriate Dutchman resident in Paris called Springer. Springer had the car restored by an Amsterdam company, and it still survives in this modified form.

Of course, more conventional vehicles were also offered: and it was the 1905 range which was to earn the marque its famous soubriquet 'Dustless'.

Spykers were carefully streamlined underneath, and fitted with an undertray, which certainly minimised the raising of dust on the unmade roads of that era: and when Spyker achieved an outstanding result in the Luton Dust Trials of July 1905, their reputation was sealed as well.

It was around this time that the marque acquired the famous round radiator that was to remain their hallmark until the end of production; and the 1906 range consisted of a 12/18 hp of 2799 cc, a 15/24 hp of 3456 cc, a 20/30 hp of 4562 cc and a 30/40 hp of 7964 cc. It was almost certainly one of these models that the motor novelists C. N. and A. M. Williamson described as being typically Dutch: 'It made so little noise, yet moved so masterfully, and gave an impression of so much reserve power.'

By 1907, there were 800 workmen at Trompenburg, and the order books seemed comfortably full. That year the range consisted of a diminutive 1810 cc 10/15 hp, the 15/24 hp, the 20/30 hp and the 30/40 hp.

An engaging scoundrel named Godard wheeled a Spyker out of the factory to enable him to compete in the 1907 Pekin-Paris Race, falsely claiming that *Le Matin*, the organiser of the event, would pay all expenses. M. Godard managed to scrounge his way across two continents until the exasperated Jacobus Spijker had him ejected from the car when it reached Berlin.

But this was just about the only light relief in a gloomy year for Spyker: in February 1907 Hendrik Spijker had been drowned in the wreck of the SS *Berlin*, and when the books were examined after his death it was revealed that the finances were in a parlous state. A slump had hit the car market that year, and the French agent had unexpectedly cancelled a big order for chassis, which could not be placed elsewhere, with the result that Spyker were considerably in debt.

Though they survived the crisis, they never fully recovered from the blow. Models were little changed for 1908, except that the bore of the 15/24 was reduced, making the car a 15/20 and its swept volume 2799 cc, the same as the 12/18 which had gone out of production a year earlier. And there was—briefly—a sports-racing 40/80 hp at the head of the range, with a massive 10,603 cc power unit. This was only produced

during the 1908 season, but all the other models soldiered on until 1910, when they were replaced by cars of more radical concept. These had power units designed by Laviolette, with short *transverse* camshafts driven by worm direct from the crankshaft. There was one camshaft to each pair of cylinders, carrying two cams to actuate four valves; in 1911 Laviolette even delivered himself of a six-cylinder model built on these curious lines: it was not, apparently, a success, being subject to catastrophic internal derangements.

Surprisingly, the transverse camshaft Spykers were noiseless as well as dustless: and Queen Wilhelmina bought two of the new 4589 cc 25 hp models and a 7238 cc 40 hp landaulette, which was very likely the Queen's first car.

Smallest of the range was the 1791 cc 12 hp, which had its gearbox incorporated in the back axle, but with a brake *between* clutch and transmission, which meant that it did not act when the car was in neutral, a factor which apparently contributed to a number of accidents.

As Holland was neutral during World War I, production continued, though at a level greatly reduced by shortages of raw materials. A handsome vee-fronted radiator, still circular, was adopted in 1914, but most of the wartime production of the firm was sold for military use.

Spyker also made Clerget rotary aeroengines during the war, and adopted the image of a propellor superimposed on a wheel bearing the Latin motto *Nulla Tenaci Invia est Via* as their badge to signify their move into a new dimension.

At the beginning of 1918 Spyker announced that they were abandoning car production until after the war; but by the end of the year they were back in the market with an all-new 13/30 model of 3.6 litres. Its side-valve four-cylinder engine was built in unit with a three-speed transmission, and was obviously influenced by current American design trends: quite unique, however, was the 'aerocoque' coachwork fitted to a number of these chassis. With flared wings which

appeared to be flapping ready for takeoff, a tiny tailfin, and bodywork styled like a fuselage, these cars were unkindly nicknamed the 'Flying Hens': their looks, it seems, were more impressive than their performance.

Only 330 13/30s were built before another new Spyker model took over. This was the 30/40 hp, designed by Frederick Koolhoven, who was better known as an aircraft designer. It used a German Maybach engine of 5.7 litres, and the impression the car gave was one of ponderousness—even the open tourer scaled well over two tons.

'Guaranteed for ever,' was Spyker's proud boast about this car, and in July 1921 S. F. Edge chose a specially-bodied 30/40 to attempt to beat the 24 hour record which he had established in 1907 at Brooklands on a Napier.

The engine was slightly modified, a straight-through exhaust was fitted, as were Hartford shock-absorbers, augmented at the rear by bungee straps between the axle and the frame; driving for two periods of twelve hours, Edge averaged 74.27 mph, a great improvement over the 65.91 mph he had achieved fourteen years earlier, considering that he was now 51, and the Spyker's engine was far smaller than that of the Napier.

At the same time that Edge was circulating round the track, the wife of the British Spyker concessionaire, Colonel Janson, was also indulging at some record-breaking at the track, with a Trump-JAP motorbike: Mrs Gwenda Janson (née Glubb) would later achieve lasting fame as a lady racing driver under the name of Gwenda Hawkes.

The big 30/40 was hardly a best-seller, and for a time Spyker toyed with the light car market, importing Mathis cars from Strasbourg and selling them as 'Spyker-Mathis,' but the venture was short lived.

Probably around 150 of the 30/40 Spykers were made, and it was obvious that, despite continued patronage from Queen Wilhelmina, the company was no longer viable: in 1925 the Trompenburg factory closed its doors for ever, and the stock in hand was auctioned off. DBW

Below: a 1911 Landaulette; this was Queen Wilhelmina of the Netherlands' first car

ADRIAN SQUIRE'S $1\frac{1}{2}$ litre sports car was probably the best looking British two seater to be built in the 1930s. The low, rakish and perfectly proportioned Vanden Plas bodies (that had more than a whiff of touring about them) gave the cars a thoroughbred ambience they richly deserved. The thickly slatted and deep set V shaped radiator considerably enhanced the front of the car while raising one side of the finely louvred bonnet revealed a supercharged twin overhead camshaft engine, complete with heavily finned induction manifold. Because the Squire looked so good it is probably a little difficult to accept that there could be anything wrong with it. Alas, the impressive looking, but over stressed British Anzani engine that under the bonnet, was the thorn in the Squire's side.

Adrian Morgan Squire first dreamed of building his own sports car in the 1920s during his schooldays at Downside, the Roman Catholic public school. Such was his enthusiasm that at the age of sixteen he even produced a six page catalogue of the 'all British' $1\frac{1}{2}$ litre Squire. One of the car's attributes was a low centre of gravity 'which ensures maximum stability on corners' and a 68×103 cc 1496 cc engine.

Although he seems to have been totally dedicated to the motorcar, Adrian studied electrical engineering at Faraday House, London after leaving school. However, his stay there was destined to be a short one, as

GREAT PROMISE UNFULFILLED

Adrian Squire's untimely death meant the end of a promising company and a potentially great career

Below left: the impressive twin-camshaft Anzani engine in a long-wheelbase Squire

Below right: Adrian Squire, seen on his wedding day

Bottom: Val Zethrin's long-wheelbase, Ranalah-bodied car

he soon left and joined Bentley Motors as an apprentice. Then in September 1929 he left Cricklewood and went to the MG Car Company at Abingdon as a design draughtsman. In 1931 he was on the move again, for wealthy young G. F. A. 'Jock' Manby-Colegrave, who had been at school with Squire, agreed

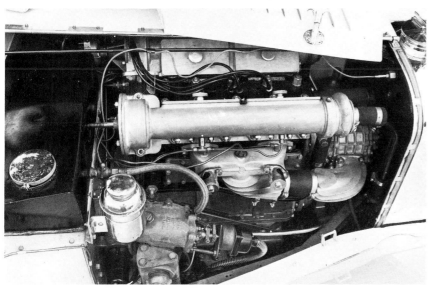

to back Adrian's plans for the '1½ litre Squire.'

It was decided that the car should be built at Remenham Hill, a few miles from the delightful Thames side town of Henley. A cottage was purchased at the top of the tree lined Remenham Hill and this was turned into a petrol station while a workshop was tucked away behind. It was in this quiet and rural area that the Squire began to take shape.

Squire and Manby-Colegrave (who were then both in their early twenties) were soon joined by Reginald Slay, a 'free lance' car salesman of somewhat maturer years; he was 27 at the time. Slay looked after the sales side of the business as a showroom had been rented in Henley. It was hoped that profits from new and second hand car sales would help finance the production of the Squire car slowly taking shape at the Remenham Hill works. In view of his limited facilities, it is unlikely that Squire was thinking of building his own engine, but in September 1932 an announcement in the motoring press caught his eye. Details were being released of a twin overhead camshaft engine of 1½ litres capacity that had just been announced by British Anzani. It wasn't long before Squire and Manby-Colegrave found themselves in the office of Anzani's young managing director, Douglas Ross, hearing details of the new engine. Squire said he would have the engine and promptly ordered twelve.

Had the R1 been left in unsupercharged form it would probably have been reliable enough, but Squire was intent on performance as well as good looks. Therefore the Anzani was supercharged at 10 psi, a compact David Brown roots type blower being driven off the front end of the crankshaft. This, coupled with other modifications was said to boost the bhp from 70 to 105, but blowing at this pressure helped sow the seeds of unreliability that dogged the Squire for its two year production life. For although Ross had intended the R1 to be supercharged from the outset he was thinking of a blower pressure of around 6 psi. As a result gasket blowing and overheating proved a major and recurring problem. Also the valve gear was incredibly noisy; a symphony of double

helical gears and tappet clearances of thirty and forty thousandths of an inch. No doubt with an eye to aiding acceleration, Squire used an ENV 110 pre-selector gearbox. There was no clutch, a hardworking bottom gear band having to do duty as such. A conventional channel box section chassis was used, suspension being by half elliptic springs all round. Squire favoured the use of sliding trunnions on these springs, a reminder of the time he had spent at MG; the arrangement being used on the C type Midget of 1931. Starting and lighting were looked after by a Rotax dynamotor mounted between the two front dumbirons, another inheritance from his schoolboy doodlings. He designed brakes with 15⅛ in drums that filled the entire internal diameter of the wheel. The trouble was that these brakes proved, on occasions, almost too efficient. They used Lockheed actuation. On at least two cars, strengthening flitch plates had to be added to counter the vicious retardation.

When the Squire was announced in September 1934, two body styles (either open or closed) and both by Vanden Plas were listed. The car was available in two chassis lengths, even the shorter of the two cost

Below and right:
Kenneth Rush's drawings of a 1934 works-demonstrator Squire

Far right: a typical British-sporty dash-board of a 1936 car

£1200, making it almost Britain's most expensive sports car—twice the cost of a 2 litre Aston Martin.

If there were some doubts about the reliability of the Squire's engine, the same couldn't be said for the roadholding, for which the young designer deserves full praise. *Motor Sport* had no doubts about the car. 'Even the straightest roads are not without their fast bends, but one could take them at 75 mph.' 'Even when we took fast bends at what seemed excessive speeds the car declined to slide or display any other

instability.' Each car was sold with a BARC certificate saying it had exceeded a timed speed of 100 mph at Brooklands. Once the prototype, the aforementioned works demonstrator, was completed the next car, naturally enough went to Jock Manby-Colegrave. Then the Hon Sherman Stonor, who lived at nearby Stonor Park, purchased the third short chassis Vanden Plas bodied two seater, but then there were no more orders. No doubt with an eye of getting some publicity on the race track, Squire decided to enter a single seater version for the British Empire Trophy race at Brooklands in July 1935. Unfortunately the car, driven by Luis Fontes, only lasted nine laps as the crankshaft broke, although as a face saver it was announced that a big end had run. It was another two months before the single seater was seen at the track

again and that was in the BRDC 500 mile race. On this occasion the Squire managed to soldier on for 54 laps before the chassis fractured. However, it was a case of third time lucky in October when Fontes was placed third in a Second Mountain Handicap race.

Meanwhile in the Autumn of 1935 another Squire was sold, this time a long chassis version. Val Zethrin of Chislehurst, Kent had seen the cars being tested at Brooklands and to this day maintains that the Squire was the safest car he ever drove. The road holding of the long chassis car was even superior to the short chassis, in Zethrin's view. A second long chassis was sold in 1936 to Sir James Walker of Faringdon, Berkshire. Another short chassis car was also built up during that year, but alas, the end was in view and a creditors meeting was held in July 1936 and the Squire Car Manufacturing Company went into voluntary liquidation. During the two year period only seven cars had been built: two long chassis and five short.

Work also stopped on a $1\frac{1}{2}$ litre racing car for the Duke of Grafton, with a Squire designed twin cam $1\frac{1}{2}$ litre six cylinder engine with twin superchargers being driven from the centre of the block, a la P3 Alfa Romeo. The chassis used Porsche independent front suspension, while a de Dion rear axle was also planned. Although this car was designed for the then current *voiturette* formula there seems evidence to suggest that the Duke had record breaking aspirations for this car. Unfortunately he was killed at the wheel of his type 59 Bugatti in August 1936. However, this was not quite the end. Val Zethrin, who, it will be recalled, already owned one of the two long chassis automobiles, bought all the remaining spares and chassis. Two mechanics remained at the Remenham works, and in 1937, a Corsica bodied Squire emerged. Zethrin built his own body on the last chassis which remains in his ownership.

Adrian Squire later re-joined W. O. Bentley at Lagonda and subsequently went to work at the Bristol Aeroplane Co. He was killed at the age of 30 in a daylight raid on the factory in 1940; his promise, one feels, unfulfilled. JW

FLYING THE BRITISH FLAG

The Standard flag was lowered just after the company's diamond anniversary

Top: a Standard 6 hp single-cylinder of 1006 cc of 1903

Above: a 1906 Standard Tourer

THE HISTORY of the automobile and of automotive engineering is crowded with stories of patrons supporting brash young men trying to make a bid for the great new transport market. One such man was Sir John Wolfe Barry, the designer of Tower Bridge. After his young assistant, Reginald Walter Maudsley, was left in financial straits by his father's death, Barry provided a cheque for £3000 to enable him to leave civil engineering and establish himself in the nascent British motor industry.

Maudslay formed the Standard Motor Company in Coventry on 2 March 1903, with his total capital of £5000, a small factory in Much Park Street and offices in Earl Street. Chairman of the tiny company was Maudslay, while his chief engineer was Alex Craig. The car that they produced incorporated only those principles which had been thoroughly tried, tested, and found to be reliable (indeed many of them seemed to have already been tried in Craig's designs for Lea Francis and Singer). Because the car was built on proven principles, Maudslay named it the Standard.

The first Standard was a solidly built Motor Victoria with a very over-square engine of 5 in bore × 3 in stroke (available in both single- and twin-cylinder forms) mounted under the driver's seat. The two-

cylinder version cost £367 10s.

Total 1903 output was six cars; the workforce consisted of six men, who the following year increased production to the staggering total of nine cars.

For 1904, a three-cylinder version of the over-square engine was available in a motor Brougham costing £415, whilst the company advertised that they could improve the performance of low-powered cars by fitting one of their 12/14 hp four-cylinder engines at a cost of £85.

Although business slackened off during 1905, the little firm (at that time there was a labour force of sixteen) kept up with the times by producing an 18/20 hp six-cylinder car. They also made their first export sale, when a gentleman from Canada walked into the works and bought a car on the understanding that it would be shipped immediately. Such high-powered business amazed the press, who described it as a 'bold bid for the export market'.

Standard cars were exhibited at Olympia in November 1905, and Charles Friswell, a London motor agent, was so impressed that he offered to take the entire output of the factory.

Friswell subsequently was appointed sole distributor, and the rate of production stepped up. A larger

factory at Bishopsgate Green was taken, in order to turn out the 18/20 hp six-cylinder model at a rate of at least ten per week, and the labour force enlarged.

Despite some financial anxieties, production went on at a steady rate. In March 1906, the 18/20 was replaced by a 24/30 hp six, and by a 50 hp luxury model. With the increasing demand for Standard cars, the company took over the works of Pridmore and Co, elastic web weavers, in Cash's Lane, the Bishopsgate Green factory now being concerned solely with the production of coachwork. The Widdrington works, in Aldbourne Road, were acquired subsequently in order to carry out repair and servicing work. A milestone in the company's history occurred in late 1908 when the soon well-known circular Union Jack radiator badge was introduced.

By this time Friswell, now Sir Charles, had become chairman of the company in addition to being sole distributor. He was a very conscious publicist, and when the Imperial Press Conference of 1909 was held, he arranged for a fleet of twenty 20 hp six-cylinder cars to be laid on for the benefit of the 'gentlemen of the Press'. They ran a total of 40,000 trouble-free miles, and received much favourable publicity.

In 1911 Friswell sailed for India. Here, he convinced the Government of the worth of his cars, and entered into a contract to provide all the cars for the Coronation Durbar celebrations to be held in December. He also contracted with the Viceregal authorities to provide cars for the Royal suite and lorries for the beaters for tiger hunting expeditions. Seventy Standards were sent to India. Fleets of cars were established at Bombay, Calcutta, Delhi and Nepal.

Friswell was attempting during this period to dictate the design of Standard cars, and offered to acquire all Maudslay's shares in the company. However, Maudslay was not prepared to sell and made a counter claim which eventually resulted in Friswell leaving the company to pursue his other interests. C. J. Band, a Coventry solicitor, replaced him on the board.

Standard had experimented with light cars as early as 1909, when they had produced a 12 hp model with the rare distinction of being able to take spacious landaulette coachwork, thanks to a 6.5:1 backaxle ratio which restricted top speed to 25 mph. And in March 1913 the company announced a real 'big car in miniature' in the shape of the 1087 cc 9.5 hp S model, or 'Rhyl', which proved so successful that it virtually dominated the output of the Standard factory, approximately 1300 of these little cars being built during the period 1913–16. A modern touch was the 3-year guarantee offered with each Rhyl, which was the first car to employ the classic Standard radiator with the shouldered header tank of the early models rounded off and mounted on a tubular cooling element with no side panels.

When war broke out, the Standard factory was turned over to the manufacture of munitions, and it was decided to undertake aircraft production, for which a new factory was constructed at Canley, in the

Top left: a 1912 model 20 six-cylinder of 3620 cc

Top right: another 20; this one was built in 1910

Above left: produced between 1914 and 1915 was the Rhyl; its power came from a 1087 cc four-cylinder engine

Above: a tourer, *circa* 1913

countryside outside Coventry. Here Standard built some 1600 of the angular RE-8 'Harry Tate' reconnaissance biplanes, an obsolescent machine known as the 'Rigger's Nightmare' from its cat's cradle of flying and landing wires.

But when peace came, and Standard relinquished the production of 'Fokker fodder', they had a nice new factory all ready for car manufacture, and henceforward Canley was the centre of their operations. The first post-war model was the 1328 cc SLS, which was a modernised, long-stroke version of the S, but it was not long before this was replaced by a truly postwar design in the shape of the 11.4 hp SLO, which, as its initials denoted, was an overhead-valve model. This dated from 1921, and with it was launched Standard's famous advertising slogan: 'Count them on the road'. An enlarged variant of this model was introduced in 1922 as the 13.9 hp SLO 4.

This was a period of expansion for the Canley factory: a test track now encircled its buildings, and there was now a production line for coachwork. The early vintage Standards were innovators in the field of all-

Below: the 1935 9 hp four-door saloon

Below right: a 13.9 hp saloon of 1923

Bottom right: the Big Nine Swallow of 1932

four-seated fabric saloon coachwork. It proved an instant success and the saviour of the company; 1928 saw the announcement of a larger power unit (1287 cc) and a longer wheelbase as options for this model, and there was also a sports version with raised compression ratio and wire wheels.

In August 1928 *The Autocar* tested a Standard Sports Saloon, with coachwork by Gordon England 'fitted out rather in the manner of expensive and luxurious town carriages intended for much larger chassis'. This bodywork included a proper luggage boot at the rear, and there were also two nicknack containers concealed in the rear seat armrests. Top speed was 51 mph, fuel consumption was 40 mpg, and the magazine concluded: 'With four passengers the car is considerably more comfortable than with two, owing to there being a slightly choppy action of the

Opposite page, above: a 1934 drophead 9 hp

Opposite page, below: a 1926 14 hp Charlecote two-seater

weather coachwork, for the tourers had rigid side-screens which could be swung away into the interior of the doors, a distinct advance on the detachable side-screens fitted to many of the SLO's contemporaries.

The popularity of the new Standard models was shown by the 1923 production figures, for over 5000 of the SLO variants were delivered that year. For 1924, model names were allotted to the various incarnations of the SLO: on the 11 hp chassis there were Canley and Coleshill two-seaters, Kineton and Kenilworth four-seaters and the Piccadilly saloon, while on the 14 hp chassis were Leamington, Warwick, Portland and Pall Mall bodywork.

Expansion continued at the Canley Works, but demand for the company's products suffered an alarming downturn in 1926, and the following year Standard introduced its first six-cylinder model since before the War. This was the 18/36 hp, which replaced the 11 hp Standard in production. The rapid development of this model was illustrated by the state of the car on show at Olympia: its bonnet was locked, thus excluding the prying enthusiast from discovering that the car was devoid of an engine. In any case, this wasn't the right model for the times, and sales continued to slump. Hastily, Standard moved in the opposite direction, developing a new 8.9 hp light car, the 1159 cc Standard Nine, normally supplied in 'Teignmouth' form, with

springs, possibly due to the short wheelbase (as noticeable with other small cars of about the same size). This is really only experienced on abnormally bad roads, and is damped out by extra load. . . . Generally speaking, the little car would be ideal for town work, because it is very easy to handle, economical to run, and not large enough to be awkward in car parks or in traffic.'

The success of the Nine staved off the financial crisis until 1929: but then the company had to be drastically reorganised to escape bankruptcy. Captain John P. Black, previously in charge of Hillman, was appointed managing director of Standard in 1930, and under his control the product range was completely reorganised. For 1931 the Big Nine of 1287 cc acquired a 'smart new radiator' and a 'remarkably roomy body finished both inside and out in good style and replete with every modern appointment'. The cheapest of the

Big Nine range was the Popular six-light, four-seater, four-door fabric saloon, while the most expensive was the Special fabric saloon, which for £245 offered a four-speed 'twin-top' gearbox, leather upholstery, safety glass, bumpers, wire wheels and sunshine roof.

There were now two ranges of six-cylinder models: the Ensign light six was virtually an enlarged version of the Big Nine, with a 2504 cc engine, while the 2552 cc Envoy was 'a full five-seater of the commodious type popular overseas, and had a chassis up-to-date in all mechanical details'. Standard were also supplying chassis to specialist bodybuilders like Avon and Swallow; the Swallow Standard eventually grew into a distinct marque, the SS, progenitor of the Jaguar. Total Standard production for 1930 was 6000 cars.

A new small Standard, the Little Nine, with a 1-litre engine, appeared at the end of 1931, costing only £155 in coachbuilt saloon form; the Big Nine was improved in appearance and the specification of the two six-cylinder models was upgraded. Demand for these 1932 Standards was such that the entire output of this model year was sold by July 1932.

Consequently, the 1933 models were introduced ahead of schedule: new to the range were two small sixes, the Little Twelve and the Big Twelve. The Little Twelve was basically a 1337 cc derivative of the Little Nine, with the chassis lengthened to accommodate the two extra cylinders, while the Big Twelve had a 1497 cc power unit. At Olympia, it was announced that the Big Nine and Big Twelve models would be available with the Wilson self-changing gearbox, and most models offered the Bendix automatic clutch control as an optional extra. The design of coachwork was rationalised throughout this rather complex range, while the 2552 cc Twenty now had a new design of chassis incorporating cruciform cross-bracing, and was available with seven-seater saloon coachwork.

The year 1933 saw the start of a thorough reorganisation of the Canley works, with extra facilities being constructed to enable the company to concentrate all its production here. By the middle of 1935 the factory had been completely mechanised, with overhead con-

veyors in all departments; and in 1936 alone, over £350,000 was spent in enlarging and re-equipping the plant to cope with an output of some 34,000 cars.

Sadly, Maudslay did not live to see the fulfilment of this programme of expansion, for he died in late 1934 at the age of 63, and was succeeded by John P. Black.

Design of the Standard cars was completely revised for 1934: now all models had cross-braced chassis and flexibly mounted engines. There was a new Nine, available in saloon form at only £135, which featured an underslung chassis, as did the Ten (£168); all the year's Standards now had four-speed transmissions with synchromesh on the upper three ratios (the Wilson box was still available as an extra), while all models save the Nine and the cheapest Ten had a free-wheel incorporated in the transmission.

Only modest changes were made to the range for

Right: this striking-looking prototype was built on a 12 hp chassis in 1934

Below: a Standard small saloon *circa* 1934

1935, though the Twelve now boasted 'Tri-Comfy' coachwork, the centre section of the rear seat sliding forward to accommodate a third passenger. Streamlined sports saloons known as the Speed and Speedline were available on the 10–12 hp sports chassis, which had an aluminium cylinder head and twin carburettors.

Much of 1935 was spent in the development of radically new models, which were announced on the eve of the Olympia Show: these were the famous 'Flying Standards', with streamlined swept-tail coachwork developed from the 10–12 hp Sports. To keep the overall height to a minimum, the chassis was sharply cranked over the rear axle, which thus operated inside an arched slot in the frame. At first, only 12 hp, 16 hp and 20 hp Flying Standards were available, at prices ranging from £259 to £315. Standard waxed eloquent about their manifold virtues: 'A car of astonishing beauty with flowing lines simplified for practical reasons only: to give comfortable seating within the wheelbase . . . to make cleaning a simple easy matter, to remove every obstacle to silken, silent, unbroken speed . . . it's called the "Flying Standard" because at speed it is as silent as a bird on the wing . . . it combines brilliant speed, family roominess with economy.'

The new styling became universal on the 1937 models: there were the Flying Nine (£149), the Flying Ten (£169), the Flying Fourteen (£249), the Flying Twelve (£199) and the new Flying Twenty (£349), with a 2686 cc V-8 power unit. Only 200 of these V-8s were actually produced, though its 'fencer's mask' radiator grille was to set the style for the following year's production, and the power unit was also used

in the ephemeral Raymond Mays car.

At the 1938 Motor Show, three new models were exhibited: these were the 8 hp, Super Ten and 12 hp Saloon De Luxe. All had independent front suspension by transverse leaf spring. Conventional semi-elliptic springing was retained on the continuing models, the 9 hp, the 14 hp and the 20 hp, and the 'Flying Standard' styling was on the way out, as the 9 hp, 10 hp and 12 hp models could be ordered either with the sloping tail of the Flying range, or with a more square-tailed version with luggage lockers built in the rear panel.

When World War II broke out, the Canley factory once again turned to the manufacture of aircraft: this time over a thousand De Havilland Mosquitoes were built as well as Airspeed Oxford trainers. Component manufacture included items as large as complete Bristol Beaufighter fuselages and as small as bomb

Below: a 1938 Flying Twelve; this car was powered by a 12 hp engine

Bottom: a 20 hp of 1936

releases; 20,000 Bristol Hercules aeroengines were built, and 417,000 cylinders for Bristol Mercury and Pegasus engines. Vehicles were produced, too: some 10,000 light utility vans were built for military use, based on the pre-war Flying Standard 14 chassis, as were 2800 examples of the curious Beaverette. This was a light armoured car on the 14 hp chassis, intended mainly for use by groups such as the Home Guard in the event of invasion. Powered by the Standard 14 engine, the Beaverette was about as basic as an armoured car could be: early examples had armoured

Left: produced between 1937 and 1938 was this V8 of 2686 cc and 75 bhp

bodywork, but retained the far from bulletproof radiator grille, wings and bonnet of the civilian Fourteen. Later models had full frontal armour, though the wheels were still exposed. Armament consisted of either machine guns or anti-tank guns, and the armour was $\frac{3}{8}$ in mild steel plating protected at the sides by a backing of oak planks; the floor, apparently, consisted of petrol tins beaten into shape.

Experiments were also carried out with four-wheel-driven military scout vehicles—'jungle jeeps'—which could have formed the basis for a postwar utility car costing no more than £100–£140, but the project was dropped when the fighting in the Far East came to an end.

Once the fighting was over, Standard quickly resumed production for the civilian market, as the necessary tools had all been carefully stored during the war. In 1945 the assets and goodwill of the Triumph company were acquired: this firm had gone into receivership just before the war, and its factory had been destroyed in the blitz, so the new Triumphs were also produced at Canley.

Standard's immediate postwar lineup consisted of the Eight, Twelve and Fourteen, but these were all swept away in 1947 when production was concentrated

on one new model, the Vanguard. It was intended that this rather bulbous unit-constructed car should be offered in only one body style, a four-door saloon: it was powered by a rugged four-cylinder engine with wet cylinder liners which was also used in the Ferguson tractor, another Standard product.

The transatlantic styling of the Vanguard made it relatively easy to sell in the export markets, and in the early years of its production it was a relatively rare sight on British roads. By 1951 an estate car version was available, as was the option of a Laycock de Normanville overdrive, the Vanguard being one of the first British cars to offer this facility.

The 1952 Vanguards underwent a mild styling improvement, with a lower bonnet, new radiator grille and larger rear window: this was known as the Phase I Vanguard, and was replaced the following season by the Phase II, which incorporated a more radical restyling, including the provision of an extended boot to replace the rounded back end of the original Vanguard.

In 1953 a new Standard Eight appeared, though this was a very different animal from its namesake of the 1939–47 period. With unit construction and bland styling and the most basic equipment, it was intended as a kind of sub-economy model. This idea was soon dropped, and a more lavishly appointed variant appeared in the spring of 1954, as did a 948 cc Standard Ten.

These models, intended to establish Standard in the

lower-priced popular car market never quite made the grade, handicapped possibly by somewhat vague handling characteristics. An estate version of the Ten was originally to be marketed as the 'Good Companion', but it seems as though the marketing department at Canley lost its nerve at the last minute, and the car was eventually named merely the Ten Companion.

For 1956, the Vanguard was completely restyled, with all-new Phase III bodywork, and the following year there was also a Sportsman version, with ugly two-tone paintwork, an MGA-like grille and a high-compression twin carburettor engine.

The 1958 season saw a more expensive Ten, the Pennant, and a cheaper Vanguard, the Ensign, but it was becoming apparent that the name 'Standard' was now a very debased currency. Originally it had signified a yardstick by which others should be measured:

Far left: the 803 cc Eight of 1954

Right: produced in the early 1960s was this Ensign

Below: the 1948 2088 cc Standard Vanguard beetle back

now it was applied by other makers to their basic models, and meant the opposite of 'de luxe'.

Rebuilding was taking place at Canley to provide production facilities for a new family car, but this was to be built under the Triumph label as the Herald.

The announcement of the restyled Vignale Vanguard in 1958 was little more than a stay of execution, and once the merger between Standard and Leyland Motors took place in April 1961, there was no hope for the continuance of the marque, beyond a new six-cylinder Vanguard that appeared in 1962. This engine later powered the Triumph 2000, but it was to feature in few Standards. The last car to bear the Standard name, an Ensign De Luxe, was produced at Canley in May 1963, though the marque's demise didn't become official until the autumn of 1963, after all the cars in stock had been sold. DBW

SYNONYMOUS WITH STEAM

Stanley built, without doubt, the most successful steamers ever

THE MOST SUCCESSFUL STEAM CAR of all time was the Stanley. Its production life of over a quarter of a century was at least a decade longer than that of any other external combustion car: and even after its demise there were attempts to revive the marque.

Francis E. Stanley and Freelan O. Stanley were identical twins, born in 1849 in Kingsland, Maine, whose principal boyhood hobby seems to have been making violins. They turned this hobby into a business, mass-producing violins which, while a little roughly finished, were acceptable musically.

Though they came of farming stock, the Stanleys' interests were more technical than agricultural; they had a natural talent for mathematics, and indeed taught this subject in school when they were young men, all the while picking up sufficient scientific knowledge to be able to invent and patent an early type of X-Ray apparatus.

Their first patent, however, was for a new type of photographic dry plate, and they established a photographic factory in the 1890s at Newton, Mass.

The Stanley Dry Plate proved so successful that eventually the Stanleys were able to sell the business to the Eastman Kodak Company at a handsome profit.

One day in the autumn of 1896 the brothers attended the Fall Fair at Brockton, Massachussetts, where the star attraction was a demonstration run by a 'horseless carriage'. However, the carriage proved so unreliable that it was unable to complete even one lap of the track. The Stanleys were convinced that they could do better, and F.E. is reported to have told his friends: 'Well, boys, before another fall I will show you a self-propelled carriage that will go around that track not only once but several times without stopping.'

The Stanleys reckoned that the entire car should weigh no more than 500 lb: but when the engine arrived from the Mason Regulator Company of Milton, Mass., it weighed more than 400 lb. And the boiler, made by the Roberts Iron Works Company, scaled over 200 lb. So the finished car was grossly over its design weight: but, apart from a tendency to frighten the local horses, it ran well. The first trial run, from Newton to Newtonville, took place in September 1897, easily meeting F.E.'s deadline.

Now they designed a lightweight firetube boiler capable of withstanding pressures of 2000 lb yet weighing only 90 lb: its strength was imparted by three layers of steel wire wound round the exterior of the boiler shell. And J. W. Penny & Sons, of Mechanic Falls, Maine, supplied an engine which weighed only 35 lb. During the winter of 1897, the Stanleys built three more cars—two runabouts and a surrey. They dismantled the Surrey, but each took a runabout and used them for the next year, refusing all offers for the vehicles. The Stanley brothers still considered automobiles as only a hobby.

One would-be buyer, a Bostonian named Methot, was more persistent than the rest, and eventually persuaded F. O. Stanley to part with his car for $600: Stanley, knowing full well that he and his brother could easily build a better machine, was not unduly perturbed at parting with the car.

Then F.E. entered *his* steamer for a race held on the Charles River cycle track in connection with New England's first motor show and outran the other competitors (a De Dion, a Haynes-Apperson, a Whitney steamer and a Riker electric) so convincingly that within a fortnight the brothers were inundated with orders for 200 cars of identical pattern. So they decided to become car makers.

The Stanleys' friend, Sterling Elliott, offered his bicycle factory and the brothers bought the premises,

Above: one of the Stanley twins' early cars, this little two-seater was built in 1898; over two-hundred cars of this type were manufactured

installed machinery, and began manufacture.

In February 1899 one car was completed and the other 199 were in varying stages of manufacture when, arriving at work around 7 am one morning, the Stanleys found a stranger sitting in their office. He was John Brisben Walker, publisher of the *Cosmopolitan* magazine, and he wanted to buy half the Stanley automobile business.

The brothers did not want to take on a partner: but a few weeks later Walker was back with another offer. This time he wanted to buy the entire operation. To scare him off, the Stanleys thought up an outrageous price. 'We want $250,000—cash,' they told him, knowing that the entire operation to date had cost them under $20,000.

'Exactly the figure I had in mind, a quarter of a million,' replied Walker, and wrote out a $500 cheque as a deposit.

Walker in fact did not have the $250,000, but aimed to raise it by interesting wealthy men in the business, and eventually sold a half share to one Amzi Lorenzo Barber. The conditions of the sale included an agreement. (Recalled F. O. Stanley: 'We found it difficult to understand, and quite ambiguous. But on the whole safer for us than for him, so both parties signed it.') that the Stanleys should not engage in the manufacture of steam cars for one year from 1 May 1899. Nominally they were on the board of the new company, but that was the limit of their involvement. Within a fortnight the alliance between Walker and Barber had gone asunder: Walker began manufacture of the Mobile

Above: looking more sophisticated than the 1898 model is this 1904 car, now in the Grandson museum, Switzerland

steam car at Tarrytown, N.Y., while Barber built the Locomobile of almost identical design at Westboro, Massachussetts. The Stanleys began developing a superior steam car which circumvented all their old patents, ready to go into production when the year's suspension came to an end.

In fact, they didn't begin manufacture under their own name again until 1901, when Locomobile moved to Bridgeport, Connecticut, and sold the Stanleys their old factory—and the patents—for a mere $20,000. Within a few months, the Stanleys had sold the rights to use two of their patents to the White Company for $15,000, ending the venture a healthy $245,000 to the good.

The new Stanley steamer had its twin-cylinder engine geared directly to the back axle, a layout which would characterise this marque for the rest of its life. At first the cars were typical buggies, but by 1906 the boiler was at the front under the easily reconizable famous 'coffin-nose' bonnet.

Right from the start, the Stanleys placed a premium on performance. They claimed that their fire-tube boiler gave a greater reserve of power than flash boilers, and remained faithful to this design throughout the production life of the Stanley Steamer. The Stanleys rarely indulged in paid advertising for their products; they could be assured of around 1000 customers every year on word-of-mouth recommendation, and did not see why they should put themselves out to increase or cheapen production.

Unfortunately, Freelan O. Stanley had little part in this revival of the Stanley, for ill-health had compelled him to move to Colorado where he eventually built a home and the Stanley Hotel at Estes Park, a noted beauty spot.

Francis E., on the other hand, threw himself into the activities of the company with gusto: in 1903 he drove the first streamlined Stanley racing car at Readville, a town just outside Boston.

But it was Fred Marriott who drove the most famous Stanley, the *Beetle* (alias *Wogglebug*), which exceeded 127 mph on Ormond Beach, Daytona, Florida, on 27 January 1906. With a standard engine, but increased boiler capacity, this car had a long, low, streamlined body, probably the first to be developed by wind-tunnel tests. Unfortunately, even the underside of the car had been faired in to decrease windage, and when the front wheels of the car bucked off the ground in a subsequent speed record attempt, *Beetle* became a 150 mph aerofoil and took off. The car was smashed to flinders and Marriott seriously injured. The Stanleys never raced again, though both brothers retained their love of high speed. Their 1907 range introduced the most coverable of Stanleys, the Gentleman's Speedy Roadster, available with three different engine sizes, and was easily capable of over 75 mph in short bursts.

It was a car ideally suited to the driving habits of the Stanley twins, who were wont to hurtle about the countryside in identical steam cars, a ploy which often caused confused double-takes by policemen attempting to operate timed speed traps. But it was his love of

speed which killed F.E. at the age of 69, in 1918. Breasting a hill at speed, he found two farm carts blocking the road and swerved to his death.

Fashion demanded that steam cars should look as much like petrol cars as possible. In addition foot and mouth disease, which broke out in New England in 1914, caused the removal of many of the roadside watering troughs on which the old non-condensing Stanleys had depended, and made the use of a condensor, which upped the range between water refills to 150–200 miles, imperative.

The condensor model Stanleys, however, were a rearguard action by a firm already on the decline, thanks to its seat-of-the-pants marketing strategies, since about 1903. A total of 743 Coffin-nose Stanleys was built in 1914, but only 126 of the more expensive and complicated condensor models appeared the following year, for the company had gobbled up all its surplus capital in development costs. Some 250 cars were built in 1916, and 500 in 1917. The 1918 output might have been boosted by an order for 160 mobile military showerbaths mounted on Mack truck chassis, but the war ended before more than a prototype could be constructed, and the order was cancelled.

The brothers had retired from the business by May 1918, and a new management, led by Prescott Warren, took over. Prices were raised in the hope of increased profits, and indeed 1920 saw the company with the biggest backlog of orders, in money terms, of its entire history. But the sudden recession in the car industry caused the cancellation of many of those orders, and

left the company with a lot of expensive orphans on its hands. Now no-one, save a handful of dedicated enthusiasts, wanted steam cars. Perhaps half a dozen Stanleys were imported to Europe at that period. Owen John Llewellyn of *The Autocar* tried one and concluded: 'Its ease of movement is superior to that of any multi-cylindered petrol car I have ever been in, and with regard to its manoeuvring qualities . . . it is infinitely easier to handle.'

The Stanley company itself averred that its twin-cylinder double-acting power unit was the equal in smoothness to a petrol-powered eight: and, of course, it was virtually silent. But these virtues were lost on a generation which had been brought up to believe that steam was synonymous with complication of operation and required special driving skills. The Chicago investment group of Prescott Warren controlled the company's ailing fortunes until 1924, when the Stanley Motor Carriage Company was sold to the newly formed Steam Vehicle Corporation of America, which sold the Newton factory and transferred the corporate headquarters to Allentown, Pennsylvania, but it seems that no cars were ever built there, and the company ceased trading in 1927. There was a brief attempt to revive the Stanley Steamer in the middle of the 1930s which from the beginning was fraught with difficulties and soon came to nothing.

The surviving Stanley twin, Frelan O., was active in his retirement at Estes Park right up until the day of his death in 1940 at the ripe old age of ninety-one—nearly half a century after the first Stanley Steamer.   DBW

Above: hardly distinguishable from an ordinary petrol car is this 1920 model 735; the car's double-acting twin-cylinder engine drove the back wheels and gave the car a top speed of 50 mph